D1127321

Nothing But The Truth

Taken at Kazachinskoye in 1952 after the author's release from the
Tayshet labor camp

JOSEPH BERGER

NOTHING BUT THE TRUTH

THE JOHN DAY COMPANY · NEW YORK

The John Day Company, 257 Park Avenue South, New York, N. Y. 10010
An Intext *Publisher*

Published in England under the title Shipwreck of a Generation.

Library of Congress Catalogue Card Number: 75-155021
Printed in the United States of America

Contents

Names followed by an asterisk will be found in the alphabetical index with a short biography as well as page references.

Names not followed by an asterisk appear in the index with page references only, but these personalities are either minor characters or sufficiently well described in the text not to require further elucidation.

Biographical Note

JOSEPH BERGER was born in Cracow in 1904 of Jewish parents. In 1914, after the beginning of the First World War, when Russian troops occupied Galicia and threatened to capture Cracow, the family went as refugees to Vienna. They returned home in 1916 and settled in Bielitz in Silesia. Brought up as an orthodox Jew and a Zionist, Joseph, at the age of fifteen, went as the leader of a group of young emigrants to Palestine where he worked, first on road construction and then as a translator in an engineering firm, and where he became converted to communism. In 1922 he helped to found the Communist Party of Palestine and became its Secretary. When the Party was admitted into the Komintern in 1924 he went to Moscow where he spent a few months and met his future wife, Esther, a Russian Jewess. In the middle of 1925 he returned to Palestine where his wife joined him; their son was born the following year.

Living mainly in Palestine, Berger travelled to Egypt, Syria, the Lebanon and Transjordan, where he helped to found Arab Communist Parties, while continuing his work as Secretary of the Communist Party in Palestine. He was several times summoned to Moscow, where in March 1929 he had a five-hour personal discussion on the Palestine question with Stalin. Later, after the 1929 Arab rising, the Palestine Party's Central Committee was reorganized by the Komintern to include an Arab majority but Berger was directed by Moscow to stay on as its General Secretary.

In 1931 he was recalled to Moscow and sent from there to Berlin as Secretary of the Anti-Imperialist League (founded in 1927 in Brussels). Already closely in touch with the leaders of the Komintern, among them its representative in Western Europe, Dimitrov,* he now met such prominent members of the League as Pandit Motilal Nehru, and for some time edited the journal of the League in cooperation with Clemens Dutt. He also spent a few months in Berlin jails (Moabit and Spandau) at this juncture.

Summoned back to Moscow by the Executive Committee of the Komintern in 1932, he was put in charge of the Komintern's Near-East Department, a post which he held for two years. In 1933 he was given Soviet citizenship and the name Joseph Berger.

Before the change of climate in 1934 Berger, by then doubtful of some aspects of the régime but still a loyal communist, was dismissed from the Komintern and simultaneously, in February, expelled from the Party (no reasons for this were given or discovered even in 1956 on his rehabilitation). For some months he worked in a printing house. Then, on the night of the 27th of January 1935, he was arrested at his home and taken to the Butyrki prison. Ten days later he was summoned for interrogation and charged with being a Trotskyist agitator. Some disparaging remarks he had made about Stalin had been reported to the authorities by a Russian professor. The interrogation lasted for two months; during this time he was kept in the Butyrki, sometimes in solitary confinement, sometimes in a cell with other prisoners. Psychological but not physical pressure was brought to bear on him (torture was not yet in frequent use); as he refused to "confess," Berger was labelled "an ideological enemy who refuses to disarm" and finally sentenced *in absentia* by the special board (OSO) of the NKVD to five years in a labor camp for counter-revolutionary Trotskyist activity.

In April he was sent to the camp of Mariinsk in Siberia, where a spirit distillery was being built. At the end of the year he was transferred to Gornaya Shoriya, a camp near the Mongolian frontier, where he worked on the building of a new strategic railway to Tashtagol.

In April and May 1936 he was brought back under special convoy to the Lubyanka prison in Moscow as a potential witness in the trial of Zinovyev. The attempt to use him in the trial was given up, but his own case was re-investigated and his sentence changed from five years in camp to eight years in prison. On the point of being sent back to Siberia in July 1936 he refused to leave Moscow without seeing his wife and won his point after forty-four days on hunger strike. In August 1937 he was transferred to a prison for hardened criminals in Vladimir and from there, in December, to a similar prison on Solovki.

Solovki was evacuated in August 1939 as it was close to the Finnish border and Berger was sent by the ship *Budyonny* (following an ice-breaker) to Dudinka, at the mouth of the river Yenisey, and then to a camp at Norilsk in Northern Siberia (69° N.).

In July 1941 he was re-arrested in the camp, charged with organizing a group of prisoners to overthrow the authorities, and sentenced to death. (Without knowing it at the time – he discovered this only in 1956 – he had already been condemned to death once, in 1937, but the sentence had been mitigated owing to the intervention of an official who knew him.) Berger refused to sign his own death sentence (as the regulations required) and again went on hunger strike, this time for fifty-six days. Moscow refused to ratify the sentence owing to a formality, and in 1943 he was condemned instead to ten years in camp as from 1941.

He served his sentence in Norilsk until September 1948 when, after the assertion of independence by Tito, he was transferred as a particularly dangerous political prisoner to the top security Alexandrovsk prison near Irkutsk; there he stayed a year, and was then sent to the "special" labor camp of Tayshet. Prisoners from this camp began to construct the Bratsk hydro-electric power station. At the end of his term, in 1951, he was released, only to be sentenced simultaneously and *in absentia* to lifelong exile in Siberia. For the first time in fifteen years he was allowed to see his wife and son, who came to visit him in Kazachinskoye (300 kilometres north of Krasnoyarsk), where he was working on a collective farm. Then he moved to Maklakovo, near Yeniseysk; too weak for physical work, he was kept alive by parcels from his wife, while he devoted his spare time to translating Chekhov into German.

In February 1956, three years after Stalin's death, he was rehabilitated and after a delay caused by food poisoning and temporary blindness he returned to Moscow. His wife and son, who had suffered a great deal as relations of a political prisoner, were anxious to leave the country. This was now possible because Poles were permitted to resume their former nationality and return with their families to Poland. After a year in Warsaw, where he worked at the

Polish Institute of Foreign Affairs, Berger emigrated with his wife to Israel, to which their son had preceded them. He is thought to be the only top-level pre-war communist to have survived imprisonment in the Soviet Union and come to the West. He now lives in Tel-Aviv and lectures at the University of Bar-Ilan.

Author's Note

FOR the sake of brevity and in order not to repeat material already published elsewhere, I have preferred not to give a chronological account of that part of my life covered in this volume. Instead I concentrated my attention on just a few of the thousands of people whom I met in the Soviet prisons and camps, and for the sake of convenience grouped them according to their political or other affiliations. However, it should not be thought that I am thereby making any generalizations about these categories – I am writing about individuals as individuals and trying to preserve as open a mind as I can.

Introduction

ONE difficulty about beginning to write a book of this sort is to decide upon its scope. For however short a human life and however insignificant compared to the immensity of the universe of which it is a part, it seems itself to be limitless, and one life alone can appear to raise problems which concern the lives of all the millions of people who fill the world.

A second difficulty is that because of all that has happened in the past half century, the reader may well ask himself at the outset: 'What conclusions has this man reached? What has he deduced from the facts? How does he evaluate them?' He may perhaps even start by looking at the last page rather than the first, and he may have his own predetermined view of events and therefore expect me to be either his ally or his enemy. I should like to say at once that such a reader will be disappointed: partly because, after all that I have seen and lived through, I have reached very few conclusions, and partly because even those I have arrived at I feel unable to wrap up neatly in formulas or to treat as final judgments.

It is my sincere wish that my book should not be regarded as an attack on anyone. I do not intend to play the role of either prosecutor or counsel for the defence. I feel that what is most needed in our time is a knowledge of the facts and an objective, unprejudiced and, if possible, dispassionate attitude towards them. If enough people will honestly describe what they have seen, as they have seen it, sufficient evidence will be accumulated in the end for a judgment to be possible. My own task, as I understand it, is to state what I saw and felt and lived through. This, I believe, is the most that I can possibly do, and even this task is difficult enough.

One danger I am keenly aware of is that of selecting evidence in such a way that, although every part of it is true, the sum fails to convey the truth: the danger of presenting a partial truth as though it was the whole picture.

Another problem which troubles me is the risk of making my own life the centre of attention: for all the subjectivity of my judgments and impressions, I would think it very wrong to write a book focused on my own fate. What *is* important for me is to describe what happened to the hundreds of thousands, indeed the millions of people who found themselves in the same position as myself. This was the attitude I took up even in the thirties and forties while I was in the labour camps and it was fundamental to my whole resistance to our oppressors. The official explanation then of the purges and repressions was that they were necessary for the general good, for mankind as a whole, and that it was only an occasional individual who was struck down unjustly, dishonoured and condemned. Such a victim was called upon by his interrogators to concentrate his whole attention on his own case. But I found this to be both impossible and wrong. I thought it my duty to try to understand the reason for the blows which had hit me along with many others, and to discover why there were so many others. I thought it wrong that each of the accused should speak only for himself. In this I often differed from other prisoners, who were agonizingly concerned to prove that they were either wholly innocent or at least innocent of the particular crimes with which they had been charged. I refused to sign any declaration which tended to show that my own fate was exceptional, or that I would regard a change in the official attitude towards myself alone as sufficient reparation.

What concerns me now, as it did then, is the fate of that whole generation whose destruction I witnessed. For it was not merely individuals, or groups, or even tens of thousands of individuals who were destroyed. It was a whole generation – the generation which brought about the greatest revolution in history and which, twenty years later, had been either physically annihilated or swept aside in such a way that only a few traces of its work were left. This multitude included not only the men directly responsible for the Revolution but also the millions who took part in it less actively and less consciously, as well as the many more who gave it merely the passive support caused by their hostility to the 'former classes'.

I was not myself an eye-witness of the October Revolution. I was not in Russia at that time and I would in any case have been too young to take part in it; but judging by what I heard from hundreds of its friends and enemies, I think it impossible to see it as the achievement of a small group only, however active. What I learnt convinced me that the Revolution was the work, not even of the Russian people alone, but of all the peoples who then lived on Russian territory.

In this I differ from what was generally thought in Russia under Stalin and is still thought, as far as I can judge, outside the communist world today. For example, I remember a meeting held by the leaders of the Moscow Party Organization in 1933. I think it was in preparation for some purge or other. One of the speakers was relating his autobiography and said: 'And so in 1917, when the Revolution took place, I . . .' At this point he was interrupted by the chairman, an old Party member who had worked for the pre-revolutionary underground and who was often referred to as 'the conscience of the Party'. He struck the table with his fist and said: 'Stop! What do you mean when you say that "the Revolution took place"? Comrades!' he turned to the audience, 'remember that the Revolution did not "take place", it was *made* by Lenin and a group of devoted Bolsheviks: they prepared it, they organized it and they carried it through to victory.' In essence this view, which was taught later in all Soviet text-books, was the same as that of many foreigners: the Revolution was not a nation-wide movement, but the action of a small group which succeeded in seizing power.

This picture struck me as false, and it still seems to me false even now, after my quarter of a century's experience of Russia and of people who had lived through the Revolution and the Civil War. Indeed, I think it is a naïve interpretation and fit only to be classed with slogans such as 'No fortress is impregnable to the Bolsheviks' – slogans aimed at bolstering up conceit and not at explaining history.

I think that the idea we had in the early twenties of the Revolution as the work of the masses, and of the Bolsheviks as playing only a secondary role, was closer to the truth. Even if Lenin and the men around him can be said to have 'made the October Revolution', it is still more true to say that they were made by it. I honestly believe

that there was a movement which nothing could have broken or
stopped – though it could have been directed differently – and it was
this movement which brought Lenin and his disciples to the fore. I
do not wish to minimize the work of preparation carried out for
decades by the Russian revolutionary movement, but the reason
why, at a given moment, the Bolsheviks came to power is, I believe,
because at that moment they had the people behind them. This is
not the place to speculate on why the masses did not make their
will prevail at other moments – in the Constituent Assembly, for
example, or in the course of the Civil War; other factors intervened
then. All I maintain is that in October, or rather from July 1917
until a few weeks after the October Revolution, the Bolsheviks did
have mass support for many of their aims. Peace, the distribution of
the land, government by workers' and peasants' soviets – all this, I
think, was in accordance with the people's will, and in fact the
Bolshevik slogans were formulated in response to it. It is clear from
the Bolshevik literature of the period that their ideas until then had
been purely abstract and that they became realities only when they
were changed to gain popular support. This was why the Bolsheviks were able to seize the leadership of the country.

Thus, when I speak of the generation which 'made the Revolution',
I mean the whole generation of Russians who were between the
ages of fifteen and thirty in 1917 – a whole people, just like the
people on whom Robespierre relied in France or Cromwell in
England.

This generation was virtually destroyed within the next two
decades; and to explain the reasons for and the manner of its decline
is what I see as my prime task.

A few words about the readers whom I should like to reach. I have
talked about my subject with myself for over thirty-five years; now
I must leave out of this interior dialogue whatever is uninteresting
to the reader whom I have in mind. Who is he? First I must mention
one group of people who will never read my book but of whom I
have never ceased to be aware as I wrote it. They are the thousands
of men who travelled with me on my way and who lost their lives.
I have no right to speak for all of them, though many of them
thought and felt as I did. But I am conscious of their presence and I

would not say anything to hurt their memory. I should like to dedicate my book, in the first place, to them, to what they did and to what they hoped for.

Secondly, I address myself to those in Russia who have become adult since the death of Stalin. To many of them what I have to say will seem strange, for the interval between the first revolutionary generation and the third was a time of successful falsification, aimed not so much at justifying certain crimes as at confusing the issues. For this reason they need to be enlightened about certain things which were understood instinctively by the second generation, the one that replaced the first, stepped into its shoes and accepted the falsifications. The young men of today are not committed to these lies, they are not forced to believe them, and they can face the truth.

Finally, I should like to reach a much wider public – men of good will, however young or old and wherever they may be. To my great comfort I found, when I returned to life, that many people, whether consciously or half-consciously, whether deliberately or merely through the force of events, had developed a thirst for facts and for unbiased judgments. In contrast to the situation of twenty years or so ago, there are today many people in every country and perhaps in all political parties who are unwilling to become dogmatists. Not only in the West but in the communist countries and even in the Soviet Union itself it is now the fashion for decent people to begin what they have to say by declaring: 'I don't want to be dogmatic'. Whatever differences of approach lie behind this common attitude, dogmatism is discredited on all sides. Everywhere I have found people who are interested not in theses or in Resolutions, or in making facts tally with the Resolutions, but in what is really happening or has happened so that they can draw their own conclusions. This gives me the hope that the past as well as the present may be better understood.

In days gone by this approach was thought to be characteristic of materialism. Materialists felt superior to other men because they believed in accepting and in analysing the bare facts. But in the fifty years of Soviet power, including the quarter of a century during which one large part of Soviet society was isolated from the rest, things have changed. What came to matter was the formula; what

'Comrade Stalin said' became the definition of reality. The important thing was not reality but whether it was in keeping with this or that quotation from a text.

During this tragic quarter of a century attempts were also made to set up similar schools of thought in the West. It is true that the Fascists and Nazis did not begin by adopting the principles of materialism and therefore did not have to trample on them; but they started from the alleged need for dogma, which was once and for all established and which could then be followed with a good conscience. In the West and in much of the East this period is now over. Nearly everywhere there is a hope that people may be found who simply want to know the facts.

It is to them primarily that I address this book.

CHAPTER I

'FORMER PEOPLE'

I WENT to live in Moscow fifteen years after the October Revolution, by which time Russian society had undergone vast changes; men who had been important in the past had been removed from public posts and had lost all political and social influence, while many other people had risen from the bottom. The circles in which I found myself knew practically nothing about Russian society as it was before 1917; they were either foreign communists like me, from almost every country in the world, or Russians who were working in the Party apparatus. We derived our knowledge of 'former people', as members of the old, deposed upper class and intelligentsia were called, from the printed word and from the fantastic stories still told about them. We, the young generation of communists, envisaged them as blood-suckers, exploiters, and opponents of all reform. Occasionally we ran into them working, owing to the absence of other adequately trained personnel, as specialists, technicians and translators in the Commissariat of Foreign Affairs or the Communist International. But what were they really like?

Not until my first arrest in January 1935 did I expect to find myself in prison with 'counter-revolutionaries'. I was in for a considerable surprise. Although mass arrests had not yet started most of my fellow-prisoners were of peasant or working-class origin. Only a handful matched my preconceptions of the 'counter-revolutionary'. After my release in the fifties young students, largely ignorant of the past, were astonished when I told them that the prisons during the thirties were not crammed full of bankers and noblemen. I had difficulty in convincing them of this, and of the fact that the Terror was already then directed not against any special class but against the people as a whole.

In my opinion collectivization was the turning point. Everybody,

Party members included, had to take sides over the crude coercion of the peasants at a time when even opposition in theory provided sufficient grounds for arrest.

The paucity of 'former people' in no way surprised my fellow-prisoners, many of them Party men of long standing, for they were well aware that earlier directives for the annihilation of the old ruling classes had been implemented with ample zeal. The only survivors from the old ruling classes were those who had fled the country (émigrés were numerous), or those who managed to conceal their past by merging with the peasants in villages or with the workers in factories. The Security Service never for an instant relaxed its vigilance towards 'former people' and their extermination continued remorselessly year after year.

Whenever I ran into them in prisons or camps I was struck by their vitality, a quality remarkable in people never before subjected to the rigours of manual labour. I had my first deep and lasting impression of a 'former person' in a 'general cell' in which I was placed after my arrest and transfer to the Butyrki prison in Moscow. In the tightly packed cell I singled out one man notable for his exceptional pallor and uncommonly intelligent face, standing in a sad and exhausted crowd suspicious of newcomers lest they turned out to be spies planted by the authorities. Two or three days passed before I had the chance of conversing with him. He told me his name was Alexander Mikhaylovich Loris-Melikov, a name instantly recognized by the few better-educated among us as that of a great liberal reformer who, while a minister of Tsar Alexander II, had prepared a progressive constitution for Russia.

Alexander Mikhaylovich explained that this famous Loris-Melikov was his uncle. His own father, who was half-Armenian, had at the turn of the century been a member of a Russian diplomatic mission to Egypt where he met and married an Egyptian lady. Alexander Mikhaylovich remarked that his own peculiarities of character were due to his being one part Occidental and two parts Oriental. His father had either emigrated or died during the Revolution, after which his mother had lived very quietly in order to attract as little attention as possible. She had returned to her native Egypt during the twenties, at which period Alexander

Mikhaylovich, highly gifted in mathematics, had taken his university degree and been appointed to the Civil Service. By 1930 he was the author of various internationally known books, had played an important part in inventing new methods of weather forecasting, and was lecturing at Leningrad University.

However, Bolshevik ideology was anathema to him and he brooded regretfully over his idyllic childhood in Egypt and the luxuries he had enjoyed in the family palace at St Petersburg, as Leningrad had then been called. Yet he had prospered under the new régime owing to the high pay his talents earned him. He argued that his style of living was far lower than a man of culture had the right to expect. Almost certainly it was lower than that of cultured men in the so-called capitalist world.

Alexander Mikhaylovich had done everything possible to get abroad and he said I interested him both as a foreigner who knew the world outside Russia, and as one who was not, in his own words, 'one of the boors' to be found in such large numbers within our prison. He was quite unconcerned about the conditions of workers in the West and his thoughts were only for the creative classes abroad upon whose shoulders he considered all cultural development rested. In his view the October Revolution had hopelessly depressed the status of the upper reaches of society without in any way bettering the situation of the poor. We agreed to differ about this vexing question, but we talked at length about science and scholarship in the West. For me he was a typical remnant of the past, hoping against hope that 'this disgraceful business', as he termed the Bolshevik Revolution, would soon peter out. He refused to believe that any state could go on existing in the conditions of Russia at that time. He was convinced that the Russia of the Revolution was bound to break up from within or succumb to a world crusade against it from without. Dismissing my own reasoning against such possibilities, he insisted that by the end of that very summer (it was then February 1935) we should be watching the extinction of the Soviet State.

Naturally I inquired how he, a corresponding member of the Soviet Academy of Sciences and a recipient of various Soviet awards, could live with such hatred aflame in his heart. He answered that neither I, nor any of our fellow-prisoners, really knew what the Russians were like. Soviet administration, conducted without an élite, was shaky, and its experience of government woefully limited. True leaders could be bred only over the generations and they formed, inevitably, a privileged minority. Soon, he observed, the people themselves would come crawling to their old rulers and beg them to resume their duties.

'Did you talk to your colleagues like this at work?' I asked him.

'I wouldn't be such a fool,' he retorted. 'I always performed as I was expected to. I was even well enough up in Leninism to give lectures on Dialectical Materialism at the University.'

'Do you really know anything about Dialectical Materialism?'

'What's there to know about such meaningless rubbish – except the patter?'

In his opinion university entrants since the advent of Soviet Socialism were of such poor quality that it made little difference how or what they were taught. The authorities would be lucky if anything came of even one per cent of them. The technical training which even in the old days produced skilled men would continue to produce them, and these skilled men could be turned into engineers. But they would never master abstract thinking and true learning, so the Soviet State did well to employ men like him because there was not the slightest prospect of true scientists emerging from the system. He assured me that employees of university faculties, scientific institutes and the press, wholeheartedly shared his views.

According to Alexander Mikhaylovich thousands of people remained barely conscious of the sort of duality which racked him but were, like him, quite resigned to the curious way of life he followed. He was one of the first who made clear to me a frequently expressed attitude. If a man fell among thieves and was forced by torture and hunger to profess certain beliefs he could yield to compulsion without in any way compromising his conscience. Was this not what happened when Turks captured Russians and made them embrace the Moslem religion? Deceit had to be the response to force. The authorities in the Soviet State were playing a game which might be unfamiliar in Italy or America. 'You yourself as a foreign communist may not understand the rules,' he explained, 'but every Russian is perfectly familiar with them. We don't express our thoughts which the authorities know full well are hostile to them, so our silence forces them to find other ways of repressing us. They start campaigns against us from time to time, thinking up pretexts for the express purpose of eliminating a given number of us "former people".'

Alexander Mikhaylovich had been arrested as a 'saboteur'. The entire staff of the Meteorological Office, with the distinguished scientist Wangenheim at its head, had suddenly been accused in 1932 of falsifying weather forecasts in order to damage the harvest. Alexander Mikhaylovich commented that in fact their margin of error in forecasting was no wider than that in other countries. Although he was never tortured he signed a confession under intense psychological pressure and because of his infinite contempt for official procedures. 'We were obliged to confirm the usual fictions', he told me. What else was there to do, as truth and falsehood were quite irrelevant? Yet he also assured me that, although he was an implacable opponent of 'their' ideology, he always carried out his duties loyally. They had sentenced him to ten years in a Siberian labour camp and he worked on the Baykal-Amur railway, known as BAM.

We met because in the middle of 1934 the authorities had appointed a special investigator, Akulov, to re-examine certain cases involving specialists. Alexander Mikhaylovich had therefore been transferred from camp to prison and was now awaiting the outcome of the fresh investigations. He observed ironically that, since errors in weather forecasting had probably increased after the arrest of the alleged saboteurs, the authorities were apparently now keen to reinstate him. He had frankly informed Akulov that he wanted neither amnesty, pardon, nor re-examination of his case. His sole wish was to leave the country since he was not a pure Russian and his relatives lived abroad. 'After all I've been through,' he said, 'I'll do everything I can to leave the place whether I'm at liberty or in captivity.' He stood his ground firmly against promises of compensation and freedom to work, write and publish again. In fact, the assassination of Kirov* at about that time put paid to any chance he

may have had of leaving the country or of arriving at some compromise with the authorities. Mass arrests and purges were spreading,
the re-examination of cases was abandoned and prisoners were
returned to their camps.

I myself still believed in the integrity of Soviet justice, so from
the moment of my arrest I adopted the policy of speaking nothing
but the truth. I never deviated from this policy even under the
rigours of interrogation. Alexander Mikhaylovich insisted that I was
shortening my life and he enlightened me about the degradations
and humiliations to which specialists of the 'former classes' were
subjected in the camps. He pointed out that, in the last resort, the
NKVD[1] always won. 'Fight them,' he urged, 'as you would fight a
gang of thieves, by guile and cunning.' Experience was to teach me
that either method could prove fatal. I ascribe my own survival
only in the smallest measure to my tactics. Whenever I was pressed
to admit false charges I went on hunger strike. Alexander Mikhaylovich was horrified. In his opinion I was doing the enemy's work for
him and bringing about my own destruction. I was being transferred to solitary confinement for declaring a hunger strike at the
moment when the authorities informed Alexander Mikhaylovich
that there could be no revision of his sentence. His last words to me
were that he would unhurriedly carry out his plans should they ever
release him but prohibit his emigration. If they returned him to
confinement he promised he would somehow find the means of
ending his life.

In 1935 he was taken away from the Butyrki prison to an unknown destination. Only in 1937, some two years after our encounter, did I learn from another prisoner the end of Alexander
Mikhaylovich's tragedy. He was sent off to a concentration camp at
Pechora in the far north of European Russia. So violent was his
resistance that they had to tie him up to get him on the train. He
continued his bitter resistance at the first transfer camp and in a fit
of madness declared a hunger strike. In transfer camps the severity
of discipline made successful hunger strikes impossible. He was
thrown into a punishment cell, dirty and crawling with lice, all by

1. Soviet Security Service, originally Cheka 1917-22, GPU and OGPU
1922-34, NKVD 1934-43, NKGB 1943-46, MGB 1946-53, now KGB.

himself, deprived of his clothes and all his possessions. He did not even have a book to read. Struck down by illness, he was refused medical assistance, grew weaker and died. The authorities viewed the Loris-Melikovs of this world as saboteurs whose incorrigibility justified their liquidation. They were little interested in the survival and the talents of such people. Even the majority of their fellow-prisoners had scant sympathy for them. Fifteen years after the establishment of the Soviet State Alexander Mikhaylovich still clung to his aristocratic heritage, and his willingness to share certain things, like his rations, hardly alleviated his isolation and in reality increased his vulnerability.

*

By contrast, however, my fellow-prisoners warmed to a man like Shefranov, whom I met at a camp in Norilsk in 1939. Shefranov, another typical representative of the 'former people', came of lesser aristocratic stock but he too was an intellectual. He had belonged to the Cadets,[2] but moved further to the left and in 1917 served in a ministry during Kerensky's* provisional government, set up after the February Revolution of that year. Briefly tolerated by the Bolsheviks after Kerensky's downfall, he worked in Moscow as a specialist in transport. In the early thirties, however, even his old friends could no longer protect him from the deepening suspicion towards the 'former classes', for whose arrest any pretext was sufficient.

Shefranov underwent no formal trial. He was simply sent to a camp for three years on the strength of a decree by a special board of investigation. Eight years later he was still in a camp! Astonishingly, he had preserved his personality; he was a large, kindly man with a stick, courteous of speech and manner and, because he was over sixty, he had been found employment in the camp administration. Eight years had in no way diminished his efficiency and he had never missed a single day's work because of illness. The successful running of the technical section depended upon his ideas and his ability to implement them. Even the Party official from Moscow

2. Party of Constitutional Democrats founded in 1905 favouring constitutional monarchy.

who was officially in charge never moved hand or foot without consulting him.

Shefranov may have been outstanding but he was by no means an exceptional example of his kind. Almost all the technical specialists in the camps were drawn from the prisoners themselves, and no projects undertaken by the Central Directorate of Camps (Gulag) could possibly have succeeded without their co-operation. To this day people are arguing in Russia about the economic advisability of employing prison labour in this way. Nevertheless, the fact remains: development projects, costing astronomical sums of money, which would otherwise never have succeeded, were carried out by means of a prisoner élite.

When I was released after the death of Stalin I saw the film *The Bridge on the River Kwai*, and noted the application of the very principles adopted by the Soviet authorities. The Japanese exploited not only the physical energies of their prisoners but also their minds and their moral strength for economic purposes. From the thirties onwards the Soviet authorities likewise exacted labour from tens of millions who supplied it for next to nothing in conditions too terrible to be imagined. Prisoners achieved the impossible. But why did they yield to the demands of their captors? Why did they not indulge in extensive and unceasing sabotage? Curiously enough they were convinced that everything they were doing was for the good of Russia. Their profoundly ingrained patriotism overcame even their loathing of the communist system. They also wanted to survive, and their efforts generally earned them some amelioration of their conditions (an amelioration granted out of pure self-interest by the State, which would need their labour in future). The privileges they managed to wrest from the authorities enabled them, moreover, to save thousands and thousands of their fellow-men from certain death. Without these little privileges all would surely have perished, as the authorities failed to provide automatically even the minimum necessities for human survival.

Shefranov himself never believed in the possibility of his own liberation which, after the extension of his sentence, was due in 1942. Two years before this the Central Directorate of Camps had proposed his formal release while planning to keep him in the area for further work. The Camp Commandant advised him that to return to Moscow could only mean re-arrest. Shefranov's sudden death from a heart attack one morning in 1940 resolved this strange dilemma both for him and for the authorities.

While Alexander Mikhaylovich Loris-Melikov had died like a pariah in utter loneliness, Shefranov's funeral amounted to a public demonstration; his past was quite forgotten in the acclaim he had earned for himself. The majority of prisoners who were of peasant or worker origin sympathized with the Shefranovs in spite of their aristocratic backgrounds and reproached the authorities for any harsh treatment meted out to them. Even a major of the NKVD was sympathetic. Shefranov was a positive, creative man who justified not only his own existence but that of his friends as well. His work was of benefit to others and the means of self-salvation. This was the difference between Shefranov and Loris-Melikov.

*

In 1936 in Moscow I was thrown into solitary for declaring a hunger strike but, as often happened, there were too many hunger strikers and insufficient space for us all. We found ourselves two, sometimes three, to a cell. One hunger striker who kept me company on this occasion was another representative of the 'former people', no more than eighteen years old and with a certain nobility of countenance. Since I could give him about ten years and as my beard must have added a slightly venerable touch to my appearance he eagerly and nervously – if not hysterically – sought my counsels as an older man.

'I am an Obolensky,' he announced with a hint of arrogance, 'one of *the* Obolenskys.' His family had escaped via Latvia, and were working through the Red Cross and especially Yekaterina Pavlovna Peshkova* (who, since Lenin's death, formed the link between the Soviet Union, the émigrés and that organization) to arrange his departure for either London or Paris. He had by now spent three years in prison, condemned as an 'agitator' in 1933 for some critical words to his schoolfellows. Luckily his youth, and perhaps the efforts of his family as well, had saved him from utter disintegration. He behaved correctly and worked conscientiously in the hope of being allowed to go abroad at the end of his sentence. The day he was due for release he was informed that fresh charges were to be brought against him. He could not imagine what his new crime could be for, as he put it, he had spent the last three years between four walls, and a hunger strike was his method of protest. He was not aware that a directive had recently been issued ordering the detention of political prisoners until further notice.The authorities therefore busied themselves with cooking up pretexts for holding on to prisoners like him.

What he wanted me to tell him was how far I thought it was his duty to be obstinate about his hunger strike. He was a healthy boy with a normal appetite. Mealtimes came and went and he was obviously in agony; clearly he wanted to find some justification for ending his strike. We probed deeper while we talked. His education and upbringing had been entirely under Soviet auspices, yet, like Loris-Melikov, he had rejected his conditioning and kept an uncommonly independent mind. While sharing his indignation at the cruelty of the camps I proclaimed my support for the ideals of the October Revolution, which was directed towards the common good and towards the elimination of privileges for a favoured minority. Jumping up from his bunk he paced up and down shouting:

'You've read Turgenev? You remember Bazarov? I agree with him. Humanity is not my business. And between you and me, *they* don't see humanity as their business either. They only pretend to, so as to mask what they're doing. It's impossible to serve humanity except through one's self-fulfilment as an individual.'

Argument between us had struck a dead end.

Unlike Loris-Melikov he believed the régime would endure for years and held to his conviction that the attempt to abandon the idea of the value of each individual in favour of humanity as a whole could result only in more misery and bloodshed than ever before. He derived his ideas, as did many others, from the Russian classics. He had soaked himself in Tolstoy, Turgenev, Goncharov and, especially, Dostoyevsky. How strange it seemed then that, decades after his death, Dostoyevsky should still be influencing the minds of young people! During our talks about *The Possessed* and *The Brothers Karamazov* he insisted that Dostoyevsky had predicted and judged 'all these things' long ago. Russians found the meaning of life in their 'mission' and in their Orthodoxy. Time would prove that this was so.

He greedily eyed the food brought in to us, and to alleviate his suffering I proposed that he should ask for paper and pencil in order to write to Peshkova, 'Aunt Katya', as we prisoners called her. If they agreed he should end his hunger strike. Since they obliged he did so and was accordingly transferred elsewhere. I heard later that he was occupying a cell reserved for those who were to be allowed to emigrate. He may have been lucky; 1936 was a turning point, and by 1937 it would certainly have been too late.

I do not claim that my portraits of these three men typify the destinies of the whole Russian aristocratic intelligentsia which remained in the Soviet Union. I ran into the mere remnants of a class only incidentally exploited by the Communist Party, whose aim was its total elimination. When this obliteration was nearly complete the 'Stalin' Constitution of 1936 was promulgated; while enfranchising everybody it in effect deprived ordinary men and women of all opportunities to participate in the affairs of state. The Constitution marked the end of discrimination against the 'former people' as a class. Oddly enough, however, the end of their special difficulties as a class, their meaningless enfranchisement and their re-qualification as people who could hold administrative posts and enter universities coincided exactly with the beginning of the new sufferings they had to endure alongside any other members of society who might have wanted to oppose Stalin. Significantly, the style of a certain dreaded official form altered towards the end of the thirties. No longer concerning itself with questions of property and possession, it asked whether the signatories, or members of their families, had ever fallen foul of the State and whether they had any relatives abroad. Now it was such matters that were to determine the distinctions between various social groups.

The struggle for the liquidation of the 'former people' had taken twenty years. The struggle to create the 'new man' and a new society still goes on.

WRITERS

In the thirties the 'new man' was an idea that kept recurring in books, pamphlets and lectures, eventually superseding all other ideas as the dominant theme of communist ideology. The reason was plain enough. The Revolution had taken place and had gone beyond its initial stages, the foundations of the 'new society' had been laid, and each year saw considerable changes in the social structure of Russia. Yet it was becoming increasingly clear that to create new forms, new conditions and new inter-relationships was not enough. The very means of re-shaping society lay within the human being. It was man himself who had to be re-shaped.

Difficulties and sacrifices were only to be expected during the initial phases of the Revolution, but after ten or fifteen years its leaders felt they had to offer a sign that the period of preparations and expectations was over. The transformation of society, the economic system and living conditions, was not enough in itself. The true objective was the creation of the 'new man'. And in the making of the 'new man' a certain class of persons were to be regarded as the experts. Politicians had to busy themselves with public affairs, economists with their figures and schemes for industrial mobilization; industrialists, doctors, teachers and others also had their allotted tasks. Why should not their combined efforts be able to create a 'new man'? The Communist Party decided that specialists had to be made responsible for showing how the 'new man' was to be born, bred and educated.

Soviet newspapers had always carried a section devoted to 'human problems'. Now *Pravda*, *Izvestiya*, *Gudok*, *Trud* and others began to print features dealing with the personality of the 'new man', forecasting the qualities he would some day acquire, and condemning those 'remnants of the past' which were impeding his emergence. People are not easily attracted to facts and figures about science and industry but a human problem which was related to the 'Soviet way of life' always commanded exceptional attention. 'Feature-writers', though they did not write the sort of features published in Western newspapers, became popular watch-dogs over the emerging 'new man'. Their articles constituted a particularly important weapon because the public regarded them as social criticism.

How far can human nature be changed? That it *can* be changed is a basic Marxist precept. That all men are born equal and changed mainly by social circumstances is also fundamental to the teachings of Marxism. The question is not new; it has been a topic of philosophical debate throughout history. No longer philosophical but political, it was now the issue debated by the 'feature-writers', whose mission it was to note the signs of change in men and women and to trace the progress of that change as time went by.

However, I came across people who even in the twenties and thirties dismissed this issue as mere sophistry. Some of them argued that the existing society could never produce the 'new man'. The heirs to the 'old society' of capitalists and serf-owners were unsuitable for the task because they bore the taint of the old corrupt society. Tolstoy had longed for a 'new society' but he maintained that it could be created only by the 'new man'. Which then came first: the chicken or the egg? Did the 'new man' have to make the 'new society'? Or did the 'new society' have to make the 'new man'? Not surprisingly, most discussion of the subject ended in deadlock.

In the early days of the Soviet state it was taken for granted that the problem would in practice solve itself. Had not history already supplied the answer? Had not Russian society already been transformed? The leaders and propagandists assumed, therefore, that the 'new society' would produce the 'new man' automatically. The writings of Lenin and his colleagues repeatedly stressed this view, which was shared for a time by the rest of the world. It soon grew evident, however, that the attainment of such an ideal was far from inevitable. The absence of private property by no means obviated greed. The elimination of an individual's economic power to exploit his fellows by no means obviated the lust for power in general and the crimes this engendered.

The Communist Party accordingly placed increasing emphasis on subjective factors. Subjective factors, it seemed, were essential both for the destruction of old social relationships and for the evolution of new social forms. Marxist doctrine proclaimed that social evolution resulted from the operation of an inner, esoteric law. But now it was reiterated that the time for the exclusion of voluntarism had not yet arrived. The inference from this premise was to have far-reaching effects. If the 'new man' still had to be created and could not emerge without the help of the 'new society', it followed that his creators had to be members of the party which had founded the 'new society', and that party members had to become his educators. The majority of Russian intellectuals who had acquiesced in the establishment of the Soviet régime now came into sharp conflict with it. If the 'new man' was to be the product of education why should his educators be selected from those whose sole qualification was the possession of political power and the means of enforcing it? As we were to see, argument alone proved insufficient for the resolution of this conflict.

'We have no need of self-appointed educators,' joked Party members. '*We* shall be the educators' – which meant turning the rest of the population into 'pupils'. So many 'pupils' found themselves unable to accept the grounds for setting their educators above them that great confusion ensued. The self-declared rights of the educators could hardly win assent from the majority of their countrymen.

The argument about whether human nature can be changed flared up within the Party itself, to be settled in the long run not by reason but by force, as political considerations dictated. The concept of the new education thus came to be discredited in the eyes of the population as a whole. Indeed, people doubted whether such education was even possible and whether it should be a Party monopoly if it were. The more honest Party members appreciated that the new education had to be based on rational concepts if it was not to degenerate into a mere system of mythology. On the other hand education based on common sense was hardly likely to suit the needs of Russia's ignorant millions only too accustomed to obeying ready-made orders from above. In this the Party perceived its advantage.

Among other things, the need to establish a monopoly over education aroused in the Party a desire to become monolithic.

*

One of the first people I met in a Siberian labour camp in the thirties was a man with whom I exchanged only a few words and never saw again. I met him one morning in early spring when the temperature, forty below zero, was subjecting the human body to unimaginable strains. This man, like the rest of us, was dressed in rags and looked utterly exhausted. Indeed his appearance corresponded exactly to my picture of how camp inmates ought to look, for I believed them all to be criminals and counter-revolutionaries. He told me that he had been arrested because he was a follower of Tolstoy, and that there were thousands like him scattered around the camps. Having outlined his views in businesslike tones he started to argue and became very excited. He realized that new arrivals like myself were communists, condemned by fellow-communists so that they, the latter, would stay in power. His chief interest was communist ideology and he evidently discussed it ceaselessly both in his own mind and in conversation with others.

'So you're a communist!' he exclaimed with an air of triumph. 'Well, there's one thing you don't know, but you soon will. Tolstoy was right. We can't build a "new society" with man as he is. First we have to re-make the human soul.' He winked after he made this statement, shook my hand and vanished. Although I never set eyes on him again I was to hear his point of view repeated by innumerable other people. The harder the State strove to create by force the 'new man', the ideal member of the 'new society', the stronger grew the doubts of its practicability. At this period repression was at its height. Compulsory re-education was a stated objective of official policy, and it was to be implemented in enormous labour camps. These camps had millions of inhabitants wrested from their usual surroundings. Their mentors were the tens of thousands of camp officials trained in the methods of re-education. Soviet society was at that moment rent by doubt. It was asking itself whether re-education not only failed to eliminate 'vices' but actually provoked fresh ones, and whether totally different methods ought not to be applied after a fresh start.

Official policy remained contradictory and confusing. Questions such as the Soviet attitude towards punishment and the character of Soviet justice, once considered answered, again seemed wide open. Was it not taught that no such being as the hopeless criminal existed? Was not rehabilitation available to all in Soviet society? It was believed that even the most vicious persons could be transformed into 'positive' elements. Yet, oddly enough, the more numerous the 'positive' elements were said to be, the larger the camps and the larger the quantity of 'material' considered suitable to enter them. To stifle opposition and stop all argument seemed the only way of putting an end to mental chaos. In camp we found that the moment conversation touched some fundamental issue the resulting conflict raised tempers to boiling-point. The only thing we could agree on was that the 'official' doctrine was wrong. Whatever the chances of providing society with new moral foundations in times to come, it was plain that the contradictions of our own day were too profound for these foundations to be laid now.

As it turned out, the State merely applied palliatives. At a given time given 'vices' were singled out and campaigns against them were launched. Often these 'vices' were described as leftovers from the 'old days'. Alternatively the régime harped upon the 'virtues' it had selected as basic and sermonized about them. But even in this restricted sense furtherance of the 'new morality' raised thorny problems. A murder remained a murder. If the victim of a murder happened to be the murderer's father or mother the offence was much aggravated. Yet if a son denounced his father or mother to the authorities at the behest of his educators and the authorities shot the parent involved, the boy was a 'hero', an example to other children and the object of adulation. A whole movement sprang up among small boys anxious to emulate the example of just such a hero, Pavel Morozov,* and become heroes in their turn.

Thus actions acknowledged by everybody as 'vices' were translated into 'virtues'. Articles were written lauding children for their denunciation of 'anti-social' parents who failed to hand over their quota of wheat, or clung to religion, or remained unwilling to break with formerly accepted moral values. Yet at the very same time other articles urged children not to disobey their parents and not to treat them harshly, and patricide and matricide were condemned as unspeakable crimes. How then could one distinguish right from wrong? To this day many Russians do not know.

Experience taught the average Russian that certain actions were regarded as praiseworthy and others as blameworthy. He was thus guided in separating right from wrong. But life is never quite so simple. Exceptions abound. The 'feature-writer' therefore stepped in to analyse such exceptions and call them right or wrong according to the rather abstract yardstick of 'political reality'. The 'feature-writer' was therefore to some degree a moral arbiter. I was anxious to meet one of them. What sort of people were they? Character was obviously of paramount importance in a moral arbiter and reliability counted for much in the absence of recognized standards. Were there enough people of character able to resolve moral dilemmas by intuition, if not according to the principles of logic and morality? Like many Russian and foreign communists I believed that argument about such fundamental matters led nowhere and that moral arbiters had to be sought out who could carry others with them by the force of example.

Such also was the 'official' line. It proclaimed the existence of such people. But these 'ideal' beings, of course, comprised the Party. Unfortunately the Party was in a constant state of change. Millions of people who belonged to it were at one moment considered 'good', and at the next moment 'bad'. The concept of a 'true' communist was therefore shown to be relative. Accordingly, if communists in general were not to be depended on, the 'feature-writers' were in a special position to offer guidance, especially as the Party had called on them to be moral arbiters.

*

Nobody could have represented the 'feature-writers' better than Agranovsky, who for many years had been a contributor to *Pravda*, the organ of the Party's Central Committee. During my internment at Norilsk in 1939 I heard that he was in the camp. Two things crossed my mind. First, the Central Committee deserved a black mark for its failure to devise more suitable retribution for a moral arbiter than internment. Second, I had a strong desire to make his acquaintance, to discover what he had been accused of, and particularly to try to understand his attitude towards himself, towards the Party and towards society at large. I had an inkling of his personality from a study of his articles, but now I also had the opportunity of laying bare whatever he concealed behind his public face and of judging how far – if at all – he had changed.

I knew he had been appointed to his post only after a long search for the man best fitted for it. Among his competitors were 'feature-writers' known both to the public and the Party: L. Sosnovsky,* an 'Old Bolshevik'; A. Zorich,* an old Party member and a brilliant and incisive writer; journalists like Ryklin, D. Zaslavsky* and Mikhail Koltsov, who joined the company later on. I did not then know that Koltsov, brother of Yefimov, one of the best Soviet cartoonists, had already been arrested because of some trouble over his behaviour during the Spanish Civil War, which he reported very sensitively for *Pravda*. Koltsov's readers knew that he had vanished but not that he had vanished behind the walls of the NKVD. We got this information later in the camp, discovering at the same time that many Soviet participants in the Spanish struggle had, like Koltsov, disappeared from view. The majority, including the recipients of decorations and distinctions, were arrested on their return from Spain and shot or imprisoned in the camps. But Koltsov was already dead when I learned these things. (Twenty years passed before he was rehabilitated and his books republished.)

My first impression of Agranovsky was favourable. He was modest in manner, gave considerable thought to any subject under review and tried to see it from many sides. Yet I must say that I expected greater depths in a Soviet moral arbiter. He told me that in 1938 he had been accused of complicity in a journalists' 'plot'. Familiar as he was with my past he realized that I had the outward formulae at my finger-tips but that I would wish to penetrate behind them. When we touched any serious problem, however, he grew evasive, drawing back into his shell like an experienced Party member. I understood his caution, for even years after one's sentence had been pronounced the danger of fresh charges remained.

An intimate talk could easily lead to accusations of making anti-Soviet propaganda. He might have wished to avoid all contact with his fellow-prisoners, but isolation was difficult in the camps and he soon became the centre of a circle in which it was tacitly understood that no-one should trespass beyond the official slogans. I therefore took it for granted that no ambiguous word should be uttered.

Agranovsky had qualified as a doctor and practised his profession for a short time before joining the Ministry of Public Health (owing to the shortage of good communist administrators). Since he could never hope to write in a camp, he reverted to his old calling and became a medical inspector. He was always ready to discuss his activities in this field even though a camp doctor invariably had to face a variety of moral issues. He insisted that his work had a social aspect and that part of his task was to improve the morale of prisoners. Yet he went about this task in a distinctly odd way. While he was prepared to assist the camp authorities in enforcing their rules, he was not prepared to help his fellow prisoners who pleaded for the amelioration of their conditions. The older Party members remembered him kindly as the author of influential articles in *Pravda*, but the rest, who looked to him as a doctor with a responsibility for easing their lot, came to hate him. Although serving a twenty-year sentence himself, he was regarded by them more as part of the administration than as a victim of it.

Agranovsky had not pleaded guilty to the charges laid against him. He and the others involved had been named by the NKVD, which at that time was controlled by Yezhov.* Not all of them had been arrested at once. A few at a time were brought in, since the 'confessions' of each group served to incriminate others and provide grounds for further arrests. During the second half of 1938 Yezhov's position was weakening and in an effort to strengthen it he stepped up the number of arrests. Harsh sentences fell upon those whose dossiers had been completed. Yezhov was brought down shortly afterwards because Stalin decided to replace him and discard some of his methods. With him went the heads of his departments, including the man who had invented the journalists' 'plot'. The eclipse of Yezhov and his colleagues saved a number of prominent journalists from impending arrest, among them Zaslavsky of *Pravda* and many people on the editorial boards of *Izvestiya* and its associated magazines.

News of these events reached Agranovsky in camp through letters he received from members of his family who were working for his release. He drew laughter from most of us because he thought his case would be dropped, a thing quite unheard of. But he had the last laugh. The changes in the NKVD following the dismissal of Yezhov and his team reportedly saved some fifty thousand people in the Soviet Union. It was as though a new manager had taken charge of a factory, discontinued production of a certain line of merchandise and cancelled existing orders for raw materials. In this manner thousands of cases were discarded.

Agranovsky, it seemed, was better acquainted with the workings of the NKVD than we were. At once he began writing appeals, not to Stalin or Vyshinsky,* like thousands of others, but to friends of his within the inner circle. After eighteen months his sentence was quashed. The reason was that Lavrenti Beria,* the new chief of the NKVD, either had to round up all those on Yezhov's lists or declare that the affair of the journalists' 'plot' was a mistake and free those already in prison and camp. Agranovsky was released in January 1941, rehabilitated and handed back his Party card. He did not return to Moscow but remained in Siberia. During his stay there war broke out and large numbers of people were evacuated eastwards from Moscow. He acted as correspondent of a Siberian newspaper and, although in poor health, continued to write articles about Soviet life and morals until he died several years later. *Pravda* published an obituary and he was buried with full honours. That his death at fifty-four was hastened by arrest and the treatment he received during the investigations and months of internment went unmentioned.[1]

The case of Agranovsky demonstrated to us how small the practical value was of discussions about Soviet ethics. He was a man who on orders from above had been elevated to the upper ranks of the Soviet hierarchy. He was arrested, tortured and sentenced on equally flimsy grounds. He was then freed and his good name

1. Two sons of Agranovsky became journalists in their turn and they are still well-known in the USSR.

restored merely because of changes within the apparatus of the NKVD. A few years later he was dead as a result of his experiences. His fate, shared by many others, emphasized the futility of philosophical debates of the kind which went on throughout the twenties and thirties and during the Second World War, and which have been revived since Stalin's death.

*

In 1936 when I was in the Butyrki prison I met an interesting man. We were in the same cell. He told me that his name was Parfyonov, and added, 'Don't mix me up with that swine of a writer Panfyorov who's always licking the boots of the régime.' A man of medium height, stocky, broad shouldered and typically Russian in appearance, he was of peasant Cossack stock but had grown up in Siberia. Everyone treated him with respect and I soon learned that he was a poet, an old Party member and in the past one of the chiefs of the Red partisans in Siberia. He had led his unit against Kolchak* and against the Japanese, and had acted as liaison officer between various Siberian Partisan H.Q.s and the Communist Party Centre.

After the Civil War was over he lived by writing novels, short stories and in particular popular songs, for which he wrote the music as well as the words. In 1935 he published a novel, *Public and Private*, in which he described the lives of various heroes of the Civil War and the difficulties they encountered when they had to face Soviet reality. It aroused both enthusiastic praise and harsh criticism. Eventually he was arrested and charged with Right-Wing deviationism.

When I first met him his case had been under investigation for nine months. He was very popular among the prisoners both on account of the stories he had to tell about life during the Civil War and because he used to hum his songs to them, although only in a low voice as it was forbidden to make a noise in the cells.

He had a particular reason for singing to us, for he claimed that many of his songs had become immensely popular and had been published with the alteration of only a word or two under the name of Lebedev-Kumach* or other writers. He often mentioned a partisan song which concluded with the words 'And our campaign ends at the Pacific Ocean'. This plagiarism made him very indignant; indeed he had good reason to be furious, for not only was he being defrauded of fame but also of the tens of thousands of roubles which these songs earned when broadcast and sung at concerts. (Not that he actually mentioned the financial side of the racket, but it certainly added to his anger.)

Parfyonov was a stubborn, irascible man, and he told us that he had had many quarrels with the Writers' Union and also with his publishers. He said that he had frequently written letters to the press defending his authorship, but that in spite of all this many of his works continued to circulate under the names of other writers. He was something of an anti-Semite and believed that Soviet literary circles were dominated by Jews and that his arrest was due to the wish of the literary clique to steal his fame and silence him for ever.

He had known most of the well-known Soviet writers; he was a friend of Yesenin,* had been patronized by Gorky* and had met Fadeyev* during his time in the Far East. A pre-revolutionary writer he much admired was Nikolay Leskov;* indeed he was so enthusiastic about his work that I got some of his books out of the prison library and also became a devotee, not because I liked his ideas but because I enjoyed the richness of his style.

Parfyonov had been on the board of the Moscow branch of the Writers' Union and gave me a lot of interesting background information about their hopes and squabbles. It seemed that these writers felt they were being victimized because of their attachment to the Russian tradition. But when Bukharin* appeared at their Congress in 1934 they took heart, believing that their views might now find support.

One thing they had wanted from the early days of the Union was that a special *Russian* Writers' Union should be created. The Leningrad and Rostov delegations were particularly forceful in support of this plan, arguing that, since the Union had Uzbek, Kirgiz and Ukrainian sections, it was reasonable that there should also be a Russian section which would not be submerged in the whole body of the Soviet Union of Writers. The proposal, however, came to nothing as it was regarded as chauvinistic in its implications.

Parfyonov's views on the subject seemed to me not very clear, for while he agreed with me that a Ukrainian writing in Russian would belong to the Russian section, he proposed to exclude Ehrenburg* because he wrote in French, and when I pointed out that he also wrote in Russian this did not make Parfyonov change his view.

In his interrogations Parfyonov could not refrain from criticizing Stalin on the grounds that his methods were not in keeping with the Russian spirit. Curiously enough, he was full of praise for Lev Trotsky,* whom he had met during the Civil War; he disagreed with his political views but had a high opinion of his character.

As for the other leaders the one he really admired was Kirov. He told me that Kirov's attitude was in keeping with the Russian cultural tradition, that he had stood up for Parfyonov and his friends on a number of difficult occasions and that he surrounded himself with literary men whom he helped. Another of Kirov's assets was that he was extremely hostile to Kaganovich,* whom Parfyonov considered to be the evil genius of the Central Committee, and whom he described as a petty, vain man who tried to push himself ahead at other people's expense and who was cruel, not only because he was carrying out a Stalinist policy but due also to his natural harshness. Parfyonov insisted that Kaganovich did not even know Russian properly, was totally ignorant of Russian literature, either modern or classical, and had no understanding of the cultural values of the Revolution or of the psychology of the intelligentsia. Parfyonov believed that Kaganovich had achieved his position only thanks to the part he had played in collectivization, which he had directed in the name of the Central Committee.

Parfyonov told me that during his interrogations he had attacked Kaganovich on all these counts but had been assured that no use would be made of it. This was no doubt due to the fact that in those days, while no criticism of Stalin was permitted, other leaders could be criticized with impunity. Unfortunately Parfyonov had also criticized the tyrant-in-chief; yet he regarded himself as a faithful member of the Party, hoped for support from those who had encouraged Russian nationalist writers, and believed that in the end he would be released. Meanwhile he continued to compose verses and tunes but, as writing material was not allowed in the prison, he had to behave like a mediaeval bard and only recite or sing his works to his companions.

His optimism about the future proved ill-founded; as a result of the pressure brought to bear on him during his interrogations he fell ill and was sent to hospital. I heard that for a long time he was moved from one hospital to another, still believing that one day he would be cleared. Then it was decided to use him in the Bukharin trial, after which he died; possibly he was shot.

In 1962 I read a strange article in the *Literaturnaya gazeta*. It stated that the copyright of one of the most popular partisan songs, a song that concluded with the words 'And our campaign ends at the Pacific Ocean' had been restored to its author, and I realized that Parfyonov's obstinacy had at last – *post mortem* – borne fruit.[2] Readers of the *Literaturnaya gazeta* must have been rather astonished to learn that the copyright of a song that was over forty years old and which had been sung innumerable times all over Russia, and abroad too, had at long last been attributed to its rightful composer. It is possible that Sholokhov,* himself a Cossack, was instrumental in seeing that this piece of posthumous justice was done, for Parfyonov used to tell me how critical Sholokhov's attitude had always been towards 'the people at the top'.

If we are to believe him, Parfyonov was not the only victim of literary pirates; even some of the leading writers were not beyond resorting to this practice. The reason is not far to seek, for popular songs brought with them fabulous renown and immense profits. Nor should anyone in the West, where serious writers cannot compete in these fields with pop singers, be too surprised that this should happen in Russia. Indeed, in the Soviet Union very mediocre culture had, besides its natural appeal, the direct support of Stalin. He was no doubt partly influenced by the low level of culture of those around him but he was also very anxious to please popular taste. Accessibility to the masses was his criterion for judging all creative work, which is why Stalin was so much against any experimental art, which could be appreciated only by the few. Everything that was written had to be understood by everyone, and to point to the glories of the régime.

2. This particular work had been appropriated by Sergey Alymov.

To some extent he was successful in getting the novels he wanted written; he was less successful in the field of drama, for it seems that lies are not very effective on the stage and plays which bear no relation to people's lives do not inspire the audience.

The songs Parfyonov wrote while he was still free were a gift to the régime, for they were both popular and, since they were based on partisan actions, celebrated real heroes. Those he wrote in prison were of a different order. I cannot quote any of them, but I remember that they were very sharp satires on life in the Butyrki prison and on what happened in the course of the interrogations.

I wonder whether any of them have survived. He told me that only once had he had the chance of writing a few down on paper, but that the guards had later confiscated them. They may still be in his file and perhaps one day they will be found and valued for their documentary interest.

*

Among the other writers whom I saw in prison in 1936 there were some who were wholly imbued with the Party spirit, who had followed the Party line in all their works – whether published or unpublished – and who had made every possible effort to say what they should and still more to avoid saying what they should not. How did they come to grief? Evidently the directives issued to purge this or that milieu included writers, not by name but by number. This was made clear to me not only by victims of this policy but also by a man who stood at the centre of the NKVD and who was responsible for carrying out its policy in regard to scientific workers, academicians and prominent literary figures.

This is not the place to go into the details of my meetings with him. But he was a highly educated man who had graduated in philosophy as well as literature, who had some literary taste and had no prejudice against intellectuals as such. His job was not to interfere in the writers' creative work or private lives; their morals were not his business any more than was their material welfare. He had only to look out for anti-State manifestations among them. I spoke to him not only in the thirties but in the fifties too, at a time when he could discuss these events in retrospect and could, if he wished, have put the blame on Beria, Merkulov,* Yezhov, or the police system in general. He could speak objectively because he had an alibi. But even then he argued that, in order to fulfil his task of protecting State security, he sometimes had to 'lock up' certain writers whom he knew to be legally irreproachable. Unless writers knew, year after year over a long time, that the slightest deviation would attract severe repression, he could not guarantee the virtual unanimity and 'rightness of thought' which were achieved in the thirties and forties. He argued that to ensure the complete security of the State there must be total unanimity of thought. This could be established only by the sense of total insecurity which terror alone could induce. There were many difficulties, according to this man. If, for instance, Kirshon* was arrested for specific words which he had actually written, and this was made known to other writers, the aim would not in fact be achieved, for the event would merely be a proof of an added need for caution. For the required 'fear of God' to exist, writers – especially important writers who could not be accused of anything – had to vanish for no known reason; later it was said that they had been shot as spies, diversionists and so forth. It was precisely this incomprehensible element, the fact that punishment fell at unexpected times and on unexpected victims, that created the general sense of insecurity and fear which was an incomparably stronger deterrent than any concrete accusation. In my meetings with arrested writers I became fully convinced of this, and an added proof is the fact that *all* of them were rehabilitated later, after Stalin's death, by the same Soviet authorities which had repressed them. The investigation and repression were *ad hominem* – not *ad rem*: a given number of people had to be eliminated from a given milieu; this was being done in every sphere. In the case of writers, these were generally to be people who had a potential moral influence over their colleagues.

It is true that some of those who were arrested had actually committed 'deviations', but such cases were treated lightly: they might be sentenced to three years and then released. A well known case is that of the script-writer Erdman; his crime was real – he had told some anecdote – and he was released after a few years. Much worse was the situation of those against whom there was nothing and who were arrested merely in order that tales could be spread about them. Such was the fate of Babel,* Pilnyak, Kirshon, Tarasov-Rodionov* and many others – writers who had a *good* Party reputation, who in their writings had tried their hardest to find ways of adapting themselves, and who were sentenced to long terms in concentration camps or even shot. The number of writers who escaped *all* forms of repression was very small, perhaps only a few dozen.

Playfully, or as a joke, members of the security services referred to their task as 'vaccination' or 'immunization': a man who had not had a taste of the Lubyanka in Moscow or the Kresty in Leningrad, who had not felt the hand of power upon him, was not immunized – not filled with the necessary fear. It was the obvious intention that arrests, but not the reason for them, should become known to the victims' families and circle of friends; the aim was to create the myth not only of the omnipotence and omnipresence of the NKVD but also – this I believe to be the essential purpose – of the incomprehensibility of its motives. It was a strange paradox: for twenty years all notions of a superhuman power presiding over human destiny had been extirpated by every means; now the notion had come back, not in an abstract but in a very concrete form. Just as people in the old days used to say 'we all walk under God', so now they said 'we all walk under the NKVD'. This summed up the popular sense of 'inscrutable ways', of the possibility that anyone might be struck down. Such were the methods which in the thirties confirmed the changes which most writers had voluntarily accepted in the twenties.

How painful the process of adaptation from the old to the new life had been I realized in the course of countless meetings over the twenty-odd years of my wanderings. The essence of what I discovered did not emerge so much from the conversations I had *with* people, in which they were explaining things to an outsider, as from conversations they had between themselves but at which I was present. My circumstances during these years were such that there could be virtually no secrets between the people I met. Life went on before the eyes of all and it almost needed more effort not to know what went on in the minds and hearts of one's friends than to find it out.

To illustrate the crisis and the change in the mentality of writers at that time I will speak of two of them who were then well-known and whom I first met in prison in 1936. They were there as the result of a 'gathering in' of authors of various sorts, abilities and opinions, some of them Party members and some non-Party.

One of them was a man whom I will call Nicholas Ivanovich and who had been through the First World War and the Civil War and had joined the Party in about 1917. He was thus a senior Party member, a man of some experience who had been encouraged in his literary work by such important writers of the time as Serafimovich,* Seyfullina* and Alexander Fadeyev. In the twenties he wrote for various Soviet papers and had already published several books. I must admit that I had not read him before and I got to know him only through our conversations. It became clear to me at once that he was a man of very strict principles. Indeed I felt a little doubtful about his fitness for his chosen career because he had so little humour or scepticism in his make-up. He took on trust whatever he was told by people whom he considered to be authoritative and he in his turn wished to be regarded as an authority by others.

The other writer, 'Peter Grigoryevich', had started his career in a more roundabout way. He did not tell me much about his origins, but he clearly did not belong to the worker or peasant class. He might have been the son of an official, doctor or lawyer in Tsarist times, for he had received a good education and a thorough grounding in literature, and for him the point of departure for his later work was the golden age of Russian writing which ended in the nineties. He was also keen on the literature of the early twentieth century, on symbolism, acmeism and particularly such writers as Blok* and Bryusov. However different the backgrounds of my two friends were, they had both found themselves in the same circumstances as early as the twenties. Peter Grigoryevich was a much more sensitive man than Nicholas Ivanovich, who was always pulling out the ideological stops. Nicholas believed that the main task of literature was to reach the 'broad masses' and he therefore considered that it was a waste of effort for writers to polish their work.

'What is important,' he said, 'is that the reader should really get my point, that he should be convinced.' 'In that case,' Peter broke in, 'for you the task of the writer is in no way different from that of the propagandist.' Nicholas thought a little and said: 'I wouldn't say that they were exactly the same. But I see no reason why a propagandist who is a good journalist shouldn't become a good writer. Indeed, a writer is a journalist who has developed to the maximum his capacity to be accessible to the broad masses.' Peter objected that, on the contrary, it was the writer with little talent who could easily become a journalist and a propagandist, and that what was essential in literature was something altogether different. This conversation brought out the essence of the difficulties of that time. Although both men stood with both feet firmly on the foundations of communist ideology, they could hardly open their mouths without discovering great differences in their attitude to letters. For Nicholas the essential point was the effect on the masses; for Peter the writer's purpose was to express his thoughts with as much clarity and beauty as he could achieve.

The interesting thing was that each believed his view of the function of the writer in society to be the one approved by the authorities. Indeed, until their arrest both had been in favour and had enjoyed the full approval of the publishing concerns and, so far as could be judged, also of the public. As a Party writer Nicholas could not, of course, remain outside the Party debates concerning literature in the twenties. In 1925 he was in Leningrad and when trouble arose between what was called the Zinovyev* Opposition and the general line of the Party he found himself, like many other Leningrad officials, on the side of the Opposition. Not that this had much effect on his writing, for arguments within the Party did not find open expression in literature. The Party apparatus had enough control over both authors and publishers to prevent anything that was obviously outside the general line from appearing in print. But the struggle became increasingly acute, and Nicholas found himself in danger of expulsion from the Party. He avoided this, and was merely sent for a time to a remote region. When he came back he was able, like many others, to resume his work.

Nevertheless, it was his participation in the Leningrad Opposition which served as a basis of the charges made against him ten or eleven years later, when I knew him. He argued that, whatever may have been his views, he had never in the preceding ten years infringed Party discipline or deviated from the 'general line' of the Party in his published or unpublished writings. The authorities' answer to this was 'Just you try', meaning that his conformity was taken for granted and proved nothing. The interrogators then read out to him a long list of his friends – past, present or merely potential – who supposedly belonged to various underground and terrorist groupings. It was on this that he was tried, without reference to what he had actually done. For this reason he believed himself still to be a champion of the Party line in literature, regardless of the fact that the Party already regarded him as a dangerous enemy.

Peter had joined the Party later, in about 1920. He had less Party experience than Nicholas, his origins were not as satisfactory and he had received less political training. For these reasons he took no part in important discussions within the Party. A man with a proper Marxist training would know exactly what tactics had been prescribed and how Marxist theory was to be applied in practice, but Peter knew only enough to be able to repeat the formulas by heart and quote the right statements from the papers. He was of course better educated and better read than men like Nicholas, but his training in Marxism was not sufficiently thorough. That is why he had avoided the danger of finding himself on the wrong side in inner Party arguments. His trouble was that he had taken an active part in discussions about literature. It was not that he had any doubts about the right of the Party to exercise its authority, or about communist principles. By 1934 that would have been unthinkable for the great majority of people engaged in any public activity. Indeed, Peter played a prominent role in forming the editorial policy of the magazine *Krasnaya nov* (*Red Virgin Soil*), which greatly affected all the current literary tendencies. He would not have been tolerated for a single day in any editorial office if he had had any doubts on matters of principle.

But there were other differences of opinion between the writers. One concerned the question of the origins of the Soviet literary tradition and of the authors to whom Soviet literature should look as examples. Even after the first Writers' Congress and when general agreement had been reached on the minimum credo to be accepted by anyone who wished to take part in Soviet literary life, there still remained a fairly wide sphere in which writers could differ among themselves.

The Magna Carta of writers was the speech made by Gorky at the Writers' Congress, echoes of which had reverberated throughout the Soviet Union and even abroad. In this 'Charter' Gorky had asserted that it was legitimate and indeed necessary to hold widely-ranging discussions among writers and students of letters, in which the various problems of practical creative work should be argued out. In this field Gorky was very liberal, and even twenty years later his views were being quoted in defence of such freedom of discussion and of tolerance of conflicting views.

Gorky, however, made the reservation that the criterion by which legitimate expression of opinion should be judged was loyalty to the Soviet State. What he said in effect was: 'Anything can be discussed. We will not hamper anyone or prosecute him for his views so long as he is loyal; such a man has as much right as we have to discuss any questions.'

The writers placed the widest interpretation on this statement, as Gorky probably intended. Gorky meant to create a large reserve of literary men on whom Soviet art could draw. It was only later – in 1935 and 1936 – that his magic formula turned out to be less simple than it looked and to contain an important ambiguity. The difficulty was to define 'loyalty to the State', of which there was no objective test.

An author might be working for the State, he might never have written anything disloyal or expressed a disloyal thought in a discussion, but this was still not regarded as an 'objective' proof of loyalty. Theoretically, it was impossible to know even oneself whether one was loyal or not. At any moment a writer's loyalty might be called in question, not by his fellow writers or the public, but by the Security Services of the State. This was the hidden meaning of the formula, and it was because of this that the formula itself was seen to be a trap. This was firmly believed by scores of writers I met in the thirties. There were even some people, especially among the younger generation, who insisted that Gorky must have

known what he was doing or else he would have added something
to define loyalty. Others excused Gorky on the grounds that, though
he did set the trap, he fell into it himself. They thought that in his
conversations with the authorities, perhaps with Stalin himself, he
had been convinced that his formula would be interpreted with
fairness, and the misinterpretation only came later, independently of
his wishes.

However this may be, it is a fact that countless writers who were
caught by it persisted during their interrogation in quoting Gorky
in their defence, but to no avail. The answer, given with a cynical
smile, was: '*You* may think that you are loyal, but *we* think differently'; or, 'We have material proof of your disloyalty'; or even,
'You will yourself give us the proof of your disloyalty'. So it went
on, and any pretext turned out to be good enough.

The question of the loyalty of a writer could easily be connected
with the question of the extent to which the disputes of the forties,
fifties and sixties of the nineteenth century still remained relevant.
The most important of them was the one between the 'Slavophils'
and the 'Westernizers' – a subject which might seem as abstract and
as remote from current politics as an argument between two schools
of archaeologists. But this was by no means the case, although Peter
was still naïve enough not to realize it. Even Nicholas was amazed
at how little Peter – in spite of his experience in the Party and in
spite of being a Russian born and bred – was aware that in everything that was said there was something unspoken and assumed.
Peter could only see the text – not the 'sub-text' – of what was
stated publicly, and he believed with complete sincerity that his
views before and after the Writers' Congress were irreproachable.

Even I had by now realized that there was already a tendency to
favour 'Slavophil' ideas. The idea was gaining ground that pro-
Western tendencies were inevitably 'bourgeois' and opposed to the
'popular' (*narodny*) element in the arts. Thus the Slavophils could
claim that they were closer to the people and better able to with-
stand influences from the West. This issue is still not resolved even
today.

But in the early thirties a man of letters could still think that
whether he chose to be a 'Slavophil' or a 'Westernizer' had nothing

to do with his loyalty, and that he could prefer Turgenev to Aksakov or Aksakov to Turgenev without this reflecting on his loyalty as a citizen. Alas, it was not so. Not only the case of Peter, but of many others I came across, proved that this was an issue over which a writer could easily break his neck.

Sometimes the investigators would simply resort to sophistry. 'True', a writer would be told, 'you wrote about the West as it was in the last century, but we know that all the time you have your eye on the West as it is today. You thought you were praising the Western Europe of the 1860s, but in fact you were defending the agents of our enemies.'

And so, despite his declarations of loyalty, his support of all official resolutions, the orthodoxy of the views which he expressed in articles and books, Peter was arrested in 1936, and the basis of the charge against him was his admiration for the Westernizers of a century before.

Here, then, were two men with very different backgrounds. One had been long and closely connected with the Party, and seemed almost too well aware of what went on inside it. The other had few such connections and had not been sufficiently aware of what was going on. The causes of their simultaneous downfall were very different, but the result was the same.

Whenever they argued in the camp about some basic problem, Nicholas still played the role of the 'Party organizer' watching over a man whose Party training was deficient and who was consequently mistaken on many points. Over and over again they came back to the same fundamental issue, which has still not been finally resolved today: is it merely the ability and the will to portray the truth which marks a genuine writer? Both agreed that truth was indispensable and that without it literature would be not only useless but something to be ashamed of. But whenever it came to defining truthfulness in the expression of ideas or the portrayal of events, the conversation became extremely vague. They talked as though they were unconscious of each other's statements, like two deaf men having an argument.

After many hours of discussion, back they were again at the question: 'Are we talking about the same truth? Or are there several truths?' And here Nicholas stood firmly on ground which Peter had willy-nilly to share: he defended what he called 'Party' truth. He asserted that in the Soviet Union, especially for a writer carrying the torch of enlightenment among the masses, 'Party' truth was the only truth that could exist. Peter would counter by asking why truth needed an adjective: was there not such a thing as truth in general? But Nicholas would quote from resolutions and indeed from Peter's own works to show how 'narrow' and 'inadequate' was the concept of absolute truth – of truth in itself – a concept often used by 'our enemies' to undermine the very foundations of the Party.

Yet when Peter was forced to agree that Party truth was indeed the only truth, the highest truth, the sum of all existing truth, neither he nor Nicholas found it at all easy to define what this truth was and how it differed from truth in general. Nicholas believed that in any conflict between the great and grandiose Party truth and the petty *truth-as-such* the one was bound either to evade or crush the other. Though Peter admitted that Party truth was the ground to be defended above all, he tried desperately in practice to preserve at least the remnants of the humble *truth-as-such*.

Here I must make a short digression: The discussion about *pravda* ('truth') and *istina* (also 'truth') went on endlessly in the camps and prisons. Russian was not my mother-tongue and I could not at first fathom the distinction, but a philologist explained it to me. The equivalent of 'truth', '*vérité*' or '*Wahrheit*', is *istina*, which denotes the correspondence between the notion and the objective reality. *Pravda* is a unique and specifically Russian concept: it means the higher concept of truth, a truth elevated to the rank of an idea. It is etymologically linked with *pravo* ('right' or 'law') and with *pravo-sudiye* ('process of justice'). A Russian who 'stands for *pravda*' or who 'struggles for *pravda*', does not stand or struggle for the sum of all kinds of truths, big and small, but for that truth which needs to be attained, truth in action, the ideal of conduct, the correspondence between acts and the demands of ethics. Perhaps in English one would have to say 'the right truth', or 'knowledge plus righteous-ness', but this splits the concept – and in the thirties this split created an abyss.

In the rooms of the NKVD and at Party meetings, *istina* was nothing – it was relative and it could easily be changed: only *pravda* was absolute. It seemed to me, as it must do to millions of others who have not been through this school, hard to understand how a philological distinction could have such an effect on the lives of so many. But in fact this small difference – this tyranny of *pravda* over *istina* – was the lever by which white was turned into black; no such dialectic had existed since the Inquisition. The notion of *pravda* was the basis of power.

In 1936 I eventually succeeded in persuading one of my most intelligent interrogators to answer my question: 'Are you not in the least interested in what actually happened? Do you really only want the pre-selected truth which is the "Party" truth?' He gave this trenchant reply: '*Pravda* is what appeared in today's leading article in *Pravda* [the newspaper]. Anything that doesn't fit into this framework is, for us, *objectively*, *not* true. What have we to do with your petty *istinas*?' And here followed the misquotation from Pushkin which one so often heard in the prisons and camps: 'The *pravda* that uplifts us is dearer to me than the mass of petty *istinas*'. Pushkin's verse in *The Hero*, about Napoleon, runs of course, 'The deception [*obman*] that uplifts us is dearer to me than the mass of petty *istinas*'. The epigraph to this poem is 'What is truth [*istina*]?'

For the interrogators the main thing was not to know the mass of *istinas* but to turn the lie they needed into *pravda*. A scholastic trick? But when such an abstraction has behind it the colossal power of the State and immense psychological pressure it becomes very concrete and hard to resist. This question, which has tormented Soviet intellectuals for decades, is, I believe, far from being solved either in Russia or in the outside world. And perhaps in the talks between Russia and the West the ideological differences will be seen to be reduced to this. Is there indeed a court of appeal which can distinguish between *istina* and *pravda*, which is empowered to choose between them? In Russia people feel this problem must be tackled, but so vast are the ruins that the work of restoration after chaos is difficult, and whether the problem can be resolved elsewhere I do not know.

Nicholas and Peter repeatedly arrived at deadlock, trying to define the relationship of *istina* to *pravda*. Yet Nicholas had certain advantages. It seemed at first as if Peter had both feet on the ground, while Nicholas relied on Party principles. Nicholas made pseudo-scientific analyses while Peter insisted that day is day and night is night. But in the course of their discussion it became clear that things were not so simple. Peter had to recognize that when, fifteen or so years previously he had become a Party man, he had in fact gone over to the position held by Nicholas. So although he insisted that he was a realist, that he started from *istina* – from what he actually saw and heard – he had in fact lost the right to say this. And Nicholas drove him to admit that in many instances he had acted in accordance not with *istina* but with *pravda*, with his duty as a member of the Party. He could no longer cling to *istina* because as a writer he had often followed and expressed the 'Party' truth. It was easy for Nicholas to prove this by quoting from Peter's work or from that of other writers whose whole task had been to leave aside the petty *istinas* and to make the reader conscious of *pravda*, by which was meant the 'Party' truth.

However, even when Peter had been forced to agree that *istina*, the factual and, as it might seem to foreigners, objective truth, was of little moment as compared with *pravda*, they still found it difficult to define what exactly *pravda* was in a given case, and they still differed on the exact relationship between the two. As Nicholas saw it, *pravda* was not only to be preferred but, where the two clashed, it should obliterate *istina*. Peter was always anxious to preserve a semblance of *istina*; he wanted either to avoid a head-on collision with *pravda* or to bring some *istina* in through the back door.

Of course, in their discussions neither writer in fact solved any concrete problem. It turned out later that neither Nicholas, an irreproachable Party propagandist, nor Peter, who had been the head of a department in the editorial offices of a literary journal, had been able to avoid their fate: both were forced to sign what the interrogators put before them and were sent to camp on precisely the same charges. I do not know how much they admitted or denied – in 1936 this made no difference – but their cases show the official attitude towards writers in general. Once it was decided to eliminate this or that author, he was arrested, his fate was sealed, and all the others were left to draw appropriate conclusions from his case.

I should add that neither the *istina* nor the *pravda* of what they were accused of was made public, and I am sure that when, twenty years later, their cases were re-examined (at a time when 'Party truth' required something different) the charges proved to be as empty as all the others. But at the time they were put down in the archives and the decision was regarded as final, and every such decision was a brick in the edifice of Soviet justice. The existence of such bricks has a great bearing on the whole of Soviet literature and thought, even now that the bricks have been shown to be hollow and to weigh so little.

CHAPTER 3

COMMUNISTS

THE natural reaction of a communist arrested in 1935 was to take it for granted that he was the victim of a misunderstanding which sooner or later would be cleared up. It was still believed that the population of Soviet prisons and camps consisted overwhelmingly of class enemies and counter-revolutionaries. The idea of finding oneself among such people was horrifying in itself and added to the shock of arrest.

After I had been sentenced to five years in camp I started on my journey east. The train was made up of *teplushkas* – goods wagons which were little better than cattle trucks; they were divided into cells holding eight prisoners each, and had a separate compartment for the guards. In charge of the convoy was a Colonel Arakcheyev; in spite of his name[1] he was not an unkindly man, and when a prisoner in another carriage asked for permission to talk to the 'foreign comrade' who was on the same train, Arakcheyev agreed.

The prisoner was a tall, broad-shouldered man with a weathered face, white beard and childlike blue eyes. He wore a Russian shirt, a

1. A Count Arakcheyev was Minister for War under Alexander I, and his name has become a byword for harsh discipline and strict control over personal freedoms.

peaked cap and trousers tucked into knee-high boots. I did not at once recognize his name, Nikolay Yemelyanov.

The reason he was anxious to meet me was that he belonged to that generation of worker communists who felt a close bond with the international communist movement. In return for what I could tell him about it, he told me the story of his life.

Yemelyanov was a worker who had lived on the shore of a lake near the small station of Razliv, not far from St Petersburg. He had been a Social Democrat since the 1890s and joined the Bolshevik party as soon as it was formed. In 1905 he was working at a factory near St Petersburg and took part in the revolutionary strikes and demonstrations, as he did again in February 1917. That summer Kerensky's Provisional Government, threatened by workers' and soldiers' demonstrations, this time in favour of the Soviets, decided on energetic measures against the Bolsheviks. On the 20th of July they ordered the arrest of several of the leaders, including Lenin and Zinovyev.

Yemelyanov, an experienced conspirator, was entrusted by the Party with the task of ensuring their escape. He hid Lenin and Zinovyev in the loft of his cottage in Razliv and later built them a shack on the shore of the lake. The whole family helped – Yemelyanov's wife, Nadezhda, who was herself a Party member, and most of his seven sons; only the youngest were outside the plot.

When the hay was in about the middle of August Lenin shaved off his beard and he and Zinovyev, disguised as firemen, were put on the engine of a night train to Finland. They returned by the same route on the eve of the October Revolution.

Lenin remained grateful to Yemelyanov to the end of his life. Yemelyanov was treated as a member of the family; he had a permanent pass to the Kremlin, and if he gave no sign of life for some time Lenin or Krupskaya* would enquire after him. The Zinovyevs also kept closely in touch with him.

After Lenin's death Yemelyanov's sons, now grown up, became involved with Zinovyev's Opposition group, but their connection with it was brief. They allowed themselves to be convinced of the wrongness of their stand and became genuinely loyal to the Stalin leadership.

Yemelyanov himself had ceased to be active in politics. His cottage and the shack had become a museum of which Yemelyanov was the guardian. An authority on the early history of the Party, he occasionally lectured on it to young communists, including members of the GPU. But as times changed he was considered less and less fitted for this task, since many of the names he mentioned were those of people who had fallen into disgrace. A still blacker mark against him was that he was suspected of having been given a copy of Lenin's 'political testament' – the notes in which Lenin had criticized most of the members of the Politbureau, Stalin in particular, and which the Politbureau decided to suppress.

In 1935 Yemelyanov and all his sons were arrested as oppositionists and received the usual sentence of five years in camp. Yemelyanov was tortured during his interrogation but admitted nothing.

*

After four days' journey we arrived at Mariinsk, a village in Siberia between Novosibirsk and Krasnoyarsk. It was April; the *taiga* was covered with snow and the rivers were still ice-bound. It was not the remoteness of the countryside that frightened us but the astonishing number of prisoners we found already in Mariinsk and saw arriving by every train from the West.

Mariinsk was divided into a transit camp, through which thousands of prisoners passed on their way to other camps, and into a small special camp (*osoby lagpunkt*) for some 250 men accused of KRTD (counter-revolutionary Trotskyist activities) and KRZD (counter-revolutionary Zinovyevist activities). It was there that Yemelyanov and I remained. We were housed in cattle-sheds. The cattle had been removed but nothing else had been done to make the sheds fit for human habitation. There was no floor and our bunks stood on the trampled snow.

We were woken up at six in the morning and marched off to work at seven with the usual warning from the guards: 'One step to the right or left and we shoot.' We worked on a building site where a spirit distillery was being put up, clearing the forest, building the roads, digging the foundations. We went back to our huts in the evening, had a meal and went to bed at ten.

We worked in sections of twenty-five men, each with its elected section leader. After a good deal of wrangling between the various political factions among the prisoners, Yemelyanov was elected to this post. His function carried various privileges: he received a bigger ration of bread and was not obliged to work as hard as the others. But he insisted on doing the same work as the rest of us because he wished to share our hardships.

I was given the additional function of 'welfare officer' (*kulturnik*), which meant distributing the mail and parcels. Because of this, my bunk was next to Yemelyanov's and we had, between us, a rare piece of furniture indeed – a cupboard. We became very close. One day Yemelyanov showed me his simple poem, entitled 'The Mysterious Shack'. It was all about Lenin's stay in Razliv, which had so influenced his own life. He often spoke of the past and puzzled about the future. What we had seen at the transit camp had given us the beginning of an idea of the colossal scale of the deportations and the huge number of the camps scattered throughout Siberia. We could no longer delude ourselves that, except in individual instances, the mass of the deportees were enemies of the people.

One night Yemelyanov woke me up to ask me what the international proletariat would say about this situation once they realized what was going on. Half asleep, I muttered that it was all a misunderstanding; it would soon be cleared up. This was the line which Party members still invariably adopted.

'You needn't say that to me,' Yemelyanov said. 'You and I know better.'

After a few months, the camp was inspected by a delegation of high-ranking security officials from Moscow, led by one of the heads of the Gulag organization, Belenky. Several of us knew the visitors – until recently we had been their colleagues in the Party apparatus, holding ranks similar to theirs. We exchanged a few words with them. As they were leaving the barrack, Yemelyanov barred their way.

'I want to ask one question,' he said.

'Yes, what is it?'

'Why am I here?'

They all knew who he was. They shuffled and muttered in

embarrassment among themselves. 'Don't you know?' one of them finally asked.

'No, I don't.' Yemelyanov's voice was full of despair. 'I'll die without knowing why I was sent here.'

The delegation pushed its way past him and left.

After the inspection, conditions in camp were slightly improved. Some of us received parcels. Yemelyanov got parcels and letters from Krupskaya and from Lenin's sister, Mariya Ulyanova. In one of her letters Krupskaya wrote: 'I wish we could do more for you, but we can't.'

In the summer, Yemelyanov fell ill. The camp authorities, who respected him, urged him to stop working, but he refused. Later in the year I was transferred from the camp and lost touch with him. It was not until 1954 that I heard of him again. He had been released and rehabilitated earlier than the rest of us and that summer the newspapers carried the news that he had been awarded the Order of Lenin. I was still in Siberia. I wrote to him and received a friendly answer from his son, Alexander, the only one who had survived the Terror. He said that his father was ill, but that he remembered me very well and hoped to see me soon. I was released in 1956 but had no chance to see Yemelyanov in Moscow during the short time I spent there before leaving for Poland.

By that time, Belenky and the rest of the delegation who had visited us in Mariinsk had themselves vanished in the purges.

*

Communists are accustomed to think big, and we had heard much about the gigantic plans for exploiting the natural resources of Siberia and the huge plants going up as part of the general industrialization of the country, which was to be achieved in record time. The reason for putting up the spirit distillery in Mariinsk was that this remote region offered exceptional facilities for growing countless acres of potatoes, but the idea of working on it was not inspiring, even when we learnt that more vodka was to be produced here than in any other place in the Soviet Union. We were driven as hard as though we were building a dam or a power station.

I spent eight months in Mariinsk. Our team was shifted from job to job. For ten hot days in July we carried loads of cement to the upper floor of one of the unfinished buildings. The men in the team were paired off, two to each load; they had to be carefully chosen according to size, strength and skill. An ill-matched pair could hold up the work of the whole team. Vasily Yurkin and I were a perfect match – equally short, equally unused to manual work, and though Yurkin had evidently once been stout, he had spent longer in prison than I had and now looked equally puny. To these ten days I owe a friendship which was of great value to me at a turning point in my life.

Ideological discussions in camp were forbidden. This had not always been so. Although, in the early years of the régime, its ideological opponents, such as Mensheviks[2] and Socialist Revolutionaries,[3] had been put in prison, the aim – at least in theory – was not to crush them physically or to put an end to their intellectual life but merely to segregate them from the rest of the population and prevent them from spreading their ideas. But the experience of Tsarist days had shown – as it was to show again under such reactionary governments as Pilsudski's* in Poland – that when communists and other socialists were imprisoned together in conditions where they could exchange their views and write, they created what were virtually universities for the disaffected. Stalin had learnt this lesson and when, at the end of the twenties, new 'corrective camps' were set up and began to fill with communists who were suspected of disagreeing with the new régime in the Party itself, very different instructions were issued to the prison and camp authorities. Any privileges which political prisoners had traditionally enjoyed were abolished. To justify this, it was explained to us while I was still at the Komintern that the new prisoners were not genuine ideological opponents but 'two-faced' criminals of a particularly vicious kind who merely masqueraded as communists; no treatment was too harsh for them. Under the new system of slave labour created in the camps intellectuals were put to the same crushing physical work as the rest, they were forbidden to

2. Originally applied to minority section of Russian Social Democratic Party in 1903. Russian socialist of the more moderate faction, and later party.

3. Party founded at the beginning of the twentieth century.

discuss their views and, to make sure that the orders were obeyed, an elaborate system of spies was created in the camps.

What prisoners usually talked about was food, their families, the chances of a letter or a parcel from home. Yet here and there, in spite of all the dangers, men who trusted one another talked about their abstract problems. They spoke in riddles, hints, quotations, aphorisms; they whispered in the barracks at night; they talked during the occasional few minutes' 'smoke' allowed in the course of the ten-hour working day, or during the hour's march to and from work. Had Yurkin and I had a longer experience of camp life and been more aware of its dangers, we might not have spoken as much as we did. As it was, from the moment we realized how much we had in common we seized every opportunity during the months we spent together in the same team and in the same hut. The passionate interest we found in this unending dialogue comforted us in our difficulties – the privations, the unfamiliar work, the jeers of our mates, who were exasperated by our weakness and inefficiency. I even remember looking forward to the next day as I thought out what subject I would raise with my older comrade and what questions I would ask him to try to relieve the intolerable pressure on my mind. We talked between one load of cement and another, during the 'smokes', on our way to and from work and on our rare days off.

Yurkin had been a Party member since 1914. As a student in Moscow before the war he had joined one of the revolutionary groups in the University. Though sharing the anti-war views of the Left, he later fought at the front, was decorated and made an ensign; he was also engaged in underground activities. He fought again and was wounded several times in the Civil War, while working as a Party propagandist. Then he went back to the University, took his degree and would have stayed on at the Philosophy Faculty had he not been directed to a post at the Ministry (in those days, the People's Commissariat) of Education. There was an acute shortage of communists who were university-trained men and well versed in the Party line; his services were valued accordingly and from 1925 he worked closely with Lunacharsky.*

At the end of the twenties the atmosphere changed at the Ministry as everywhere else. Lunacharsky was ousted, and so were most of his protégés. The new chief, Bubnov, until then Head of the Political Department of the Army, put in his own men. Yurkin returned to the Philosophy Faculty and to his work on Hegel. He published several books.

He continued to attend Party meetings and occasionally spoke and wrote on Party themes. But the current policy distressed him. His heart was no longer in politics – he preferred, he said, to 'cultivate his garden'. In his position, this was quite enough to make him suspect. He realized that he was more and more under a cloud and he was gradually relieved of his remaining responsibilities. Nevertheless, his arrest surprised him. He had not expected things to go so far. The charge was extremely vague and, exceptionally, no attempt was made to discredit his work as a scholar; yet he arrived in camp under special guard, as a 'dangerous criminal'.

An old communist, a philosopher and a native-born Russian, Yurkin was a boon to me at that time. He and I faced the same problem. We remained convinced communists. We felt that not we but the Party had changed. We were sure that the other communists in the camp were as puzzled as we were. There were too many of us, and the shock of the arrest had been too great for us to be satisfied with the explanation that each case was an 'individual mistake'. But only Yurkin and I knew each other sufficiently well to go into it more deeply, and we might have taken longer to get to the point if it had not been for an incident which took place early in our friendship.

One day we were summoned back to the camp in the middle of the afternoon. All the prisoners were assembled and the camp Commandant addressed us.

That morning, before dawn, we had been woken by two rifle shots. As soon as we were up, the rumour flew round the camp that one of the inmates, Conrad, had been shot by a guard. We saw his body on our way to work; it had been left lying in the yard for the investigating commission to examine when it arrived.

Conrad had been a good worker, a simple peasant from the Volga German Republic, and had only recently arrived in camp. The shock of his arrest, for no reason he could understand, and the sudden separation from his home and family had unhinged his mind. We had seen him wandering about the compound, muttering prayers and protesting his innocence; he could not sleep at night and often left his hut to walk around the yard. We were forbidden to go near the fence which surrounded the compound. That night, Conrad had wandered to within two yards of it. The guard had challenged him and fired a warning shot. Conrad paid no attention, and the guard shot him down. The whole camp was agog with the news but we were sent off to work without any explanation of the incident, though we were told that one would be given later if necessary.

This was the subject on which we were now addressed by the Commandant. The commission had established that Conrad had been shot while trying to escape. The Commandant urged us to be warned by this example: all infringements of Soviet law would be punished with the same severity. He then sent us back to work.

The prisoners dispersed in silence, picked up their tools and got into rank. Yurkin and I said nothing. Nor was there any conversation in the barrack that night.

We realized that the investigation had been a farce, for Conrad had never dreamed of breaking any law. He was too confused to know what he was doing. A few words from the guard would have sent him quietly back to his hut. But the guard had orders 'not to spare his bullets'. He may have hoped to gain promotion by his action. At any rate, the commission had approved it. We knew that at any moment any of us might share Conrad's fate. We also knew that neither in our camp nor in the countless others in which such tragedies must be taking place, would a single voice be raised in protest – not even the humblest appeal would be made for a re-examination of the evidence. The time for making protests was long past. Later it became clear that this passivity and submissiveness were widespread not only in the camps but throughout the country. The whole population was already then, in 1935, in such a state that any idea of revolt or even protest against any act of the authorities could hardly be thought of.

It was not until the following day that Yurkin spoke to me about it. I can still see him puffing furiously at his cigarette.

'Can you conceive of such a thing happening in 1917?' he asked me angrily.

I reminded him that I was not in Russia at the time, but that, surely, many people had been shot without trial and often by mistake.

'We were fighting the class enemy,' Yurkin said. 'We killed Tsarist officers, land-owners, bankers. But to kill a simple, innocent peasant in cold blood – we would never have dreamed of it. It was for the sake of such people that we knew we must crush the power of those who oppressed them, once and for all.'

I said that this indeed was the way in which we communists abroad had understood the Terror. It had shocked us by its cruelty but we defended it because we believed it to be unavoidable.

'It *was* unavoidable,' Yurkin said. 'But what is happening now would have filled Lenin with horror.'

Whenever he spoke of Lenin, Yurkin was transfigured. He had met him several times, had known Krupskaya at the Ministry of Education, and had many stories to tell about them. But what he talked about so much were not the details of Lenin's life but his views. He said that they had been totally distorted within a few years of his death.

It was true that at a superficial glance it was possible to think that nothing had changed. The State, with its organization, Security Forces and prisons, existed then, under Lenin, as it did now. Yet the whole content of the notion of the State had altered, and with it the relations between the Party leadership and its rank and file, between the Party and the people, and between the workers and the peasants. Lenin had stood for collective leadership. Whatever his disagreements with his colleagues he would never have settled an issue by himself or given an order in his name alone. The Party had genuinely stood for the vanguard of the people: it could never have brought about the October *coup d'état* if the people had not been behind it. There was only one enemy whom both were determined to fight – the outsiders, the bourgeoisie.

Only perhaps once or twice did Yurkin admit to me that the roots of the present evils might possibly go back to the earliest period after the takeover of power. For him, as for almost every Bolshevik

I spoke to before and after my arrest, the first years of the régime were a golden age. How then could the change have come about? How could the Revolution have turned upon itself and become the instrument of its own destruction in the hands of the man whom the revolutionaries themselves had put at their head?

I remember once asking him if the possibility of such a danger had ever occurred to them in those early days. 'Never,' he told me. 'We were too concerned with other dangers – dangers which had threatened every revolutionary movement in the past.'

In 1917, he explained, the leaders were obsessed by the lessons of history. Every popular uprising, from the days of Spartacus through the mediaeval peasant revolts to the Paris Commune of 1871, had foundered on two rocks: the disunity of the leaders and their unwillingness in the last resort to be sufficiently ruthless and use every means at their disposal to crush the enemy completely. As a result the enemy had always triumphed, the old order had been re-established and the costly work of overthrowing it had to be begun again. Each of the many Russian rebellions, down to the Revolution of 1905, had borne the same marks of what Pushkin had called 'meaningless Russian rioting'. This time the revolution was to be meaningful; it was to achieve its end. The leaders had learned enough from the past to make sure that the effort would not be wasted and the sacrifices would not be made in vain. It was this, Yurkin explained, that made them doubly stubborn in the face of every danger from outside and at every sign of inward weakening or of a wish to compromise and relent. 'There was no room in our minds,' he said, 'for the thought of a possible stab in the back.'

Yet this, it seemed, had been the real danger. How had it come about, and when? All we knew for certain was that it was now too late to ward it off.

I listened avidly to Yurkin. My own doubts about the rightness of the Party leadership were a torment to me: did they mean that I was not and never had been a genuine communist? But such a question addressed to Yurkin was unthinkable. He was one of the 'makers of the Revolution', one of those whose deeds were a legend to us. He had known the minds, the intentions and the plans of its leaders. Nor was he a simple man like Yemelyanov who had largely taken these plans on trust: he was an educated man and a trained ideologist.

*

We rarely had a day off. Officially we were supposed to get three a month, but, particularly in summer, we were lucky to have one in six weeks. We owed the one I remember to torrential rain which made work on the site impossible. It was evening. Some of the men were mending their clothes, others were playing cards (though this was forbidden), or sleeping, writing letters or, for all I knew, making up poetry. Yurkin lay on his bunk smoking, and we were talking as usual when we were joined by Belousov, a stocky, grey-haired man with work-roughened hands and slow in his speech.

I had noticed him before, particularly once when the letters were being distributed. Few of the prisoners had been in camp for long and most had kept up links with their families and friends. The arrival of the post was always a tremendous occasion. The men crowded together impatiently, shouted, grabbed their letters and went off to read and re-read them. They read them to each other and discussed them, looking for hidden meanings and hints of what was going on outside. Belousov was one of the few who remained unmoved. 'Don't you ever expect a letter?' another prisoner asked him. 'No,' Belousov said gruffly. 'Haven't you any family?' 'No.' 'No friends?' 'I've forbidden them to write to me.' He had evidently broken all his connections with the outside world.

Yet he was, on the whole, a cheerful, even-tempered old man. He was not in our brigade – he worked in a team of carpenters – but he often seemed on the point of speaking to us. On this occasion he dumped himself down on Yurkin's bunk and said:

'I've often heard you talking, comrades. You're educated men. I'd like to ask you some things I can't puzzle out for myself. Perhaps I can be useful to you as well. You always seem to be talking about theories. I can tell you facts you may not know about.'

We made him welcome and, as was the custom, he immediately launched into the story of his life.

That evening and the other conversations we were to have with him have stuck in my mind. Whether or not we helped him, he certainly helped me to understand many things.

Belousov was a peasant from a village near Tver, not very far from Moscow. Village life in his childhood was wretched, and many young men went off to the nearest town or as far as St Petersburg to try to earn more than the starvation wage they could get at home.

Belousov went to St Petersburg and at first was not much better off. But he was industrious, anxious to improve himself, and his needs were modest. In time he became a skilled metal worker and, in the early 1890s, got into touch with one of the newly formed Social Democratic Workers' groups. He soon showed that he had gifts as an organizer. He also found that he was being followed by the police, and moved to Moscow. In 1905 he was one of the founders of the Metal Workers' Union which was to play an important part in the revolutionary movement. The Union survived the reactionary years from 1906 to 1909, but Belousov, as its Chairman, was put in prison.

'So you got your first taste of prison thirty years ago!' said Yurkin.

'I was always in and out of prison. The odd thing is that when I was arrested this year they put me in the very cell in the Butyrki in which I was kept the first time. But in 1905 I wasn't there for long. They put me in for organizing strikes and distributing leaflets, but the only evidence came from Government spies and in those days that wasn't considered enough. That first spell in prison was part of my education. There were many interesting people to talk to. One of my cellmates was Kalinin* himself! We became great friends.'

'That's an influential friend to have! Have you tried to get him to help you now?'

Belousov frowned and shrugged his shoulders. 'A lot of water has flowed under the bridge since then.'

During the First World War Belousov, as a metal worker, was in a reserved occupation. He was sent to an ordnance factory, where he once again became a member of a revolutionary group. In 1916 the Metal Workers' Union was torn by a struggle for power between Bolsheviks and Mensheviks. Belousov was on the side of the

Bolsheviks and, from then on, became a professional Party organizer and propagandist. When he came to the Civil War I hurried him on: as two veterans, he and Yurkin could have spent the night exchanging reminiscences. What I wanted to know was the mood of the workers when the Civil War was won.

'To tell you the honest truth,' Belousov said, 'there were things that troubled some of us even before then.'

What troubled such worker communists as Belousov, it seemed, was that the Revolution had been made but the social order had not sufficiently changed. They put questions about this to the leaders who addressed them at political meetings. The leaders said: 'Wait! First we must crush our enemies.' This calmed some of their doubts, but did so less and less after the Civil War was over. 'We had won,' said Belousov. 'We were told, and we told ourselves, that we were living in a workers' State and that everything was in our hands. Yet how much power did we really have? It was difficult for us to understand. We were simple, uneducated people who had suddenly risen to prominence. We continued to ask questions, but the answers seemed ready-made and often too theoretical. Not Kalinin's though,' he grinned.

Belousov had kept up his contact with Kalinin. In *those* days, he stressed, Kalinin was still accessible. He encouraged people to talk at meetings, and he sometimes asked a group of his old friends to tea. The last time Belousov saw him was at such a gathering, at the beginning of NEP.[4]

'He was a good old man,' he said reminiscently. 'I bet you he had his own doubts about what was going on. How he resolved them I don't know. Certainly not by theories. He was not much better at that than we were.'

On that last occasion the friends talked as usual about the Civil War. Like other leaders Kalinin had toured the front and given pep talks to the troops. Exhausted, ill-fed and ill-clothed, they were sometimes difficult to handle. Kalinin never prepared his speech but he always found the right words to boost their morale.

Belousov recalled one turbulent meeting when a Red Army man

4. Lenin's New Economic Policy 1921–28, which favoured the peasants and permitted some measure of private trading.

had gone so far as to point at Kalinin's feet and ask why, if the government could afford shiny new gum-boots for him, the army was still going about with sodden and frozen feet. Other soldiers joined in, and Kalinin heard everyone out, asked permission to speak, got into his armoured car and took off his gum-boots. 'Here you are,' he said, throwing them into the crowd. 'Here's one and here's the other. Now, are you satisfied? I'm going home and I'll tell them: "The people have set up a people's state, they've elected their President, but they're too mean to keep him in gum-boots".' The joke was a great success. Everyone laughed and cheered.

This incident reminded Kalinin of another one like it. He was receiving a deputation of peasants. They had many grievances. It was true, they said, that they owned the land, the old masters were gone, but they were no better off than before. As usual, Kalinin tried to keep the conversation light, but one of them, who came from his own village and had known him as a child, broke in roughly: 'We're not here to be sidetracked by your jokes and proverbs. Just look at your feet. You've got good strong leather shoes – all we have are our old birch-bark sandals. Do you call that right? Is this what we fought for?' Kalinin changed his tone at once. 'Yes,' he said seriously, 'I do call it right. We've made the Revolution, but the way ahead is still hard and long. We have plenty of birch-bark but not enough leather. We must industrialize the country. When leather shoes are made by the million you'll all have them. Until then, it's shoes for me, bark sandals for you. You can go back to our village and say so.'

After telling us this story, Belousov sat silently looking at the rain outside the window.

'Did you think it was the right answer?' Yurkin asked him.

'It was and it wasn't . . . I never went to see him again . . . It was the way he said it that was wrong, somehow – with a hard look at *us*, as though the message was meant for us as well. But we were his old friends – he wasn't addressing a meeting of oppositionists. We went away feeling depressed – I more than the others, perhaps. All they felt at the time was that it was no use for a peasant to come to an important man who had been his childhood friend to talk to him about his troubles. It had become an impertinence. I ought to know better. In a way, I did know better. I was an old Bolshevik after all; I understood what politics is about. I knew that, Revolution or no Revolution, so long as there was not enough to go round, it was those who did the responsible work who ought to be secure from want. And Kalinin was a good man. He had suffered for the people. But how many of them were there like him? And how long would they keep the others in order? Already we could see that there were others, thousands of others, who were putting themselves above the people and abusing their privileges. Kalinin's shoes didn't bother me of course – but if even he could take the peasants' bark sandals so much for granted, what of all those others? Altogether, more and more this seemed to me the picture of what was going on around us. The Party was no longer a band of comrades and equals. There was an impassable gulf between us and the high-ups, just as there was between us – the Party – and the rest of the workers . . .'

'And what conclusions did you draw from all this?' Yurkin asked in a tense voice. 'What did you propose to do?'

'That's just the trouble . . . we didn't . . . When I talked to my friends I realized after a while that they felt exactly as I did. But we were simple, uneducated people. It was people like you, comrade, who ought to have given us a lead.'

'But you were an adult, experienced communist,' said Yurkin. 'You were working in Moscow. You must have known that you were not alone. You must have heard of the groups within the Party – Shlyapnikov's,* or Sapronov's and Smirnov's. What you are talking about is exactly what they were criticizing too – the inequality, the growing power of the apparatus, the fact that the voice of the ordinary workers was being suppressed or not sufficiently taken into account.'

Belousov shook his head. 'You're not a worker yourself, but you ought to understand the workers' mentality. We would have joined anyone – Shlyapnikov or Sapronov or Trotsky himself – if we had thought it would do any good. What we thought was needed was a shift of power or at least a change of attitude towards the workers. But whichever group won, it would only mean a change of personalities at the top. And there was something else. It seemed to us that already then, and especially after Lenin's death, it was too late. They were doomed to fail because a new order was already established. The Party was no longer the Party we had known. We no longer had its confidence. But the last thing we could do was to stop trusting it. It was our whole life. It was still the Party.'

'But what was it? An abstraction?'

'What do you mean?'

'A word. An idea. You could give it whatever meaning you chose.'

'Yes, if you like . . . It was what we believed in. Anyone who came to us in the name of the Party's Central Committee, we trusted in advance. He would solve our problems in the long run. It's difficult for me to explain it to you, especially to a comrade from abroad, but that's how it was. We *were* the Party and the State, and yet the State and the Party were somehow outside us. They were our religion, but they were no longer ourselves.'

'Wait a moment! This was before the struggle with the Opposition broke out. But already then you saw the Party and the Central Committee as two separate things? You believed it was the Central Committee that must do the thinking and the rest of the Party had only to obey?'

'Yes . . . We had our own ideas of course. But it was only when they were put into words by someone from the Central Committee that they became clear to us and carried authority. It was the Central Committee that established the general line, and the line must be right for everyone. We realized that this was a change of style – we old communists who had known what things had been like before the Revolution and immediately after it. This was just what we found so worrying.'

'And what did you propose to do?' Yurkin asked again.

'Not much . . . The one thing we could not conceive of was changing sides. The Civil War had divided the country, it had divided towns, villages and families. It was inconceivable for us to be on the wrong side of the dividing line – outside this State, this Party we had set up, on the side of those who had fought it and tried to restore what had been before it. It would have meant denying our whole lives. There were different personal solutions. One was to

"slide down the slope" – stop thinking about policies and social
justice, do what one was told, approve everything without reservation, and beyond this, look after oneself as best one could. People
fussed about their food, their clothes or their housing. Some of them
– a few – "degenerated", as the Party called it: they took to drink,
or extravagant living, or all the habits of the old upper class. For
them, when Lenin died the only problem was to find another
leader, and when Stalin rose to power they never asked themselves if
he was fit to take his place. For them obedience to him and to the
Central Committee was the whole of a Party member's duty. The
number of old Bolsheviks who did this was small but their example
was important, and it seemed that often it was precisely the
"degenerates" who got on. It was they who knew in advance which
view would prevail and become the general line. It was they who
got the jobs, the honours. A few others went to the opposite
extreme and sacrificed their jobs and positions; they protested, they
joined this or that opposition group. And others waited in doubt,
and tried to understand. There were also those who fell into despair.
They were some of the best. There were more suicides than is
generally known . . .'

'Can it be that you thought of this yourself?' Yurkin asked.

'No. I would have thought it cowardly, unworthy of a Bolshevik.
I was too well trained through years of underground struggle: a
Bolshevik never despaired, he looked to the future. But at that time
I had a great personal blow. I had a friend – Nadya. She was a
wonderful girl. I had known and loved her since 1917. During the
Civil War she fell into the hands of the Gaydamaks.[5] She was
tortured. It was a miracle that she escaped with her life. Then she
came to Moscow. She lived modestly in a small room in a flat
confiscated from one of the merchants. She studied at the Sverdlov
Institute. Just when all this confusion in the Party began she seemed
to drift away from me. I saw much less of her. I thought that there
was some misunderstanding between us. One day I went to see her.
Her door was locked and I could get no answer. I called the neighbours. They said she had not come out of her room for two days.
Finally we broke in. Nadya had shot herself the night before – she

5. Ukrainian nationalist soldiers.

had kept her revolver from the Civil War. The room was cluttered up with books and papers. Sorting them out, I came across her notes. I realized the struggle she had been through to understand what was happening and try to justify it to herself.'

The sense of disaster never left Belousov after Nadya's death. It prevented him from forming any close ties again.

Outwardly he prospered. By 1926 there was an acute shortage of experienced communists to replace those in the upper ranks of the administration who had been dismissed as Trotskyists or Zinovyevists. Belousov had never taken part in any opposition. He was promoted and given better pay and a better flat. All seemed to be going well with him. He decided to accept his lot. If everything he read in the papers clashed with his secret, ideal image of the Party, it also convinced him that to swim against the current was not only unpleasant and dangerous but utterly futile. What the Central Committee wanted it would achieve. He could only hope that somehow, mysteriously, what they wanted was good for the country.

'Had you no one to talk to?' Yurkin asked. 'Apart from Kalinin, you must have had other old comrades who were able to form an overall view of what was happening.'

'There was the Society of Old Bolsheviks, of course. It was a kind of club for us. It gave us a framework. It even gave us a lot of advantages. When food was short we had special rations. If we were ill we were sent to the best clinics. The Central Committee was anxious to show that there was no break, that they honoured the past.'

'You belonged officially to the "Old Guard"!'

'Yes. I had my place and my function. It all helped me to feel that I needn't go beyond it. And yet, you know, as the years went by, we gradually noticed that there was a change in our attitude . . . It's difficult to describe . . . Can you believe it – when, finally, in 1935, I was arrested, I felt a measure of relief! The fact is that for years past we Old Bolsheviks who lived in this new society, in this new State we had created with our own hands, had been living with fear and horror in our hearts – a horror more intense than anything we had felt in Tsarist times.'

'You! An Old Bolshevik! A founder of the Metal Workers' Union! You really thought it was worse than Tsarism?'

'Yes, I admit it to you now as I admitted it to myself even then. I knew that I could no more harbour anything against the State than against myself. But I also felt that every doubt, every thought in my mind was known. It was as if I was controlled by some unseen power, something that was waiting in the darkness. And when it finally pounced – when they came for me from the NKVD – I knew that this was what I had been waiting for all this time. At least it was some solution.'

We were silent after hearing this confession. It was the first one of its kind I had heard but I was to listen to many more from the communists I met in other camps and prisons. One thing struck me. Of those who were terrified long before their arrest, it was the simple people who felt the most vulnerable and defenceless. But once arrested, those who had not been in the Party for long believed that they would prove their innocence and be released. It was those like Belousov, who had been through the Revolution and Civil War, who had not a glimmer of hope from the first. However innocent their record, however long and faithfully they had served the Party, they were not surprised at being treated as dangerous criminals – they expected to be punished, kept in prison, and even put to death. They even expected their completely innocent friends and relations to be punished on their account. Such was their unconscious conviction that the State they had created was dangerous, and particularly dangerous to the men who had created it.

We heard the rest of Belousov's story on another evening. There wasn't much of it left to tell.

One day, shortly before the Party Congress of 1934, he had gone to see an old friend, Timofey, a Party member since 1902.

By this time Stalin's war against the peasants had been won. Collectivization had been achieved at an unimaginable cost. There were some small signs of improvement in agricultural production. But the workers' standard of living was still going down. Labour discipline was inhuman. Industrialization was in full spate and, once again, the human cost was not a matter for consideration.

As we now know, this was also the time when, although both the

Left and the Right had been defeated, there was a faint stirring of resistance from the 'moderates' among Stalin's supporters: they believed it was time to relax and make peace with the country. They must also have realized that, so far from slackening the pressure, Stalin had already made up his mind to unleash a Terror against the Party itself.

After tea with the family, Timofey took Belousov to his study and began to talk politics. Belousov was evasive. At last Timofey lost patience and asked him outright how he proposed to vote at the Congress. Wasn't it time, he suggested, for the Secretary, Stalin, to be replaced? Belousov looked at him in terror, rushed for his hat and coat, and left the house. Whenever after this he ran into Timofey at the Society of Old Bolsheviks he looked the other way.

Belousov was arrested in February 1935 and charged as a counter-revolutionary. He told us that, unlike many others at that time, his interrogator was an intelligent, educated and experienced man. No physical pressure was applied to the prisoner. He was told that it was useless for him to deny the charge – the weight of evidence was too great – and that, rather than play cat and mouse with him, the interrogator preferred to confront him with the chief witness against him.

Timofey was brought in. Belousov could scarcely recognize him. Clearly, his treatment had been very different from Belousov's. Equally clearly, he had given in and, though bitterly ashamed, could now only repeat what he had already told his accusers. He described his meeting with Belousov with complete accuracy.

Belousov's first reaction was that it proved his innocence. It was Timofey who had insisted on airing his views. Belousov had broken off the conversation at once and had thereafter avoided him like the plague. But the interrogator merely gave him a pitying look: 'Think of the times we live in! Kirov has just been murdered. We are having to investigate the highest in the land. Do you think that at a moment like this we would be doing our duty if we left our secret enemies at large?'

As soon as Belousov had learnt Timofey's views, the interrogator pointed out, he ought to have hurried to the nearest telephone and rung up the NKVD. His failure to do so proved that he was himself an oppositionist in his heart of hearts. After several months in prison he was condemned to five years in camp.

And yet, what had Timofey done? He had criticized one of the Party leaders and suggested that the Party Congress ought to exercise its constitutional right of replacing him. In the early days of the Party this could not conceivably have been regarded as a crime. Every communist was bound by a majority Party decision, *once it was made*. If the issue was prejudged today it was because loyalty to the Party was no longer anything but loyalty to its existing 'leadership', i.e., Stalin. In fact, Congress was being summoned less and less often and, as early as 1927, Stalin had told his intimates, from some of whom I was later to hear it, that the 'leadership' (his own) could no longer be changed except by force of arms.

And what about Belousov? From the interrogator's point of view his failure to denounce his friend had 'unmasked' his state of mind. From all Belousov had told us it was in fact clear that for years past he had done his best not to think about politics for fear of recognizing his own doubts about the wisdom of the leaders. It was this doubt that made him a 'hidden criminal', no less dangerous because his criminality was partly hidden even from himself.

Of course, in the early years this reasoning would have been recognized for the nonsense it was. In those days the doubts, the difficulties of a simple man, a communist who asked nothing but to serve the cause and the country, would have been the concern of his comrades. He would have opened his mind to them and they would have talked things out among themselves. Today he could not have confided in anyone without endangering his friends as well as himself: his doubts were the concern of the NKVD. Nothing could have been a clearer illustration of the change in the character of the Party, the change which so preoccupied Yurkin and myself.

It was late. Everyone else had gone to bed. We thanked Belousov warmly for telling us his story so frankly, and he left us. I wanted to be quiet but Yurkin kept nagging me in his schoolmasterish way:

'Now you see what we have come to. Mind you take this story to heart. This is what the Party is, and it's no good mixing it up in your mind with what the Party was. If you do, you're not a Marxist.'

At long last he wrapped himself in his blanket and said goodnight. But I couldn't sleep. When, occasionally, I dozed off, I had terrible dreams. A common theme ran through all of them: my best friends had ambushed me, fallen upon me and were trying to tear me to pieces with their teeth and nails. In between the nightmares I lay staring into the darkness, arguing endlessly with myself. What indeed had we come to? Yurkin was right. The situation must be faced. What did the new state of affairs mean for the Soviet workers? What were its implications for the proletariat of the world?

Just before dawn I heard people moving behind the partition; Belousov and most of the men in his team slept on the other side of the barrack. Here and there around me a man woke up, grunted, turned and went back to sleep; every moment of sleep was precious.

I tip-toed to the door and looked out. Some of the prisoners were being removed by the guards. They moved swiftly, speaking in whispers. I guessed what was happening: a convoy was setting off for another camp. Whenever prisoners were transferred they were rushed away quietly, suddenly, at night, so that they should not take advantage of saying goodbye to their friends to accept messages for other camps. Often a man, on waking in the morning, would find that his best friends had gone and know that by now they must be far away and he would probably never hear of them again.

An officer was picking names from a list. He had come to Belousov, and two guards were shaking him, but they could not wake him up. Tired after talking to us late into the night, he was sleeping like the dead. Finally one of them pinched him and he leapt up with a shout.

'Ssh . . . Quiet!' the guard hissed. 'Pick up your things and come along.'

Belousov stared at him, trying to collect his thoughts. The guard swore.

'Sorry, sorry, Your Honour . . . I'm just coming, Mister Supervisor.'

'*What* did you call me?'

Belousov pulled himself together. 'Sorry, sir . . . comrade, I mean

. . . It's just that I was having a dream. I thought I was back in the Butyrki in 1905 . . .'

The guards moved towards the door and I hurried out of the way. I could see nothing more. I only heard the old man grunt and walk heavily across the room.

In the morning I told Yurkin what had happened. After the two evenings we had spent with Belousov we both felt as though we were losing an old friend. Yurkin grinned:

'There you are, comrade. Comrade Belousov was here, Comrade Belousov has gone. Time to go to work.'

*

Soon after Belousov's departure the mood in the camp worsened. The weather was foul. There were rumours that we were all to be transferred to various other camps. The unremitting work had already told on the weaker of us; we were now pressed harder than ever. The distillery was nearly built, and the authorities were anxious to get the job finished on time.

' We did not in fact leave until December. It was bitterly cold – thirty-five degrees of frost already and the temperature still steadily going down. After a particularly gruelling period we were given a bonus for 'shock work' of up to twenty-five roubles; even Yurkin and I got five roubles each. We would have preferred a couple of days off. For weeks past, we had not had a moment to talk. Our problems remained unsolved.

Finally one morning all but a handful of the strongest, who remained to finish what was left to do, were marched off to the station. The usual string of *teplushkas* was waiting. The station was crowded with men from the transit camp as well as from ours. Yurkin and I tried to keep together, but we were separated.

The journey was a nightmare. The *teplushkas*, with nothing but their tightly shut and barred windows to distinguish them from ordinary cattle trucks, were unbearably crowded and stuffy. We were all of us exhausted when we started out, and many were ill. The sick received no attention on the journey; they were refused so much as a drink of water by the guards.

We arrived on a sullen morning and tumbled out of the stench and heat of the wagons into the frost. It hit us like a blow in the chest. People fainted, came to, picked themselves up and got into rank. I had found Yurkin in the crowd but I could scarcely recognize him. His face was green and he was almost too weak to lift up his bundle. I managed to remain beside him.

Our destination and even the direction in which the train was moving had, as usual, been kept a secret. We were now in mountainous country. When we got our breath back and looked round we were struck by its beauty. The road wound through a snow-covered valley; hills overgrown with forests of fir trees rose on all sides. The view reminded me of some parts of Switzerland. We discovered later that we were on our way to the large camp of Gornaya Shoriya, which lay in one of the most beautiful districts near the border of Siberia and Mongolia.

The convoy was almost a mile long. Of the handful of guards, armed with rifles, one walked in front showing the way, a few marched alongside and a couple followed with police dogs. If any one prisoner had tried to escape he would have been shot down at once, but if we had all banded together, even unarmed, we could easily have overpowered the guards. Needless to say, no such attempt was made.

We had shuffled on for several miles when the order was given to stop and rest. We were allowed to smoke. Yurkin fumbled in his pocket for the last of his tobacco, rolled a cigarette, and inhaled with pathetic eagerness.

'What are you thinking about?' he asked me with a smile.

'Nothing.' I was too busy gulping the fresh mountain air.

'Are you surprised there are so few guards?'

'Not particularly. They know we aren't going to escape.'

Yurkin coughed and spluttered, but his eyes had lit up with interest.

'That's just it. I've been thinking about it. I've got a theory.'

It was just like a continuation of our previous talks. His brain was ticking away as usual, and I prepared to listen as we sat shivering on the verge of the icy road.

'You know us, Russians, pretty well for a foreigner. But you didn't know us at the time of the Revolution or before. Of course we're fundamentally the same, but certain things have changed.

'For centuries the Russians had been meek and obedient to established authority. Occasionally there was an outbreak of violence, but its failure confirmed us in our belief that it was wrong to rebel. Then came the Revolution, the greatest revolution in history. It began in 1905: it was the same movement that reached its zenith in 1917. What the world saw now was not Russian rebels but Russian revolutionaries – Russians who had had enough of obedience and were prepared to break, destroy and uproot whatever stood in their way. The Party of Lenin, Lenin himself, embodied the revolutionary aspirations which had been suppressed for centuries past. For years the struggle went on. Then there was a moment of fatigue. It coincided with Lenin's death. It was time to pause, to rest, to look round; to re-assess the past and the future. The people had had enough of chaos, they wanted a framework again for their lives. They had had enough of destroying, and now they wanted to build. Not that they could have gone back or even wanted to go back to the old basis of society: they wanted to build on a new foundation. So the new state, the new order was built. Great changes took place very quickly – every year at such a time counts for a decade. The character of these changes was determined by two things. First, the old cadres were disappearing: they had always been in the forefront of the struggle, they had suffered great losses, and they were swamped by a great upsurge from below. Secondly, the revolutionary energy of the masses was exhausted. The people were no longer rebelling, they had gone back to being the meek, the unquestioning, those who accept authority. Look at us today. Several people died in the train. But did one of us struggle, protest, insist on a bit more air or a cupful of water for the sick, which might have kept them alive? Not one. A few years ago such a thing would have been unthinkable. This is the real essence of the change, the basis of the new order.'

'All of it imposed in the name of the Revolution and Lenin!'

Yurkin laughed. 'Well, you wouldn't expect it to be imposed in the name of the Church and the Tsar! The old order has vanished for ever – it can't come back because the people, the classes who supported it are no longer here. That's plain to everyone. That's why the new régime couldn't act in the name of the old even if it wanted to – but that doesn't mean it hasn't got a lot in common with it. Not everything, mind you – the Revolution was a great, momentous, irrevocable step. But nearly twenty years have gone by since then, and what replaced Tsarism has vanished in its turn – only that isn't nearly so clear to the people at large. We can't fight the régime of today in the name of the October Revolution – it's the régime that uses the name and the slogans of October to impose its own will and make the people obey and work: it's always easier to do this if you keep the appearance of continuity with the past. And it does get the people to work, it gets miracles out of them! And if it's busy liquidating October at the same time, that's something we've got to be realistic about and accept.'

'How can you say such a thing?' I protested indignantly. 'Is this where your dialectics get you? Are you telling me that history is a merry-go-round? That after all the sacrifices we have to accept being back at square one, faced with something perhaps even worse than Tsarism? Why did you "make the Revolution" in that case? Why didn't you listen to Plekhanov,* who said it was useless because, even if the revolutionaries won, their victory would do no good? Do you now believe he was right?'

Yurkin shrugged his shoulders. 'Perhaps he was, from some purely abstract, superhuman point of view. But we live in history, we deal in facts, not theories. The facts were such that the Revolution was inevitable. The Revolution was made by the people. When the Bolsheviks took over in 1917 they obeyed the people's will, they could not have done anything else. And the people themselves were powerless against the laws of history – they, too, could not have prevented what happened. You can call it fatalism if you like – I call it recognizing the laws of historical necessity.'

'And because of historical necessity ought we to look on passively at what's happening today?'

But the order had come to resume the march. Yurkin got up wearily. 'What else can we do? There are too few of us left, and w are worn out. Come along.'

We walked about fifteen miles that day, egged on by the usual lies – we had been told that the distance was seven. Hardly able to drag our feet we arrived at nightfall. The lights of the camp were shining through the woods. We stopped on the hillside in front of a row of dilapidated barracks. While we were waiting to be distributed between them Yurkin and I looked into one. Bunks in three tiers ran round the walls; the room was already overcrowded with sweating, half-naked, emaciated prisoners. Their faces seemed to us bestial. We drew back in horror, hoping we would be directed to another hut, but as it happened we had had a preview of the one that was to be our new home.

Yurkin bent down and with an effort picked up his pack. He looked at my appalled expression and smiled. 'Think it'll be the end of you, brother? Maybe it will. But I'm a Russian. I'll get used to it!'

CHAPTER 4

TROTSKYISTS

IN the spring of 1936 I was returned to Moscow from Gornaya Shoriya under the guard of an officer and a number of soldiers. When I got to the Lubyanka I was put for a time in a cell with an old man who was a convinced anarchist and had therefore been under arrest nearly all the time since the Revolution. Before long we started talking about the mass repressions and the thousands of prisoners who had recently been sentenced for Trotskyist activity. The anarchist thought that the main reason for all the misfortunes befalling Russia was the so-called dictatorship of the proletariat. In his opinion what was now happening was a direct result of the system set up by the Bolsheviks in 1917 and he thought that the repressions against Party members were a logical continuation of the 'reign of coercion' which he said was the root cause of every calamity. 'You communists complain about the repressions,' he would say, 'but in fact you're only getting what you deserve.' He said it was Lenin and Trotsky who had established one-party rule and thereby 'laid the basis for this mockery of the people in general and people of principle in particular'.

Although he criticized Trotsky in no uncertain terms as a person who bore much of the guilt for what was happening, the anarchist had many words of praise for him as an outstanding revolutionary figure and compared him favourably with Stalin. The fact that many young people thought of themselves as Trotskyists was itself an indication of Trotsky's personal worth. Had the roles been reversed, he said, it was highly unlikely that there would have been any Stalinists – personal followers of Stalin – at all.

Quite obviously Trotskyism in the thirties was very different from what it had been in the twenties. Trotsky's exile was not only an act of vengeance on Stalin's part and a means of beheading the opposition and paralysing its thinking and its capacity to criticize; it was also a clever tactical step which made it possible to mis-represent the movement, distort its image, and indeed replace it by something *called* 'Trotskyism' but invented by Stalin with the help of the secret police and of specialists in political provocation.

Trotsky's popularity in the Party and his personal influence right up to 1929 were such that exile was the maximum measure that could be applied to him. Stalin knew that Trotsky was the only one of his opponents who could never be forced to capitulate. He knew him better than perhaps even his closest friends and allies. So long as Trotsky was in Russia there existed a centre of gravity other than Stalin, and even Stalin's supporters felt that sooner or later he would have to come to terms with it. I was later to meet many people who had taken part in the liquidation of Trotskyism, but the possibility of the assassination or trial of Trotsky himself never so much as occurred to them, and even his exile was disapproved of by many. But had he been banished to some province of the Soviet Union his following would have continued to grow, and it already included even members of the Central Committee and the Politbureau; even Bukharin, who headed the ideological campaign against him, held him in great personal respect and could not conceive of the Party without him. Before Trotsky could be killed his base had to be destroyed; meanwhile he had both to exist and not exist: he had to be discredited.

How was this to be done? A precedent was provided by Lenin's treatment of the Mensheviks. Even after they had become harmless as a movement he still thought it necessary to expel their leaders from Russia, and he took the initiative himself. Kept in prison they would have been centres of resistance, and to kill them was impracticable – Lenin was too closely connected with them, there was not a sufficient pretext, and they could easily have become martyrs. Once they were abroad and writing in *Sotsialistichesky vestnik*,[1] however, they were as good as dead, ideologically and politically. Stalin followed this example. Whatever Trotsky did abroad, Stalin, fully in control of power, could misrepresent him and Trotsky had no adequate means of defence. His exile was a stroke of genius.

As early as 1925 there ceased to be room in Russia for both Stalin and Trotsky. It is true that Lenin had used lies, but only Stalin proved capable not only of saying the exact opposite of what he was doing but of forcing the whole Party to swear to what they knew to be untrue. To enforce the duty not merely to say but to think the opposite of what they knew to be the case was his personal triumph and basic to his régime. It could hardly have been achieved with Trotsky still in the country, but once he was abroad, Stalin realized it was possible as well as necessary to begin the liquidation of Trotsky's supporters, a great many of whom were people with minds of their own who were unwilling to give blind assent to anything just because it had been decided at the top. Many Trotskyists had joined the Party before 1917 and enjoyed the prestige of being old revolutionaries; some occupied powerful positions as Party officials. All such people, who would inevitably have doubts about Stalin's suitability as leader, who knew about Lenin's testament and the 'Trotskyist' opposition programme, and could judge Stalin's actions with this background in mind were automatically dangerous to Stalin and could spread the danger throughout the Party.

One such person was Karl Radek,* whom I had got to know when I first visited Moscow in 1925.[2] He was cultured, well-read and sophisticated, and I was struck by the unorthodox way in which

1. Newspaper founded in early twenties by Menshevik émigrés in Berlin.

2. I was never a member of the Trotskyist Opposition although, like almost everyone else at the time, I was accused of this among other things when I was arrested at the beginning of 1935. But I had many Trotskyist friends and I knew several of their leaders.

he stated orthodox views. I had indeed been warned that what I would hear from him were Party truths, but in their 'Radek version'. A friend of Lenin, he had always insisted on the basic identity of their opinions but also that his way of putting them across was his own business. His position had deteriorated since Lenin's death. He was head of the Eastern Desk of the Komintern but no longer shaping its general policy. He was not at the decision-making level of affairs but, rather, a brilliant popularizer of decisions taken by others. In this and in his knowledge of the international scene lay his value to Stalin, and he was allowed a freedom of speech denied to everyone else. He poked fun at friends and enemies alike, with a confidence which came of having got away with it for so long.

He spoke to me about a controversial issue. The German Government had come to power by crushing the uprising of 1923. What should our attitude towards it be? To my naïve astonishment, he said that we should back it, and that, although the German generals were the worst reactionaries of the lot, the Soviet and German General Staffs ought to come to an agreement on the supply of arms, military training and even the co-ordination of military plans.

Russia was totally isolated, he pointed out. The German reactionaries would be in the saddle for a long time to come. Seeckt and Hammerstein had suppressed German communism, but they resented Versailles and were therefore hostile to Britain and France. They were the enemies of Chamberlain, the man of the Intervention. We must take advantage of this split in the capitalist camp and 'widen every chink'. This was in the ultimate interests of world revolution. He tried hard to persuade me, a very young and inexperienced foreign communist, that this could not in any way stain our honour. He convinced me of his sincerity in so far as it was genuinely world revolution he was thinking of, and not the narrow interests of the Soviet Union.

His preoccupation with 'widening the chink' became an obsession after the Geneva conference at which Litvinov* first proposed general disarmament. Radek was a member of the delegation. He had been included partly because of his shrewd judgment on foreign affairs and partly as the friend of the British delegate

Henderson, then a Cabinet Minister, whom he had known through the International[3] from before the First World War.

Two things struck him at the Conference. America was resisting a demand by Japan for a revision of the ratio of Japanese to American war ships, fixed by treaty in 1922 at three to five. Radek asked the American delegate what would happen if Japan did not give in. The treaty would be scrapped, the American told him. There would be open competition instead and, as America had greater economic resources, her naval superiority over Japan would increase. In his report, Radek stressed the moral that what mattered in international relations was not diplomatic approaches or treaties but the economic strength to back them.

He also had unofficial talks with Henderson, who urged the Soviet delegates to accept whatever terms they could get from Britain and France because what Russia needed above all was time. They could have no idea, he told Radek, of how bitterly all other countries hated the Soviet Union, how determined they were to crush her at the first opportunity. Radek was so impressed that he not only reported to Stalin at once but insisted on a special directive to all foreign communist parties. If Henderson, the 'arch-opportunist', thought it necessary to give this private warning, how acute the danger must be!

For the next ten years and more, the Party was to be haunted by the danger of encirclement, the need to industrialize the country before the inevitable showdown, the need to gain time at whatever cost. Whoever could do this was the providentially appointed leader – in this lay much of Stalin's strength.

I saw Radek again in 1931. Friends had warned me that he had greatly changed. A lot had happened since our first meeting. He had been in the Opposition but, like the overwhelming majority, had capitulated after Trotsky's exile. Once again I accepted his good faith. He had believed in free discussion within the Party and had sided with Trotsky, 'the baited lion'. Now he held that monolithic unity under a single leader was vital to the Party's very survival, and

3. International Workmen's Association. The First International was founded in 1864 in London; the Second International was founded in 1889 in Paris; the Third International, i.e., Komintern, was founded in 1919 in Moscow.

was writing fulsome articles in praise of Stalin. But he was no longer the Radek I remembered and I avoided him from then on.

I was already in prison when I read his article on the arrest of Zinovyev and Kamenev.* He praised the measures taken after Kirov's murder, rejoiced that 'the prison doors had clanged on the Opposition' and called on communists to rally still more closely round Stalin. Some of my fellow prisoners frothed at the mouth – it was Radek who had urged them to join the Opposition! They were convinced he was acting out of nothing but cowardice and equally convinced that grovelling would not save his skin.

It seems in fact that Stalin had begun to suspect his loyalty. He trusted Vyshinsky and Zaslavsky, whom he regarded as Mensheviks and politicians who were finished and would never try to gain personal influence. But Radek was a brilliant journalist with a large following of his own. So was Bukharin. Both were editors of *Izvestiya*. It was no longer as a Trotskyist that Radek was dangerous, but he could still be a link between the former Trotskyists and the Right-Wing led by his friend Bukharin. Radek panicked, and evidently thought his only hope lay in more and more squalid self-abasement. He kow-towed and praised in advance whatever Stalin might do.

On the 31st of August 1936 came the news that Zinovyev and Kamenev had been condemned and shot. Radek was the radio commentator on a weekly programme given out in several languages. That evening he spoke for three hours. He quoted Vyshinsky's 'Death to the mad dogs!' and anathematized the 'traitors' and 'international fascists'. Shortly afterwards he himself was arrested.

His behaviour at the trial is well known. For three months he had fought his interrogators for his life. He denied his guilt. He admitted it, and implicated virtually every communist in a master plot – one was '50% Trotskyist', another '25%', a third '10%'. He was sentenced to ten years.

For a long time rumours circulated that Radek was merely being kept 'in a quiet place' and still employed as propagandist – how could Stalin possibly do without him? Again and again, his style was 'recognized' in this or that article.

I learnt the truth in 1938, from a man who had been in prison with him and had had the same interrogators. Very soon after the trial it was 'discovered' that Radek – who had 'confessed' to more than he was asked to, and had apparently made not the slightest effort to shield anyone – had concealed some evidence involving Tukhachevsky,* and he was condemned to death, though not executed at once. According to a Soviet publication of 1962, he died in 1939. That year, in preparation for the Finnish War, there was a massacre in the camps of former Party leaders – it was Beria's first act when he replaced Yezhov as head of the NKVD.

How had a man of such great gifts been reduced to so pitiful a role at his trial? Pressures were used which transformed men so that they were no longer themselves. I am not thinking only of tortures or drugs. Reading *Darkness at Noon* I was astonished that Koestler had understood how much could be achieved by such simple means as glaring lights, endless interrogation and a few primitive psychological devices. At some point the prisoner morally lost control, and then he became confused and could be made to say and think anything. This happened to perhaps seventy or eighty per cent of the accused. A few succeeded in committing suicide in time. Some died of exhaustion or went mad. A few held out to the end, or perhaps it was their interrogators who broke down first, the interrogation might be given up as useless and the prisoner either shot at once or condemned to death but left in prison to be disposed of later.

*

Pyatakov* was Deputy Commissar of Heavy Industry. He was responsible for much of the success of the early Five-Year Plans, but too intelligent to regard his achievement as a victory for socialism. This, to him, was inseparable from better conditions for the workers, from the trend towards a classless society, from certain cultural, moral and political standards – he noted their decline with distress. When Molotov* spoke of 'moral and political unity' at the Seventeenth Congress, this was not at all the same thing – to Pyatakov it meant the destruction of the very values he treasured.

I met him rarely but I heard about his state of mind from our common friend Münzenberg.* This was soon after I settled in

Moscow in 1932, when Münzenberg was also enlightening me on conditions in the country. I had noticed a steady worsening on each of my visits and I was struck by the inflation – it reminded me of Germany. The 180 roubles I had left with a friend in 1926 – he could have lived on this for three or four months – were worth as many kopecks when he returned them in 1931. From Münzenberg I learned that the workers' living standards had fallen to fifty per cent below the pre-1914 level, that in many places the peasants were in open revolt, and that millions were dying of starvation. This was the result of Stalin's forced collectivization of the land.

All communists believed in collectivization, but throughout the twenties it had been taken for granted that this would come about gradually, the success of one collective farm encouraging the peasants to set up another. The Trotskyists had wanted pressure brought on the richer farmers and were disconcerted by NEP, which favoured them. They were labelled extremists. But never in their wildest moments had they dreamed of liquidating five million *kulaks*[4] and 'socializing' agriculture at the cost of bringing production to a standstill. The German Socialist slogan '*Bauernnot ist Arbeitertod*' went back to before the war, and was well-known to the Trotskyists. While their chief concern was the workers, and they were willing to develop industry at some cost to the peasants, they at least foresaw the effect on both classes of the 'tribute' which Stalin levied and were as horrified at it as Bukharin, whom the peasants regarded as their friend.

There was another side of Soviet life which had struck such men as Pyatakov long before – the growth of inequality.

In the early years of the régime the ascetic tradition of the revolutionaries was maintained. One of its outward manifestations was the 'Party maximum' – the ceiling imposed on the earnings of Party members. At first this was very low – an official was paid scarcely more than a manual worker, though certain advantages went with a responsible job. Lenin set the tone by refusing an extra kopeck or slice of bread. Later the ceiling was raised, more money for expenses was allowed and it was possible to earn extra on the side by writing. Some people slipped into bourgeois ways, but this was

4. A moderately well-to-do peasant.

frowned on as a sign of 'degeneration'. NEP struck a further blow at the tradition, but as long as Lenin was alive something more than lip service was paid to it. A man might earn 120 roubles a month and use the special shops and restaurants opened for the privileged, but he was still not completely cut off from the rank and file of the Party or from the masses. The change came with Stalin and his high material rewards to his supporters. In preparation for the final struggle with the Opposition, the struggle against privilege was finally given up.

This last step was a doctrinal one. The old ideals of equality were labelled bourgeois, and by 1932 society had a new tone. A candidate for a job was more likely to get it if in spite of the universal shortage he was well fed, clothed and housed and sent his children to a good school – to have managed well for oneself was looked on as a qualification for managing the affairs of others. Modesty, asceticism and, above all, a compassionate preference for sharing the common fate were profoundly suspect. This was one of the reasons why the Society of Old Bolsheviks was disbanded, for many of its members shared these qualities.

In 1932 strikes broke out among the textile workers in the Ivanovo district. Provoked by famine and low pay, they were put down with more than usual ferocity by Kaganovich. Fairly high local officials were punished as well as the strikers. I learned the reason from a local Party Secretary. Outraged by the conditions, some Party officials were not satisfied with protesting to Moscow but insisted on sharing these conditions themselves. They and their wives boycotted the special shops, wore workers' clothes and stood in the food queues. It was for this that they were punished. As Kaganovich explained, the use of special shops by the privileged was Party policy – to boycott them was therefore aggression against the Government. It was a sign of aping the workers and following their moods – a dangerously subversive attitude. The leaders as much as the led had to respect the barrier of inequality.

Most people respected it. Material squalor led to moral degradation. There were more industrial workers than before but they no longer seemed to have a mind and will, they were no longer the workers who had made the Revolution. And few leaders escaped the corruption of power and prosperity in a world of poverty and famine.

Inequality had been one of the issues raised by the Trotskyists. But the majority who now conformed were demoralized by it as well, though they believed themselves to be still pure at heart.

There was something wild about them in those days. At their famous parties, vodka flowed and an old gypsy song was sung with the refrain: 'We'll booze away the lot, but we'll keep the concertina, and we'll make the bitches dance to our tune!' The concertina was their inner freedom, their integrity, their secret ideological 'core'. It was the justification of their hymns to Stalin, of their denial of the spirit of October, which they knew they were helping the 'bitches' to bury. It was recklessly ignored that every tenth guest at the party was an agent who would be reporting what they said.

Pyatakov kept his principles but, like so many others, took to the bottle. Just because he was bold, stubborn, shrewd and could not be seduced beyond some point fixed by his conscience, he knew that he had no future. It was said that in his last year at the Ministry he was often drunk at work, that he drank himself into DTs and wanted only to die. This did not come out at his trial.

The 'bitches' respected certain decencies. A man might be accused of crimes it was impossible for him to have committed, his relations might be shot for being his relations, but his private vices and family scandals, though used privately as a means of blackmail by the interrogators, were not made public knowledge. Not only did they know the facts – a former security worker told me of the conscientious efforts made to arrive at a true estimate of the prisoner's character. Whatever the grotesque charges in his dossier were, a concise paragraph correctly summed up his disposition, his virtues and his failings.

Towards the end of the second Five-Year Plan Pyatakov was given the Order of Lenin, thanked, praised in the highest terms by the Central Committee – and arrested. He had some experience of judicial procedure. He had been an unbending judge at the trial of the Socialist Revolutionaries in 1922. They were condemned to only ten years and released at the end of two. His own case was bound to end differently.

At the trial he confessed with seeming abandon. He was not a man to have been confused by his interrogators. But he knew too much about how things were done. There was only one discordant note. Some of the lies he told were too easy to disprove, as happened later when the evidence was published and studied in France. He had met his 'fellow-plotters' at places which did not exist, or on dates when they were known to be elsewhere. It was like him to make his gesture. Perhaps he had given away everything for fear of torture, but had reserved this one message for the historians.

*

A very different character was Ivan Smirnov, who led his own Trotskyist group. Of worker origin, he had been in the revolutionary underground and had commanded a detachment of partisans during the Civil War. He rose to a high position in the Post and Telegraph Service but always remained popular with the workers and close to them in his ways. When he lost his job at a time of unemployment and could have walked into another one with the help of his friends, he put on his cap and stood in the queue at the labour exchange.

Shocked by the growing bureaucracy and feeling that the Government was less and less communist in his meaning of the word, he joined the Trotskyist Opposition as soon as it was formed. He helped to organize it, signed its every declaration, freely voiced extremist views, and was in and out of trouble from as early as 1923. Later he acted as a link between scattered Trotskyist groups and continued openly to support the movement even after Trotsky's exile. He recanted in the end, though later than others. His apology to Stalin did not save him from arrest. He too confessed at his trial, but with certain important reservations.

He admitted his Trotskyist views, and said that it was logical for men who held them to go on to anti-Government and therefore 'counter-revolutionary' action. But he denied the existence of a 'centre' and a 'conspiracy', and would not be moved from this position however hard Vyshinsky pressed him. He must have concealed his intentions from his interrogators, or perhaps they were so anxious to include him in the show trial that he had managed to make a bargain. The Trotskyists lost a sturdy supporter by his death, but his 'capitulation' harmed them less than did those of many others.

There were some who never capitulated.

I met Trotsky's son Sergey in 1937. We were both waiting to be interrogated at the Lubyanka. The waiting-rooms were small bare cells known as 'kennels'. Normally each prisoner had a kennel to himself but the Lubyanka was overworked, busy officials rang each other up in search of a place for their charges, and sometimes two were made to share. Thus we spent several hours together one night in February.

For me it was a memorable meeting. Sergey had recently been brought back from Vorkuta. His case had been re-opened and he took a gloomy view of his prospects. My own seemed little better, and before long I was in fact sentenced to death. But for some reason Sergey said he had an intuition I would survive, and he gave me a message for his parents, should I ever see them.

He was about twenty-eight, a shortish, spare young man with a round face and a moustache. Unlike his brother, he had never taken the slightest interest in politics – he had even refused to join the Komsomol. He had a passion for books and was addicted to the circus. As a child, he had once run away and joined a travelling circus.

His relations were naturally worried by his irresponsible ways and even pointed out that they could damage his father's career. But he remained incorrigible. When his father found himself in the Opposition, he thought it only proved how right he himself had been in his bored indifference to the régime. He did well at school but hesitated a long time over the choice of a career. In the end he was trained as an architect.

When Trotsky was exiled in 1929, Stalin – in one of his unpredictable moments of generosity – allowed him to take his family and even his archives abroad. Sergey heard the news in some provincial town where he was working. He received an anxious message from his parents. Trotsky took the blackest possible view of the situation in Russia and foresaw the fate of all those who were connected with him. 'Think of the worst possible thing you can imagine and multiply it by ten,' he said to the friends who saw him off from Odessa. But Sergey was at the time in love with a girl who was unwilling to leave her family, and he refused to follow his parents abroad.

For a time it seemed as though his father's fears for him had been groundless. Not only did he escape the purges of the early thirties, but family friends who still had some influence found him a job. Only in 1935, after the murder of Kirov, was he summoned by the authorities and asked to make a public repudiation of his father. They explained that he had only to tell the truth – he had never got on with his parents or shared their views, and he had not accompanied them into exile. All he need add was that he now regarded them as enemies of their country. He refused on the grounds that he had always been apolitical – this was the reason for his differences with his father – and he would certainly not join in hounding him now. He lost his job but was not arrested until some months later.

Brought to Moscow in the autumn of 1936, he immediately went on hunger strike as a protest against his arrest. But the investigation was completed within ten days. He was sentenced to five years in a labour camp. In December he arrived in Vorkuta and for the first time found himself among followers of his father. They filled him with admiration.

While the great majority had 'capitulated', there remained a hard core of uncompromising Trotskyists, most of them in prisons and camps. They and their families had all been rounded up in the preceding months and concentrated in three large camps – Kolyma, Vorkuta and Norilsk. Sergey gave me the first news I received of those in Vorkuta.

I was not surprised at the impression they had made on him. I had met several since my arrest. Most of those I knew were intellectuals to whom Trotsky's views – less cut and dried than Lenin's – had appealed from early on. The majority were experienced revolutionaries who had fought in the Civil War but had joined the Opposition in the early twenties. A larger proportion than in other parties were members of national minorities, but all of them were fiery internationalists, intolerant of the very idea of local or Soviet nationalism and scarcely able to grasp the concept of nation. Had the term 'rootless cosmopolitans' been invented by then, it would certainly have been applied to the Trotskyists.

Purists, they feared the contamination of their doctrine above all else in the world. This had been the greatest obstacle to their co-operation with other groups and, even in the camp, they tended to keep to themselves. They had inherited this attitude from Trotsky. Lenin could he hard or flexible as it suited him. But Trotsky, even in exile, with almost every door shut in his face, could still use his time and his brilliant gifts on venomous polemics with Western socialist leaders. When I accused the Trotskyists of sectarianism, they said that what mattered was 'to keep the banner unsullied'.

Their fanaticism antagonized the majority of prisoners, and even those whom it attracted were not always made welcome. But their gloomy courage was proof against all temptations and threats.

I remember a former leader of the Armenian Komsomol. He had received a three-year sentence which ran out in 1937. Every prisoner's identity card bore the date of his release. One day, to my horror, he took out his card and, calmly smiling, altered the date from 1937 to 1987. He explained that he did not of course expect to be alive by then, but that as long as he lived he would remain a Trotskyist and would therefore have to stay in prison. Stalin was right, according to his lights, to keep the Trotskyists locked up. As for them, all they had to do now was to bear witness by suffering and dying for the truth.

When I told such people that, as politicians, they were 'opting out of history', they replied: 'That's what every opportunist tells us.'

Sergey found the conditions in the camp abominable, but his companions gave him a warm welcome for his father's sake and were themselves heartened by his presence. He remained as un-interested in their political and economic views as before, but he spoke with veneration of their independence of spirit and could even say that the weeks he had spent among them had been 'the happiest in his life'. He wanted his parents to hear about their friends and of his own change of heart, and his mother particularly to know that he was sorry for all the anxiety he had given her and that he was determined to die with dignity. He was shot a few weeks later. I was released in time to write to his mother but not to see her – she died before I reached Paris in 1962.

I heard more about Sergey from a friend of his who had had the same interrogator. When he asked for news of him, the official said: 'If his father sends a wagon-full of gold we might let him go.' But this was only a cruel joke. No such offer was made to Trotsky, and Sergey's fate must already have been decided when – perhaps in order to deprive his friends of the moral comfort of having a Trotsky among them – he was brought back from Vorkuta.

Many years were to pass before the world outside heard anything about their last, heroic stand and their death in the Northern forests. The main facts were published in *Sotsialistichesky vestnik* in New York (No. 10/11, 1961). I can only add the details I was able to piece together from the stories of Sergey and a few prisoners I met much later. That the extermination of the Trotskyists was decided on and carefully planned in Moscow is shown by the fact that the same system was followed in all three camps. But I heard more about Vorkuta than the other two.

There, in the autumn of 1936, the Trotskyists put certain demands to the authorities, such as to be allowed to live with their families and lodged separately from the criminals (wherever the political and criminal prisoners were mixed, persecution by the criminals was an added torment for the 'politicals'). They insisted that the conditions generally were more degrading than in any jail in a capitalist country.

The authorities refused and threatened them with reprisals. Then in October the Trotskyists with their wives and children declared a mass hunger strike. With the onset of the Siberian winter and in conditions deliberately planned to break them, this needed almost superhuman courage.

A few sympathizers joined them. Other prisoners – bribed by an extra slice of bread a day or broken by the threat of sharing the fate of the Trotskyists, or even out of 'conviction' (I met a few such people), were induced to side with the authorities – this is perhaps the blackest side of the affair. The camp radio broadcast speeches by former politicians who had arrived at a position curiously similar to that of some of Stalin's apologists even today. Stalin was the man of destiny. His victory was a historical necessity. Obedience to his will was a sacred duty to Lenin. Judged 'objectively' – whether they knew it or not – those who opposed him were 'enemy agents'.

The Trotskyists added to their stock of jokes. One gaunt hunger striker meeting another would ask: 'Why are you so gloomy?' The other replied: 'The Gestapo haven't sent me my allowance yet.'

The strike was kept up for three months. Even the children persisted, although the strike leaders begged the mothers to stop them because the sight was intolerable to the men.

Most of the strikers survived. Some were forcibly fed. Usually a man can do without water as well as food for about ten days. If he drinks, he can last out several weeks and, if he is forcibly fed, for five or six months, though his health is ruined.[5] Camp doctors boasted that no striker died in hospital; in fact, the hopeless cases were discharged and died a few days later.

After three months nearly all the strikers' demands were suddenly granted. A minority still refused to compromise but they were overruled. When, a fortnight later, all the concessions were withdrawn, it was too late to begin again, though some tried. The camp authorities justified their trick on the grounds that a successful strike would have made discipline impossible.

The end came in the summer of 1937. A *troyka* (a special investigation commission of three people) arrived from Moscow. The Trotskyists were put on special work and lodged at the brick factory. Some were put through a new and more severe interrogation.

One day in the autumn the brick factory was cordoned off by special guards. The prisoners were given two days' rations and their transfer to another camp was announced. This was astonishing news as by then the weather had virtually cut off all links with the rest of the world.

All that was known at Vorkuta for some time was that the Trotskyists – in their rags and with their two days' rations – were marched off into the forest at night, and that two days later the guards returned with only a few prisoners who had been included by mistake. But from them the news gradually leaked out.

A day's march away, the convoy came on a set of temporary

5. I held a long hunger strike twice, once for 44 days and once for 56.

shacks. There the prisoners were locked up. Their names were checked against a list and then, group by group, they were called out and machine-gunned. Some struggled, shouted slogans and fought the guards to the last. The guards, as usual on such occasions, were half drunk.

When it was over, the guards poured paraffin over the bodies and the rags and set them alight. For a long time the bonfire burned deep in the forest.

The camp commanders were notified of the names of a number of people who had been shot as bandits, saboteurs, or Trotskyist counter-revolutionaries. A few bandits had in fact been included, as well as a number of Trotskyists who had recanted long before.

This was the first massacre on such a scale – others were to follow during and after the War. By the end of 1937 hardly a member of the Trotskyist cadres was left in the three camps – only a few individuals were spared for special reasons.

The tracks were carefully covered up, for Stalin wanted to be able to rewrite history as well as make it. As secretly as the Trotskyists, the heads of the *troykas* which had condemned them, as well as members of the execution squads, were shot in 1938. The few who escaped by chance were those who had left the service.

In 1939 came the turn of Yezhov, whose orders they had carried out and by whose order most of them had died. The only announcement was of his transfer to another post, but he vanished completely.

CHAPTER 5

BUKHARIN AND HIS SCHOOL

STALIN wanted to deal with the Left-Wing of the Party before turning his attention to the Right. The Bukharinists were anxious to escape the fate of the Trotskyists and Bukharin himself was quite certain by 1929 that a period of oppression was beginning which would not stop at the *kulaks* but lead to a terrible disruption of society. His followers tried to adapt themselves to Stalin's requirements but several of them told me later that they had realized they were doomed long before their arrest. They could have attempted to restrain Stalin only if they had managed to appeal to the masses or to find support abroad. For a variety of reasons neither course was possible.

In 1932 Bukharin told his closest friends that he could see no way out. His own programme (of very gradual collectivization, etc.) had fitted the situation of 1928 but was now impossible. The peasants were so hostile that any relaxation or compromise was out of the question for it would endanger the régime itself. Abroad, diplomatic contacts were multiplying; the recognition that could have moderated the régime in the twenties now strengthened Stalin's position. The lack of Soviet and German communist opposition to Hitler in 1932 was no miscalculation; it was an attempt by Stalin to gain time and it came off. His opponents in the Soviet Union felt that any appeal for foreign help would now serve mainly to strengthen Nazism and weaken socialism. Those in power in Moscow in the thirties represented the interests of neither the workers nor the peasants but formed a new class which despised both. They wanted the Soviet Union to become strong, realized that it was weak and vulnerable, and yet found the general hostility of the world rather useful. In this atmosphere, therefore, the Bukharinists felt that in Russia there were nothing but tyrants and victims left. There was no solution to their predicament.

I had known Bukharin since 1925. In the Komintern he was second to Zinovyev who, as Chairman, kept organizational matters in his hands. Bukharin had less talent for administration and practical politics than either Trotsky or Stalin, but he was the most outstanding thinker in the Party since Lenin's death and as such invaluable to Stalin – a genius at manipulating the political machine but notoriously weak on theory.

If Lenin represented the first revolutionary generation of Bolsheviks and Trotsky the second, Bukharin belonged to the third – he was only in his thirties when I first met him. Of all the Politbureau, he had been the one who disagreed and argued with Lenin most often. They complemented each other, and their differences gave life and movement to the intellectual leadership. But he regarded himself as Lenin's pupil and imitated his manners, his resolute air and his crisp, dramatically simple way of expressing himself. It was the fashion, set by Lenin, to reduce the most involved political and philosophical notions to the simplest formulas. However, Bukharin's ideas were less clear cut, he was less shrewdly aware of their practical implications, and he relied rather more on brilliance of style.

It was said afterwards, when the hunt was up, that he was too dogmatic. His books may support this view, but in conversation he was warm, flexible and impressionable. He digressed freely, and you could feel that he was talking partly to make up his own mind. He was interested in what other people had to say. He drew out his subordinates, and never let them feel snubbed when a decision went against them. He surrounded himself with young people and students. They liked him and he influenced their ideas (for a time this was useful to Stalin, who had none of his expansive charm).

I was put in touch with him in February 1925, when our attitude to certain colonial questions was being defined. The Soviet view has changed little. Then, as now, the agrarian problem was regarded as basic. Lenin did not believe that peasants were capable of an international outlook. The nationalism of colonial populations ought, therefore, to be encouraged and used as a weapon against imperialism. They could be weaned from it later, with the growth of the proletariat and of political life. The Anti-Imperialist League had recently been formed, and Bukharin played a prominent part in it. His ideas were wider than Stalin's, he was more tolerant, less preoccupied with strengthening the Russian Party, and less inclined to thrust his views on others or to make a pro-Soviet attitude the condition of co-operation.

To him, as to Lenin, the period of 'stability' in the capitalist world meant a 'breathing space' for the Soviet Union to put her own affairs in order. If Zinovyev believed in having his ear to the ground to catch the moods of the workers and of the Party rank and file, Bukharin thought that the masses as a whole ought to be given time to assimilate the doctrine. The masses were still overwhelmingly peasant – the industrial proletariat was small and was itself rooted in the peasantry.

Bukharin therefore wanted a long period of peace both with the West and with the peasants. His slogan to them was 'Get rich!' The land was to be collectivized slowly, by example and consent. First there would be some large mechanized farms. Then, when the tractors were seen to pay, the peasantry would co-operate in forming the large units necessary for their use. Meanwhile, given an understanding with the West, industry could be financed with the help of foreign loans and concessions and everything was to be done to cement the 'workers' and peasants' alliance'. All this meant the continuation of NEP. How long Lenin meant it to continue we will never know, but certainly Bukharin wanted it to go on for a long time.

These were the ideas of the young Right-Wing intellectuals he led. There were others which the Left-Wing of the Party shared with the Right – better conditions for the workers, greater democracy within the Party, sufficient intellectual freedom for the arts and learning not to be stifled.

Moscow in 1925 was still the Moscow of the NEP period. The shops were full. A kilo of apples cost the equivalent of twopence in the market (a manual worker earned £4 or £5 a week). I knew that there were many things which foreigners did not see, but there was an unmistakable general air of prosperity and hope and even thinking people believed that active opponents of the régime amounted to no more than ten or fifteen thousand. By and large, the system seemed to have popular support. I was often to ask myself later whether my impression had been mistaken, but even in the thirties, in prison, when I discussed this with many people of various parties and social backgrounds, most of them agreed with me that a plebiscite in 1925 would have shown a clear majority for the Government.

In 1925 Bukharin's programme could scarcely even be considered 'Right-Wing' and it was certainly not a 'deviation'. It seemed, in fact, to be the programme of the Central Committee. Had it been carried out – had NEP continued, with its foreign loans, its prosperity for the countryside and food for the towns, it would have taken much longer to develop certain industries and collectivize most of the land, but the conditions of workers as well as peasants would have improved quickly. Civil liberties would have gained ground. Intellectual freedom, art, science and literature need not have been crushed. I am still not sure if the fear of the big farmers, the *kulaks*, was a bogey or to some extent justified. A more sophisticated, more experienced régime could perhaps have dealt with this problem by such means as taxation. Nothing could warrant a new explosion of civil war or the imposition of the Terror which forced collectivization necessitated.

But if the Left as well as the Right could have fulfilled most of their aspirations within a peacefully developing socialist democracy, there was a third faction which could not have been served in this way. This faction – Stalin and his associates – provoked and thrived on violence and injustice. They wanted peace at any price, though not particularly good relations, with foreign countries, but a sort of subdued war in their own country and a speedy development of heavy industry.

The Bukharinists, as I have said, did all they could to avoid provoking the NKVD although they knew that in any case they were almost certainly finished. Curiously enough, I had a very faint intimation of the Right Opposition about a year before the great show trial of Bukharin and his alleged collaborators. This was during my third interrogation, the one that ended in my first death sentence. I was questioned on various conversations which I might have witnessed. One of these concerned Yagoda,* head of the NKVD at the time of the Kirov murder and later to be tried with Bukharin in 1938. At this time (early 1937), he had only been moved to another post – that of Minister of Communications, which had previously been held by Rykov.* Such a move boded ill, but he was still a minister when I was asked to confirm that Bukharin had claimed him to be 'one of us'. I looked up at the wall above the interrogator's head where a portrait of Yagoda still hung and naïvely asked the meaning of the question. The interrogator laughed and said: 'If we ask you, you can be sure we know what we are about.' Clearly an attempt was being made to involve Yagoda. I assumed that no concrete evidence had been found against the Right and that a far-fetched plot was being constructed. In fact, Bukharin's case was put together very crudely; it was clear on the one hand that the 'experts' in the NKVD could by now concoct anything they liked and on the other that they had found no acts on which to base their accusations. However, cautious as they were in action, the Rightists had for years talked unreservedly among themselves. Given the spy system which was now developed to perfection, this was bound to get known. From 1932, when collectivization was proclaimed by Stalin to be a resounding success and was regarded by nearly everybody else as a colossal failure, they became increasingly outspoken in private. I was asked – in vain, of course – to supply some details about these conversations. It was a whole year before the authorities felt they had enough material for the trial to be opened.

There are many accounts of the liquidation of the Right-Wing leaders. I want to mention here only what I heard about the death of Tomsky.* He was a man who was closely linked with the workers and believed in the independent role of the Trade Unions. This became apparent in connection with the Anglo-Russian Committee in 1926. I knew of this at the time through my work in the Komintern. The Committee aroused great enthusiasm abroad where it was hoped that other such forms of co-operation with the Soviet workers would follow. Purcell visited Moscow, money was collected for the General Strike, all this activity was officially encouraged, but many members of the Komintern took a cynical view of it. For my part, I hoped that the way was being opened to mutual understanding and co-operation with the Western Trade Unions and ultimately with the social democratic masses abroad. I spoke of this to Manuilsky* who listened patiently. When I stopped I realized how naïve I was; he told me that for a machine part – he meant the Anglo-Russian Committee – to be useful it had to be made of metal, but this was a machine part made of s——. Naturally, I didn't argue: it was my duty to understand what he meant, as indeed I did. The conviction had already been formed that no understanding with the British Trade Unions was possible. A couple of years later the policy of 'class against class' was proclaimed, which meant that the communist Parties were the only representatives of the working class and no understanding between workers and employers was possible. As a result, all the committees of co-operation between communists and social democrats were ultimately broken up. Had I not heard Manuilsky, I might have been completely taken in by the later attacks on the TUC, which was accused of betraying and defeating the General Strike and made responsible for the failure of Anglo-Soviet understanding. No confidence had in fact ever been placed in the TUC and the General Strike was a complete surprise, though when it broke out the Komintern did its best to take it over and spread the movement to other countries. The slogan was actually launched: 'Unity of the working class headed by the committee of unity', i.e., the committee of Soviet and English Trade Union leaders. It was at just this moment that Manuilsky deflated me. I was later to come across many examples of such double talk: whatever the outward enthusiasm of Soviet Komintern officials, their private assessment of any situation was always extremely sober, uninfluenced by sentiment and purposeful in the sense of being subordinated to the best interests of the Soviet Party.

Tomsky was one of the chief members of the Anglo-Russian Committee and appears to have acted in good faith. He was in direct contact with the English and seemed to think that there were some real prospects of Trade Union co-operation. As someone who genuinely represented the workers he favoured this. Before long he was removed from the Politbureau and from any active part in politics. When his name was mentioned at Zinovyev's trial in 1936 he concluded that Stalin had finished with him. After the trial his suicide was briefly announced. Later I met one of his Trade Union colleagues who told me of a conversation with him after he had been removed from his post. At the end of a long discussion about what was wrong with the Soviet Union in the thirties, he said: 'Well, comrades, it looked as though we were making a railway (*chugunka*) but it turned out to be an inkstand (*chernilnitsa*).' He meant that there was no hope of righting anything by reforms, because a whole generation had spent itself in trying to build a just society – this was progress, 'the railway' – but had failed: the only result was a flood of ink and empty words. I met my informant in 1937 when this saying was fresh in his mind. Later I heard it repeated by many who no longer knew who had said it first.

If Tomsky was doomed it was obvious that Bukharin had no chance at all of survival. Stalin had long disliked him as an intellectual and known that Bukharin made jokes about Stalin's Georgian accent, his ignorance of the West, low cultural level, and so on. This did not stop him from getting Bukharin to draft the Stalin Constitution for him, a chance which the former used to define communist theory in keeping, as he believed, with the proletarian dictatorship and Leninism. For his part Stalin thought that such things as the secret ballot could well be afforded in theory – given the actual practice. I am sure that when he was doing this job Bukharin was neither a 'liberal' nor a cynic, though I doubt whether he realized that the new Constitution was going to be used directly against himself and his supporters a few months later.

Bukharin had been removed from the Komintern in 1929 and in the thirties I met him only from time to time. He had virtually no power or even influence on decision-making, yet at least two facts show that in spite of his inactivity, silence and caution his very existence continued to be dangerous to Stalin. The more Bukharin was proved right by events and the Party cadres realized that he had told them the truth about the peasant situation, the more Stalin needed to get rid of him.

One indication of this was his role as editor of *Izvestiya*. Hard as he tried to show no personal initiative or ambition and strictly as he was hemmed in on all sides, within months of his appointment he raised the level of the paper so much that, without anyone trying to increase its circulation, it was clearly the best and most popular newspaper in the Soviet Union. He proved an exceptionally gifted editor. Just when *Pravda* had turned into 'Economic News', as people said, filled with nothing but figures and reports of speeches, *Izvestiya* became quite readable. Bukharin employed the best Russian and foreign journalists. He wrote little himself, so as not to put himself forward, but his editorship gave life and sparkle to every issue, and the paper attracted universal interest. The foreign editor was Bukharin's old friend and brilliant journalist, Karl Radek. The two of them made a remarkable combination. But all this proved their continued popularity to Stalin, who followed the paper jealously. Although he stayed in the background and was not at the decision-making level, Bukharin continued to threaten him by his very existence. From time to time Bukharin tried to give up his post and devote himself to academic work – he was one of the oldest Party academicians. But he always failed – the Politbureau decided against this and Stalin himself let it be known that he would regard any attempt by Bukharin to leave his post as sabotage. This happened whenever oppositionists tried to give up work which they thought too dangerous to themselves. No Party member could, of course, refuse the job he was offered; he could not even keep away from it for more than a very short time. Once in 1937, when we were discussing this in the Solovki prison, one of us pointed out that no Soviet Party member had the rights of any grocer in Vienna or Paris, even the right to pick up his hat and close his shop if he was fed up or wanted a change. Even those who had never been abroad knew that this kind of freedom existed in the West in spite of capitalist slavery. Even a rank and file member who tried to 'pick up his hat' and give up the job allocated to him by the Party would at once fall under suspicion of sabotage – even if all he wanted was a few weeks off. Clearly Bukharin could hardly take a day off from the job imposed upon him by his mortal enemy Stalin.

I must now mention an incident from that shadowy period of Bukharin's life. It was during the brief period of the brightest 'liberalism' the régime had known since the death of Lenin – between the Seventeenth Congress in January and February 1934 and the murder of Kirov in December 1934. Stalin was trying to convince the people that the régime had changed its character and that his aim was now to unite all groups and sections of society. He had just declared collectivization to be a complete success and his name was raised far above Lenin's and above anything even his own supporters had expected. One of his devices at this stage was to make use of people who had differed from him in the past, giving them responsible Party jobs. At the height of this 'liberal' period, in the summer of 1934, the first Writers' Congress was held. This was when Gorky made his famous definition of literary freedom – 'freedom for all those loyal to the Party'. Radek spoke on foreign literature and Bukharin on poetry. He was welcomed with a storm of applause, his speech was interrupted by outbursts of noisy praise and when he finished it seemed that the ovation would never stop. Bukharin stood on the platform, pale and looking as though he was frightened to death; as he was going out he said in a low voice to a few of his friends, so one of them told me: 'What have you done? You have signed my death warrant.' So indeed it was. The ovation was noted by the authorities and though they said it came from the small group of his supporters Stalin realized that in spite of being out of politics, Bukharin was the idol of the young intelligentsia.

This incident was told to me by a friend of his, a member of his 'little school'. This was a group of young people, mostly students, from Party colleges who were closely linked with him. Its best-known leaders were the brothers Slepkov, Stetsky, Maretsky and Eichenwald and it included many exceptionally gifted young people who by their training and theoretical approach were wholly on Bukharin's side. I later got to know several of the leaders of this group whose signatures under press articles were regarded almost as Bukharin's pseudonyms. I should like to say something about only one of them, Alexander Yulyevich Eichenwald, whom I met in the Far North in 1937. He was about thirty-two, one of the leading figures among the Party youth and perhaps the most outstanding pupil of Bukharin. Such young men were drawn by Bukharin into what was called the 'scholarly front'. Alexander was a philosopher who took little interest in politics as such, though when Bukharin was editor of *Pravda* and was in the thick of the fight against the Left, he worked as his assistant and was known as his right hand. Later on he took an active part in the Right-Wing discussions among 'red professors' and in various Party organizations, as did the brothers Slepkov, Petrovsky (a son of Grigory Ivanovich) and several others who were regarded as Right-Wing theoreticians backed by Bukharin. He was arrested in 1933 as a member of a Left-Right group, as it was called. He assured me that he was not in fact a member, but his name was included in a list of people whom the group had meant to write to as potential sympathizers. He was sentenced to three years in an isolator but was released from prison and sent into exile in Beryozovo near the river Irtysh in Siberia.

In 1936, without any new charge being presented, he was re-arrested and the following year was processed together with the rest of Bukharin's 'little school' in preparation for Bukharin's trial. In the Lubyanka pressure was brought on them to give evidence against him. The conversations of the 'school' over the years were to serve as proof that Bukharin, while outwardly loyal when he was working on *Izvestiya*, had in fact been a double-dealer all through the thirties and had kept his group together for hostile purposes. It seems indeed that he had continued to speak frankly to his friends and never changed his earlier ideas. This was shown by the evidence of the group. The interrogations then went further. They tried to force the group to give evidence of Bukharin's alleged terrorist attitude, his contacts with Trotskyists and his participation in terrorist acts and espionage. Some such 'evidence' seems to have been obtained; this is suggested by the shooting of a number of his former pupils, for before they could testify against him they had to confess their own guilt. This is a side of the trials to which not enough attention has been paid: as a rule, evidence against the accused man was taken only from those who confessed to participation in his crime. The evidence of a non-participant who had merely heard about the plot from others was not usually accepted. Thus the witnesses had to start by accusing themselves. Many of the witnesses in this case were confronted with Bukharin, who resolutely denied all accusations of terrorism; later on all who had confessed to terrorism were shot. Eichenwald, Petrovsky, who was also in the Solovki prison while I was there, Maretsky and perhaps several others refused to confess to terrorism. When pressure was brought to bear on them – including beatings and torture, which by then the NKVD was empowered to use – they decided to compromise: they gave evidence on Bukharin's attitude as expressed in his conversations with them but denied all the allegations of criminal activity. Towards the end, in order to break Bukharin, confrontations were arranged between him and these witnesses as well.

Eichenwald told me this at the end of 1937 on one of the Solovki Islands, to which I had recently been transferred. An old monastery had been turned into a prison with a special régime applied to those like me who were down to be shot. The prisoners were kept in cells which were strictly isolated not only from the outside world but also from one another. In my cell there were seven or eight people; one of them was Eichenwald. We were together from December 1937 to May 1938. Our other cellmates were not interested in politics. In general the rule was to mix political prisoners with criminals and also to put at least one stool-pigeon in each cell.

Eichenwald was a tall, lanky young man; he had a broad outlook on life and a many-sided culture. The son of Yuly Eichenwald (a well known literary critic who came of a pious Jewish family but became an Orthodox Christian) and of a Russian aristocrat, he was a mathematician as well as a philosopher and keenly interested in literature. He was devoted to his mother and so, as a form of pressure, he had been allowed no news of her since his arrest. What he told me about his father showed the predicament in which some of the Left-Wing intelligentsia found themselves in 1917. Yuly was well to the left of the Cadets, yet Alexander remembered him in February, even before Kerensky had come to power and when the whole of Russia was rejoicing at the bloodless revolution, watching soldiers demonstrating in the street and the crowds giving them an ovation. Even Alexander's mother was caught up in the enthusiasm but his father suddenly said sadly: 'To think that every one of these men has broken his oath!' The sight of soldiers who had broken their oath of allegiance to the Tsar threw a shadow over his happiness. When I was told this twenty years later I was struck by the realization of how divided such Russian intellectuals must have been, and I was impressed in a way which I then found hard to understand. The incident had clearly made a deep impression on Alexander, who had since become a prominent and active Party member but who recalled it when, as a philosopher, he tried to understand the meaning of his time.

Alexander was one of those who had a confrontation with Bukharin shortly before the trial. It lasted almost five hours. The interrogator questioned him on various incidents in Bukharin's life in the early thirties when he was still in the Central Committee. Alexander was asked to repeat his evidence on his various conversations with him, and this made it clear that though Bukharin did not theorize about it he saw in the peasant risings and the economic chaos a proof of the failure of Stalin's collectivization. Bukharin admitted the general sense of these conversations but tried to deny their dangerous implications and was hurt that Alexander had said so much. Alexander justified it on the grounds that this was not 'some kind of

Pinkerton stuff' – he had firmly denied any suggestion of a plot and had not linked Bukharin with anything criminal; he had merely affirmed his ideological position. After some argument about details Bukharin usually agreed to sign the statements (in a confrontation the interrogator puts each question first to one, then to the other, and both sign a statement). In the end they were completely reconciled and Bukharin asked the interrogator to be allowed to have a talk alone with Eichenwald. The interrogator agreed. He left the room, the guard was told to stand outside, and the two of them talked for another couple of hours sitting side by side and without witnesses. Bukharin chiefly wanted news of his family and of the fate of his disciples (he had recently married a girl twenty years younger than himself, the daughter of Yu. Larin, a Menshevik who joined the Bolsheviks in 1917 and was prominent as an economist). Then Bukharin told him of his present philosophical preoccupations. He had been given permission to read and write in his leisure time between interrogations, was allowed books and a typewriter, and was writing a book. When Alexander asked him the subject he was told to his amazement that it was about the nature of man. Bukharin even tried to convince him that this was all that now mattered in their lives: they should stop thinking about ideology, economics and politics and try to understand the meaning and purpose of life.

I could not make out from what Eichenwald told me the conclusion to which Bukharin had come – how far Bukharin's ideas were mystical or purely ethical or philosophical, but such were his preoccupations shortly before his death.

A few days after the confrontation Eichenwald was tried by a military court (before which all such cases came up) and was sentenced to fifteen years in prison. He stayed among us some six months. The prison authorities watched his every move and seized on every pretext for treating him more harshly. They kept putting him in solitary confinement – and in the iciest isolation cells at that. He lost a lot of weight, developed some chest trouble, which may have been tuberculosis, and was refused medical treatment and special food. Every word he said was reported to the NKVD.

One day at the beginning of March the door opened and that day's *Pravda* was handed to us by the gaoler (it was the first news we had had from outside for a long time). For two or three weeks we were kept supplied with papers: day by day we followed the trial of Bukharin, and the gaolers made sure that we read them, especially Eichenwald. Just before the end of the trial we were summoned one by one by the prison liaison officer of the NKVD and asked what we thought of it. The question was provocative and was put in the hope of eliciting something more that would incriminate us further. Eichenwald was questioned for three hours. He was of course deeply moved by the news of the trial, realizing that Bukharin's fate was sealed, but he assured me that when he was questioned he did not deny his solidarity with Bukharin's position. It was clear to me when we discussed the various incidents of the trial that Bukharin's manner influenced his disciples. His firm refusal to confess to terrorism and treason inspired them to greater dignity when their own turn came. Eichenwald thought it was a miracle that Bukharin had found the courage to resist Vyshinsky as far as he had.

Some time later we were parted and I never saw Eichenwald again. Solovki is near the border and on the eve of the Finnish war it was evacuated. I met some of the prisoners later, in other prisons and camps, but many others I never saw or heard of again. From what I could gather, they were shot just before Hitler's invasion of Poland. They seem to have included Eichenwald although he had only been sentenced to fifteen years – practically all the survivors among those who had been implicated in the great show trials were killed at that time – but he may have died earlier, for he was very ill and exhausted.

I have no reason to doubt his account either of himself or of Bukharin; he was a man of high moral character and I thought him the most reliable of those who gave me details of Bukharin's fate after his arrest.

CHAPTER 6

MENSHEVIKS

EARLY in 1937 I met Eduard Eduardovich Pontovich in the Butyrki prison in Moscow to which I had been transferred, for a new investigation, from the camp where I was being held. Such enormous numbers of people were being arrested or submitted to new investigations in preparation for the big political trials that they could not be put in solitary confinement, as the NKVD would have preferred, during their period of interrogation. The fact that newly arrested prisoners were kept together with others who had been through the experience of an interrogation before was an advantage for the freshman, as the old hands could warn him of the methods used and thus reduce the chances of his breaking down. In such mixed cells the conversation was more varied than in those where only inexperienced prisoners were held. It was not so obsessed with the tricks of the interrogators and the progress of the investigations; there were more discussions of general events and attempts to evaluate them politically. The people I met during my stay in this cell were mostly communists, but there were also members of other parties such as the Left SRs,[1] anarchists and members of national minorities. Of the Mensheviks, my encounter with Eduard Pontovich has remained particularly fresh in my memory.

Pontovich was a cultured man and widely read in Marxism. He was a lawyer who had joined the Mensheviks when he was a student during the period of the 1905 revolution. He told me much about his life and about the Menshevik leaders he had known, in particular F. Dan and N. Sukhanov.*

In 1935 he was legal adviser to the Central Executive Committee of the USSR, a State, not Party, body, and helped to draft new laws. In the summer of that year he was removed from his post, arrested and deported to Siberia. Now he had been brought back to Moscow

1. Socialist Revolutionaries; see Footnote 3, page 60.

on the orders of the SPO (the secret political department of the NKVD).

He had stopped his Menshevik activities in the early twenties. He said that at that time they became virtually impossible and 'perhaps even undesirable'. After the exile or the emigration of the chief Menshevik leaders, attempts to organize an underground were, he thought, doomed to failure and only played into the hands of the provocateurs, making it easier for them to get rid of the loyal members of the Menshevik Party. He thought that the Bolsheviks very soon understood the need to make use of those Marxist intellectuals who had ceased to struggle for power and were willing to serve in the ministries, economic establishments and the apparatus of the Central Executive Committee, retaining their convictions but loyally carrying out the tasks which were given them. Pontovich knew many former Mensheviks who had acted in this way and he kept up his contacts with them, but he insisted that this was purely personal and that he never took part in any plots or conspiratorial organizations. He spoke very harshly about the so-called confessions made by the accused at the trial of the Mensheviks in 1931; he described these confessions as 'made in GPU' and thought them the result of pressure or of the unrestrained imagination of people who had been driven to despair. I formed an excellent impression of Pontovich, though I could never make up my mind whether he had indeed behaved with complete loyalty towards the Soviet authorities. He once let slip that he carefully followed the émigré journal *Sotsialistichesky vestnik* and the illegal Menshevik publications produced in Russia. At the time I ascribed such contradictions to his distrust of me as a communist, a distrust which I often met with in the prisons and camps.

I remember how impressed I was by his wide circle of friends among the intelligentsia. He was personally acquainted with almost all the poets, writers, artists and composers of his generation. He told me some very interesting stories which showed the ambiguity of people's attitudes towards the régime and its actions. He also knew many prominent scholars, particularly those who specialized in jurisprudence.

He had got his post in the Central Executive Committee through

A. S. Yenukidze.* As I was in camp by the time the details of the Yenukidze case were published he told me many things which I did not know. Like most members of the Central Executive Committee, he ascribed Yenukidze's troubles to the hostility of the heads of the NKVD. Thanks to his friendship with Stalin Yenukidze had succeeded in keeping on a number of specialists employed by the Central Executive Committee, among them former nobles and members of the anti-Bolshevik parties like the Cadets, SRs, Mensheviks, etc. He was still trying to do this in 1935 when most departments were being purged of 'former people'. Unfortunately there then occurred a break in his relations with Stalin. Yenukidze was regarded as an expert on the history of the Party in Georgia. He made a few disrespectful comments about Stalin's role which, he said, Beria had grossly exaggerated in his book, and recalled some details which were very unflattering to Stalin. As a result, incriminating materials which had so far been suppressed were put into use. It was precisely to camouflage his personal desire to rid himself of Yenukidze, so the members of the Central Executive Committee thought, that Stalin decided to have his case publicly discussed by the Central Committee of the Party.

The decision to expel Yenukidze was a signal to the NKVD, which proceeded to purge the apparatus of 'former people'. Pontovich believed that their cases had not been examined individually, on the basis of the evidence in their personal dossiers, but that they were simply sentenced to banishment, exile, or short terms in camps. Later the SPO looked into some of the cases again, and this was why Pontovich had been brought back to Moscow. He was accused of links with the Menshevik underground, of anti-Soviet propaganda and of the fact that the 'Yenukidze group' must have had some special reason for appointing him to a leading post in the Central Executive Committee.

During the six months we spent together in the Butyrki cell we had many long conversations on all sorts of subjects. Pontovich believed that the Bolsheviks' seizure of power was Russia's great misfortune. He thought it had been possible only because of Russia's backwardness and the absence of a real proletariat. The Western proletariat, according to him, had remained Menshevik in its views.

Russia had to catch up economically with the more developed countries; she could do this either by joining the world economic system or, if she adhered to Bolshevik ideology, by maintaining her independent economic development.

Stalin, he said, had understood the need for extreme measures in order to preserve Russia as a great power. These measures were unutterably cruel but they would achieve industrialization and only after that would a 'normal' class war begin. It was then that 'a mature proletariat would recognize the rightness of the Russian Mensheviks' approach'. He regarded the current inner Party struggle in the USSR as a conflict between 'fascist Bolsheviks' and 'liberal Bolsheviks'. He hoped in the end that the sound spirit of the Russian people would put an end to its dictatorial government.

In the summer of 1937 Pontovich was summoned to an interrogation. This was after the Tukhachevsky trial when the mass liquidation of all remaining potential enemies of the Stalin régime got under way. Pontovich had to face new charges and he was transferred to a special prison. After that I got no further news of him either in the camps or twenty years later when I was released. I shall say a little more about him at the beginning of Chapter 8.

*

In 1948 I was suddenly arrested in the camp near Norilsk. The camp régime had just got worse, possibly as a result of the conflict with Tito, and, by special order from Moscow, hundreds of prisoners, many of whom had been in prison for ten to fourteen years, were isolated in special camps without any new charges being brought against them. The following year it turned out that some of them, including myself and sixteen others who were now in the Alexandrovsk prison near Irkutsk, had been picked out 'by mistake' and were now to be sent on to other camps. We never knew our destination in advance; the official reason for this was that it made it more difficult for a prisoner to escape. In reality it was done to make the prisoners feel that they were regarded not so much as human beings but as cattle being led to the slaughter. Every transfer at this time, when the new wave of terror was making itself felt, led to grave suspicions and anxieties on the part of the prisoners. I was a little reassured when, after the necessary preliminaries, I was brought into a cell where there were several others in the same situation as myself. By talking to the other prisoners it was possible to get some idea of what was happening and overcome one's fear of the unknown.

I soon realized that we all belonged to the same category – political prisoners who had been sentenced again on newly-invented charges as soon as our first terms of imprisonment had expired.

One prisoner particularly attracted my attention. He was an old man with a pale, typically Jewish face, a sharp nose and haggard cheeks, but his manners and speech showed at once that he was a highly cultured man with a great experience of life. He introduced himself as Lev Ilyich Inzhir, a specialist in financial matters. I remembered that I had heard of him before as a gifted accountant who was employed for a number of years as book-keeper for the Soviet State Bank and as chief accountant for Belomorstroy, a canal joining the Baltic and the White Seas which was built in the early thirties by hundreds of thousands of prisoners. Inzhir was famous because on the very day when the year's work ended he had the balance sheet for the year all ready to hand in to the authorities. Legends were told about him; he was said to be an exceptional organizer who was set up as an example to the whole Soviet Union by the head accountants of various huge enterprises. Inzhir and I arranged to travel side by side – an interesting companion made a lot of difference during a journey which sometimes lasted several days or weeks.

He told me that he had been arrested in 1938 and charged, as usual in those days, with deliberate sabotage, i.e., 'economic counter-revolution', and, under Article 58/10, with anti-Soviet agitation, as a result of which accusations he was sentenced to fifteen years. He gave no further details about this, but he was only too ready to talk about politics and economics in general, which was rare among old prisoners who had been cut off for so long from the outside world, and he asked me to tell him all I knew about the West. It turned out that he had worked in fairly privileged conditions in camp, had had access to various scientific publications, monthlies and fortnightlies, read all the chief Soviet daily papers, often listened to the radio and even conversed with salaried officials employed by the Central Directorate of the Siberian Camps (Siblag). It was easy to tell from what he said that his theoretical line was very different from that of the Soviets and that he was heart and soul on the side of the European socialists, agreeing with them in their evaluation of the situation in the USSR and in the world. He thought that the only chance for the success of socialism lay in the victory of America in its struggle for world hegemony. As for Soviet expansionism, he saw it as a reactionary attempt to hold up progress and hamper the future victory of socialism: this was the basis of all his political judgments. We had several arguments in which I tried to defend Lenin's approach to capitalism, although I said I disagreed with the interpretation of it on individual questions in the Soviet press. When Inzhir became convinced that he had nothing to fear from me he said that, just as thirty-two years ago, he was still against the seizure of power by the working class when it was as weak and backward as was the Russian proletariat in 1917. He thought that Lenin's seizure of power was a colossal mistake. Since 1912, when he began his political life, he had been and still was a supporter of the 'father of Russian social democracy', Georgy Valentinovich Plekhanov; he thought it an unforgivable crime on the part of Lenin to demand at the beginning of the First World War that there should be a schism in the International. The Parties which had remained faithful to the Second International were for him the only true representatives of the Marxist tradition. So strong was his conviction of this that he hated not only Lenin, as the one who was chiefly responsible for the schism, but also Trotsky and his followers who helped to create it, for on this question there was hardly any division between Lenin and Trotsky at the time of the war. He even hated Martov* and all those Social Democrats who took up a 'centralist' position after the October Revolution and did not resist the disintegration of the International.

I learned the further details of his life only after we arrived at our destination. This turned out to be the 'special camp' of Tayshet, where there were tens of thousands of political prisoners and where the régime was particularly severe. I heard the story of his life backwards. During the first years after the victory of the Bolsheviks he had given up his political activity and devoted himself entirely to economic questions. Like most Mensheviks and Plekhanovists he believed that the Bolsheviks would not hold out for long. To prevent the final collapse of the country for the sake of its future he thought that he must conceal his beliefs and join in the work of reconstruction and sorting out the financial chaos.

During the twenties he was trusted by the Government and treated respectfully as a 'specialist' in his field. While Sokolnikov* was in charge of fiscal policy Inzhir took part in stabilizing the rouble according to the gold standard and later in fixing the exchange value of the new rouble. In 1926, although he was a former Menshevik who had not made his public recantation, he was included in the Soviet delegation to the international conference on finance which was held in Holland. He later published a number of articles on its work and results.

At this time there began a struggle between the leadership and the Opposition. Inzhir was particularly hostile to the Trotskyists and Zinovyevists and their friends. He regarded them as thorough-going Bolsheviks, whereas the 'economic group', that is, the Right-Wing, were people with whom he thought those outside the Party could co-operate, people who sought stabilization and were opposed to adventurism. He realized that the Left Opposition wanted to continue the policy of Lenin in which he saw the root of every evil. He thought the defeat of the Opposition was a just punishment for all that the Leninists and the Social Democrats who thought like them had done. He endlessly stressed his loathing of Trotsky and the Trotskyists, and kept saying that historical nemesis had manifested itself in the October Revolution more than in any other revolution before, and that the blackest reaction could not have punished the Bolsheviks more harshly than the Revolution itself did.

During those years he worked loyally and thought that in the course of time, if there were no drastic changes, he and his like could adapt themselves to the new régime. It appears that many 'specialists' such as Inzhir did indeed adapt themselves and were accepted into the milieu which was created around Stalin's power apparatus. They served him faithfully, concealing their thoughts in the hope that the historical process would of itself bring about different, more peaceful times. No doubt it was precisely to ensure their loyalty and eliminate any temptation they might have to protest against Stalin's methods that some of them had to be kept in isolation and the others threatened from time to time and made conscious of the sword which always hung over them.

Inzhir first got into trouble quite unexpectedly when he was arrested at the beginning of 1930. Why precisely he was chosen from among the former Mensheviks and Plekhanovists remained unclear to me, even though I read copies of the innumerable complaints and appeals he was still writing two decades after his first arrest. Perhaps he had expressed himself incautiously in some conversation. It was apparently at the time of his first arrest that something completely changed him and left its mark on him to the end of his days. Great pressure was used to induce him to confess. In those days such pressure was generally moral and intellectual rather than physical, as it was to become later, although physical methods were sometimes used even then to obtain signatures on false confessions and accusations of others more quickly. It is more than probable that the GPU succeeded in breaking Inzhir, not only by threats (it would have been easy enough to threaten him with a death sentence without trial and right of appeal), but also by promises. He was given the alternative of either refusing the 'information' required of him, in which case he would have disappeared without trace, his flat in the centre of Moscow and all his possessions would have been confiscated and his wife and children (whom he adored) repressed, or of giving in, in which case he was promised not only a speedy release but the chance of new and honourable work with better material conditions, of a better education for his children, and of promotion and special rewards for his services. Whatever it was that persuaded him Inzhir did give in and evidently helped the GPU to mount the trial of the Mensheviks.

The moments when, twenty years later, he spoke of the methods used to make him betray his closest comrades and put his signature to lying accusations were moments of great bitterness and deep hatred for his persecutors. It was then, in 1930, that he decided that since he had been forced to behave in this base way he would devote the rest of his life to avenging himself on those who had robbed him of the most precious thing in life. And he began to take advantage of the trust which was shown him after he had fulfilled the wishes of his interrogators in order to 'undermine' the communist régime by means of the régime itself. He made it his aim to destroy as many communists as possible by means of other communists, so that in the end all of them would perish in the struggle between the factions and life would be easier for the rest of the world.

In 1931 Inzhir, who had been sentenced secretly to ten years, was freed after a new and also secret examination of his case and given an important job in the secret police itself. He became the OGPU's chief accountant for its enormous industrial undertakings which at that time were being set up in various parts of the country. This was the time of the collectivization of agriculture, which involved the deportation of five million *kulaks* and peasants classified as the abetters of *kulaks*. These mass arrests created a vast labour force which could be used in places and conditions which free workers would not have tolerated. This was how Inzhir got the chance to display his talents at the Belomorstroy and became renowned throughout the country.

For seven years he lived a double life. He devoted his knowledge and talents to the service of the régime he hated but thereby greatly benefited. He could not in fact do otherwise for the slightest act of sabotage in the kind of work he was doing threatened him with death. At the same time, as a secret informer of the political department of the NKVD, he took his revenge on the Bolsheviks by entangling and compromising Party members with whom he came into contact in the course of his work, and thereby helped to liquidate them.

In these activities Inzhir evidently found an inward satisfaction and felt that he was to some extent atoning for the betrayal of his fellow Mensheviks. As to the Bolsheviks he betrayed, his conscience did not trouble him in the least. He was sure that the strife which he helped to fan amongst them was only a small part of the punishment deserved by those who were responsible for the catastrophe which had beset Russia and socialism.

At the height of the mass arrests of Bolsheviks, and particularly Old Bolsheviks, in 1936 and 1937, and during the show trials of

Zinovyev, Kamenev, Pyatakov, Radek and their friends, Inzhir reached the summit of his career. Appointed by N. I. Yezhov, he became the chief accountant of Gulag, the central directorate of the labour camps, which had in its charge hundreds of enterprises and thousands of building sites where, in the course of the thirties and forties, it employed tens of millions of prisoners.

He owed this appointment not only to his reputation as an expert but to his links with the top people of the NKVD at the time when the man who held this job was supposed to be completely reliable. Directly or indirectly the chief accountant of Gulag came to know more than anyone else (the Gulag enterprises included some which were highly important for the security of the state, such as fortifications and secret bases), including the plans for the creation of new industries: before these were handed over to their respective ministries they were checked for years and classified as top secret. The balance sheets of the Soviet economic institutions, of which Gulag was one, revealed the whole scope of their activities, the methods of financing them and the use made of the capital invested, and it was easy, on the basis of these accounts, to follow even the most secret details of Soviet development. At the time of the early Five-Year Plans Inzhir had at his disposal all the figures showing production costs and thus knew exactly what it cost to lay the foundations of the powerful State machine. The Gulag chief accountant received daily schedules drawn up in all the labour camps of the Soviet Union over an area of more than twenty million square kilometres from Dickson Island and Spitzbergen to Kamchatka and Central Asia; in every one of them a daily check was made on the prisoners under the headings of hours of work done, sickness and absenteeism. All the data collected at each camp were sent on and finally reached the Moscow Gulag. In addition there were also daily figures on transit points, railway stations and harbours, to check on who and what was in transit, and finally a special heading showing how many prisoners had arrived at their destination and what their sentences were, how many others had been released and how many had died. On the basis of all this material the daily schedule of Gulag was put together and handed over to the chief accountant's department, which kept the information in its own books. This daily report was put on

Inzhir's desk; at the time when the purges were at their height he was one of the very few people who knew the exact figures of the prisoners in camps.

Talking about it years later Inzhir told me of the horror he felt as day by day he followed the growing figures under the headings 'Arrivals' and 'Deaths'. He and the other members of Gulag who knew some, if not all, of the figures, had the impression that the whole country was being turned into one gigantic camp. The ever-increasing mortality rate was often discussed among them and as a result orders were sent to the camp commandants. When there were thousands of deaths every day it was obviously impossible to check the circumstances of each one. But a maximum permitted mortality rate was laid down; so long as mortality remained within these limits it was considered normal. If in any place or at any time it went down a long way below the permitted maximum this attracted attention as unusual and had to be investigated so that conclusions might be drawn and praise or blame assigned. If, however, mortality greatly exceeded the norm this meant that the plan was in danger of not being fulfilled and energetic measures were taken: telegrams went out demanding immediate explanations and urgent orders were given 'to stop mortality' (*prekratit smertnost*); finally investigating commissions were sent out with the task to reduce the mortality rate to the proportions which had been laid down. Sometimes, according to Inzhir, the camp commandant himself went on trial and was either dismissed or, in extreme cases, put to death. In other words, it was not the camp system as such that was blamed (nobody would have dared to blame it), but those in charge, who were sometimes punished; this was often made known to the prisoners, evidently in order to give them some satisfaction or compensation for their sufferings.

Inzhir worked as the Gulag chief accountant for two years and all the time felt that it could not end well. The group of experts to which he belonged had replaced another group employed under Yagoda, who had been head of the NKVD from 1934 to 1936, and which was removed when Yagoda was liquidated. By the spring of 1938, after the trial of Bukharin, Rykov and others, including

Yagoda, Inzhir felt that the position of Yezhov, who had replaced Yagoda and was in constant contact with Stalin, was beginning to be shaky. He told me about a meeting he had had at that time with one of the veterans of the NKVD, a Jew whose speech was full of Talmudic sayings, and who had firmly clung to his post from the early twenties onwards despite the fact that he was originally non-Party, perhaps because he had got his appointment through the recommendation of Dzerzhinsky.* This man, who survived all the purges and who, I was told in 1956 in Moscow, retired on a pension when he was over seventy, warned Inzhir in a heart-to-heart talk that there were signs of a new storm and that he had better retire while there was still time.

Inzhir tried to follow his advice and asked to retire on grounds of health. After a while he was summoned by the deputy minister of the NKVD, Chernyshev, who had special responsibility for the labour camps, and was told that his request had been refused. As to his health, he could have a holiday for six weeks in one of the rest homes in the Caucasus and come back refreshed to his job where, as Inzhir knew, he was under constant supervision. He went to a rest home reserved for NKVD employees which was exceptionally comfortable and well run. On his return to Moscow he found the atmosphere even more threatening than when he had left. Yezhov had by then received an additional appointment as Minister of Waterways. Late one night he summoned Inzhir, who until then had had only short and strictly business talks with him. Yezhov was sitting in his shirt sleeves on a sofa behind a table laden with bottles of vodka. His hair was ruffled and his eyes were swollen and inflamed: he was obviously drunk but he also seemed excited and alarmed. The conversation was constantly interrupted by telephone calls in which Yezhov gave rude and cynical answers to the callers. He suggested that Inzhir should leave his work in Gulag and come to work as chief accountant for the Ministry of Waterways where, according to Yezhov, there was nothing but theft and embezzlement; the chief accountant there was hopeless and would have to be imprisoned, and the books were full of errors. Inzhir tried to cry off this responsible post on grounds of health but Yezhov insisted that he should immediately take it over. As they said goodbye Yezhov suddenly asked about some detail of Inzhir's past and gave him a searching look which boded no good. Inzhir suddenly realized that Yezhov hated him and that his fate was decided.

A few days later (he had been into his new office only a couple of times) Inzhir was arrested and brought to that very Lubyanka where he had so recently had his conversation with Yezhov. He was accused of 'sabotage with a counter-revolutionary purpose' in the course of his work for Gulag, and to this were added various other accusations connected with his past, including those which had been annulled when his case was revised and he had been released.

It turned out that although the order for his arrest had been signed by Yezhov himself he had in fact been removed from his work and arrested *on account of* Yezhov, as a member of his staff and his collaborator. It was not a matter of bringing charges but of getting rid of him. For the first few days he feared that because he had worked for Yezhov and had enjoyed the confidence of his assistants his fate would be the same as theirs. However, only a few dozen of them were shot and Inzhir survived. He was merely sentenced to fifteen years.

Presumably he was saved by his connections in Gulag, where his former colleagues came to his assistance when he caught their attention again, this time as a prisoner. He was deported to South-Western Siberia where the camps were considered relatively mild, both because the climate was better than to the north of the Trans-Siberian Railway and because these camps had by now a certain tradition and experience. (In general the older camps were better than the new ones, where the living conditions were appalling, the supplies unorganized and the administration poor.)

Soon after his arrival Inzhir managed to get a job as book-keeper in one of the camp departments and, as his sentence did not include the confiscation of his property, his wife and children, who had remained in his Moscow flat, were able to send him parcels. After a short time his wife even got permission to visit him in camp and came to spend several days there.

From time to time he addressed appeals to the authorities for a revision of his case. They were unsuccessful, but inside the camp he knew neither hunger nor heavy labour. He read books on economics and made notes for a book which he proposed to write after his release.

Inzhir told me all this during the journey. After we arrived at our destination we met only from time to time. We were too busy and too tired in our broken-down state of health for long conversations. As we got to know our fellow-prisoners rumours and warnings about Inzhir began to reach me. It is a tradition which goes back to Tsarist times that prisoners think it their duty to warn their comrades against informers. I was told that Inzhir was a very dangerous man and advised to have nothing to do with him. Among those who were most insistent on this was a Lithuanian whom I will call George. He had been an active Party member, was arrested in 1937, sentenced to ten years and had had another ten added on while he was in the camp. He seemed to be trying to compromise Inzhir in every way, and at first I thought he simply wanted to ingratiate himself for some reason with me (jealousies and even hatreds of this kind often develop in camp conditions). He would not desist and after a few months he came to me with an offer. He would arrange a 'confrontation' with Inzhir and get him with his back to the wall. I avoided this encounter for several weeks – it was unpleasant in itself and if Inzhir was indeed an NKVD agent it could be highly dangerous – but in the end George arranged it against my will. On some pretext or other he brought me to a barrack-block, all of whose inmates were out at work; Inzhir was the man on duty. George locked the door before Inzhir could leave and immediately went into the attack: 'When you were with me in such-and-such a camp you made notes for several years and reported our conversations to the Third Section [Secret Police] and put all sorts of lies in as well. Then when the war broke out I was arrested and your reports were read out to me and you were used as a witness at my trial and you confirmed all the accusations. Now you're going to say in front of Berger whether this is true or not. I want him to know and beware of you because I'm quite sure that you're still carrying on in the same way.' Inzhir didn't answer for a while, and then he said: 'Suppose it's true; you must also tell Berger that it was I who saved your life.' George turned to me: 'Yes, that's true as well – he saved my life.'

It appeared that at his trial George had no chance to deny Inzhir's evidence because there were other witnesses to the fact that in 1940 he had commented very adversely on Stalin's pact with Hitler. But what interested the court was something else and it was on this that his life hung: did the accused continue his anti-Soviet propaganda after the outbreak of the war in 1941? In peacetime this was a crime punishable by ten years; in wartime it fell under Article 58/10 and was punishable by death, and at that time the death sentences were invariably carried out. Inzhir said that George had not continued his propaganda after the German invasion, and thereby he saved George's life.

This dramatic scene between two prisoners filled with mutual hatred and blind rage in the dark barrack guarded by barbed wire and the machine-guns on the look-out towers in the middle of the Siberian *taiga* made me think of some mediaeval tribunal. It seemed wrong and impossible to make any judgment. George insisted that Inzhir was still an informer. Inzhir replied that it had needed only a word from him to destroy George, a man who was not only his personal enemy but who belonged to the tribe he so hated – he was a Bolshevik and a Trotskyist.

After this I avoided political discussions with Inzhir but I did not break off all contact with him. I realized that such discussions could be dangerous, but at the same time the confrontation had confirmed my earlier opinion that Inzhir still had the remnants of a conscience. He had had every opportunity to get rid of George, a person who had definite evidence against him as an informer, and he hadn't taken advantage of it. Moreover to break off relations completely could also have its dangers, as I had already told him quite a lot. A prisoner's life could be endangered not only by what he did but equally, and sometimes more, by what he refrained from doing, and also by the opinion which the authorities and their informers had of him.

Inzhir never referred to the incident again except to make it clear to me that he felt no remorse. A prominent communist who had persecuted members of other parties was fair game. He added that a number of Jews must have suffered on George's account as well (he felt himself to be a Jew and loved Jewish culture).

When the war broke out in Korea Inzhir could not withhold

his political comments. This may partly have been on the instructions of the Third Section who, whenever anything important happened, looked for adverse comments on the official version of events and started new cases of anti-Soviet agitation. The slightest discrepancy between what any prisoner said and the line taken in the newspapers showed that something was wrong with the 'mental condition' of the camp, and action had to be taken at once. When the first news of the fighting in Korea arrived Inzhir caught me with a copy of *Pravda* in my hand (*Pravda* came late but fairly often). He never doubted for a moment that the war was an act of aggression by Stalin against the US. '*He*' (this was how we referred to Stalin to avoid uttering the fatal name) 'wants to give them a fright, *he* wants to show Asia that even Truman is afraid of him, but now they'll teach *him* a lesson. The whole world will be enraged by this provocation. This time *he*'s miscalculated.' When the Americans advanced deep into Korea he was triumphant. 'This is *his* second big defeat since the end of the war.' (The first was *his* failure to deal with Tito.) 'Now the end isn't far off.' But when the war continued and the Chinese volunteers came in he began to worry. 'That Truman doesn't understand that *he* has set him a trap. *He* wants to involve him with China to divert him from Europe, especially from East Germany. *He* is very happy to make use of the Chinese. What does *he* care if 200 million Chinese are killed off instead of 50 million Russians? Someone had better tell Truman what *he*'s trying to do.'

Usually I only listened to Inzhir without replying, as I now thought that this was slightly less dangerous than saying anything, either in agreement or disagreement. In any case he was not interested in my opinions on such matters; however, once I made some criticism of Singman Rhee. A few days later Inzhir brought along a young Korean who had recently arrived in the camp. 'Here you are,' he said, pointing at me, 'this gentleman thinks Singman Rhee is a reactionary. You tell him about Singman Rhee. And you might tell him how Kim Il Sung got to power and show him how the Soviet press is lying about Korea.' The young Korean had been arrested in Manchuria and condemned to twenty-five years for espionage. He spoke broken Russian but he told me many interesting things. Inzhir was delighted, though he added: 'I don't really need to hear all this to know that the South Koreans are right. It's enough to read the Soviet papers properly. What they write about North Korea is true of the South, and *vice versa*.'

He was convinced that the communists could have no influence over the masses in Europe and America. He explained their influence in Asia by the alliance between the nationalist movements in these backward countries and the Soviet government which helped the nationalists to organize and arm themselves: this had nothing to do with either socialism or communism. The nationalist leaders were ready to accept arms from anyone but they would use them as much against the socialists in their own countries as against the colonial powers. He considered that the Soviet government was making a miscalculation when it hoped to strengthen its influence in this way.

He thought the Second International was the only institution which had inherited the real socialist traditions and represented socialism at the present time, and he greatly exaggerated its influence. This I told him but he would not give up his dream. He argued that the attempt to create a Communist International had failed, whereas the Socialist International was more than sixty years old and would go on existing for decades until it had reached its goal. He was a great admirer of Harold Laski, whom he regarded as one of the leading Marxist thinkers and a pillar of the Second International, whose activities he had followed for years. He spoke enthusiastically about British socialism just at the time when the Soviet press was furiously attacking the Labour government. The peaceful nationalization taking place in England seemed to him the realization of that socialist ideal which had been the dream of the founders of scientific socialism, whereas Bolshevism, he said, threatened not only to destroy the Russian people but to discredit the very idea of socialism.

There was only one category of people whom Inzhir thought worse than communists in general and that was *Soviet* communists, whom he regarded as renegades, traitors to the socialist movement and hired agents who had sold themselves to the Soviet régime. He was not the only one in whom I found this hatred of *Soviet* communism: 'French and English communists are not genuine communists. They are further from Bolshevism than from liberalism or reformism in the European sense. There is no communism in other countries no matter how much some naïve people want to call themselves communists and identify themselves with Soviet communism and imitate it. They simply can't grasp the *essence* of Russian communism, and it's impossible to explain it to them even if they think themselves one hundred per cent communists. Here there's an abyss between East and West that can't be bridged.' Among the scoundrels and traitors he counted Vyshinsky, who was then Foreign Minister, and the journalist Zaslavsky. Vyshinsky's speeches at UNO, which then filled the Soviet papers, always made him speechless with fury, but he was once even more enraged by an article by Zaslavsky full of jeers at Truman. Zaslavsky wrote that the Soviet Union would never capitulate to the West – this was in 1950. Inzhir was convinced that such was the balance of forces between the East and West that complete capitulation by the USSR was the only way of avoiding war, though war would mean the total defeat of the Soviet Union and the end of its 'nightmare régime'.

He thought those Western leaders who were ready to support the communists were fools who had not the most elementary understanding of even their own interests. He prophesied that they would be the first to be liquidated when the Bolsheviks seized power with their assistance. He particularly disliked Nenni* (the only genuine Italian representative of socialism for him was Saragat,* a member of the Second International). One day when I came in to his barrack I found him so deep in thought that for a long time he didn't notice I was there. When I finally asked him what he was thinking about he said with a sigh: 'It's no good – I simply can't see the difference between Nenni and Togliatti.* I keep on trying to understand, but it looks as if I'll die before I do.'

As an invalid he was not made to do hard labour and the parcels he regularly received kept him from hunger, but his health was deteriorating fast. The parcels were supposed to come from affectionate well-to-do relations, but his enemies suspected that they really came from Section Three, as often happened in the case of informers.

In the summer of 1950 Inzhir was moved to another part of the camp twenty kilometres away. There he was soon put in charge of the cultural and educational department, which was supposed to help the 're-education' of the prisoners and simultaneously reduce the chances of their 're-educating', entertaining and organizing themselves on their own, without supervision. This was an enviable post. Those employed by this department were often released from other work: they had better clothes and lived either in a small room of their own or one they shared with only two or three others. (The ordinary barracks accommodated dozens or sometimes even hundreds of prisoners.) They belonged to the camp aristocracy. One of their functions was to write reports on other prisoners. These were used in examining complaints, appeals and requests for visits from families and for the reduction of sentences. (These reductions and promises of reductions exerted considerable influence in the life of the camp; some prisoners wore themselves out in the hope of earning premature release by hard work.) Usually jobs in the cultural and educational department were given to criminals, not to political prisoners, who were regarded as unfit to 're-educate' other people, so when the news came about Inzhir's new post it was regarded as further proof that he was indeed employed by Section Three. Soon after this George too was transferred to Inzhir's part of the camp, though not to his department. Before he left he told me he felt that this might be the result of a denunciation by Inzhir and that he was being moved in order to be 'dealt with'. However, several months went by without any disturbing news and I was even told that in his new job Inzhir did much to help the intellectuals and politicals.

Then, unexpectedly, I too was transferred to the same section. I knew from experience that such transfers of several individual prisoners were always a sign that a new trial was being prepared in the camp. I decided to be exceptionally careful, but not to avoid all contact with Inzhir. He welcomed me in a friendly way. His new activities revealed that he was not only a brilliant economist but had an excellent knowledge of Russian literature and a good understanding of art. There were many Jews in this part of the camp and Inzhir did not hide his sympathy for them. He questioned them at length, especially the ones who had been outside the Soviet Union, and was very grieved to learn of the role of Jewish communists in the 'anti-peoples' democracies' of post-war Eastern Europe. He thought they were participating in a crime for which sooner or later the Jewish population of these countries would have to pay dearly. Moreover he was convinced that the communists who were using Jews today would be the first to betray and liquidate them tomorrow when 'the Moor had done his deed'.

Inzhir's real friendship with some of the Jews in this part of the camp put him in a more and more ambiguous position vis-à-vis his work for the Third Section and his organically anti-Soviet attitude which he was unable to conceal. In April 1951 I was again moved and knew of his further fate only from what I was told by others. At that time severe measures were taken in the camps in preparation for a third world war. The MGB leaders pressed for the liquidation of dangerous or undesirable elements in the camps. Inzhir was asked for more and more reports on other prisoners and at the same time himself became a target. His sentence was supposed to end in 1953 but he knew too much ever to be released. It is also possible that he became a victim of the rivalry in the camp between the MVD (Ministry of Internal Affairs) and the MGB (Ministry of State Security), each of which operated networks of agents, was extremely interested in spying on the other, and tried to outdo its rival in the number of arrests and scope of its activities. Anyway, at this time of new mass arrests in the camps, new investigations and trials and the construction of new isolators, Inzhir was arrested and involved in a case of 'former Trotskyists'. He was accused of hostility to the Soviet régime, of attempts to create a Trotskyist underground and agitation centre, etc. . . . A dozen or so prisoners were arrested with him but only three were tried. In addition to the other charges two men were accused of sympathy with the State of Israel and Inzhir of knowing this and concealing it. The interrogators tried to get evidence of an attempt to set up a Zionist organization in the camp, but nothing came of this, largely because Inzhir refused to co-operate in any way. He declared categorically that he had seen and heard nothing of the sort. In the end the interrogators gave it up, though in other camps their colleagues were more insistent. (One of the devices used was to start a rumour that Ben Gurion had died and observe the reactions of the Jewish prisoners. This revealed any tendencies towards 'Jewish nationalism' which could then easily be dealt with in the appropriate way.)

Physical methods were not much used at that time in cases where the main object was to give prisoners another sentence and keep them on in the camp for a few more years. It was different in serious cases, when, for instance, there was a suspicion that prisoners had links with the outside world and were sending out information from the camp; then there was no ceremony, people were almost beaten to death, isolated in unheated punishment cells and subjected to other forms of torture. However, the normal conditions of those held in prison during an investigation were harsh enough to be a real torment, especially for people like Inzhir whose health was seriously undermined.

His trial was held in Tayshet. The evidence against him came chiefly from his conversations with his fellow prisoner K, who came from Kiev and had been arrested in 1943 and sentenced to ten years. Inzhir did not deny that there were certain matters on which he disagreed with the Soviet point of view.

George, who was also tried, partly on the evidence of Inzhir, behaved with dignity and did not attack him. Inzhir, however, told the story of his confrontation with George and me in 1950 and claimed that the Trotskyists, who hated him because he reported on them, were now slandering him. But the court was hostile and he was sentenced to an extra ten years. (George, whose third trial this was, got only five.) This sentence was a terrible blow to Inzhir, who lost all hope of ever seeing his wife and children again.

Prisoners who were sentenced anew were moved to another camp, apparently because they would probably now know who had sent in secret reports about them, and, if they remained in the same camp, would reveal who some of the agents were, and thus disrupt their future work.

Later I learnt that Inzhir had died in one of the Tayshet camp hospitals in 1954.

*

The previous year I had met a person who seemed to me the perfect type of an extreme opponent of the Soviet régime as well as an uncompromising supporter of the complete assimilation of the Russian Jews. It was now 1953, but this man's life had come to a standstill in the early 1920s. It seems to me that only in Soviet Russia could such a type have developed and then been preserved for decades without any noticeable change.

Boris Manasovich Bukhshtab was born in 1890; he went to a Russian grammar school and became a member of the Menshevik Party. As a student he took part in the struggles of 1905 and was later several times arrested, sentenced to prison and deported by the Tsarist police. At the beginning of the 1914 war Bukhshtab was called up and continued his revolutionary activities in the army. He was never a defeatist like the Bolsheviks; his position was closer to the internationalism of Martov. At the outbreak of the February Revolution he was serving in a unit on the western front and was soon elected chairman of a soldiers' soviet. When Kerensky's government decided to continue the war and ordered an advance he happened to be in that sector of the front where the advance was to begin. The Mensheviks were also in favour of 'fighting until victory'. On the outbreak of the February Revolution they had given up the demand for peace at any price on the assumption that the situation had changed with the fall of Tsarism. It was no longer a matter of Russia and Germany being two reactionary powers in conflict – it was now necessary to defend the Russian Revolution against German Imperialism. Bukhshtab believed that the soldiers had the duty to maintain discipline and obey the High Command. The majority in Bukhshtab's soldiers' soviet were Mensheviks and SRs who supported the Kerensky government. He succeeded, though not without difficulty, in persuading the soldiers in his sector, which was near Tarnopol, where the fighting was at its height, to advance and he was himself wounded in the battle. The advance succeeded at first but was broken by a counter-attack and turned into a defeat. As a result Bolshevik influence over the army was strengthened. The partial disintegration of the front led to the October Revolution.

During and after October Bukhshtab, back from the army, carried on his Menshevik activities in the industrial region south of Moscow round Kaluga, Tula and Orel. He was active in the Trade Union movement and in the soviets where, in the first years after the Revolution, the Mensheviks still had some influence and occupied certain positions. In 1919 he was elected by a majority of Mensheviks and SRs to the post of chairman of the Kaluga town soviet, but later on the Bolsheviks got a majority and dismissed him.

In 1920 and 1921 the Mensheviks gradually lost all chances of legal activity in Russia. Their newspapers had already been liquidated. In the regions near the front during the Civil War they were already on an illegal footing. Bukhshtab too was in the underground for some time but in 1921 he was arrested and in August of that year he was sentenced to deportation.

For over thirty years from then on he was never left in peace. He still kept up his links with the Menshevik underground during the twenties but his persecution got into its stride precisely when the underground had been liquidated. At this time members of the Menshevik Party, as well as members of the other parties who were opposed to the Soviet régime, such as the SRs and anarchists, whether they were prominent or rank and file, were required to sign declarations that they had broken with the past, were ready to co-operate with the régime and regretted their former errors. Many of the former Menshevik leaders such as Khinchuk, Maisky* and others (including Vyshinsky, who up to 1920 was one of the most active Menshevik opponents of Lenin) joined the Communist Party, while many Mensheviks emigrated or were exiled abroad. Others were put under the supervision of the police. Many of them were offered the alternative of exile abroad, but for a long time the standing secret instructions of the Menshevik Centre were not to accept this.

Bukhshtab yielded neither to threats nor bribes. He refused to make a declaration in the press, which was the minimum demanded of former members of non-Bolshevik parties, and to refrain from anti-régime activities or from political activities in general. Many attempts were made to draw him into the big political trials. At such times, particularly in 1930, when a trial was being prepared in order to liquidate the remnants of the Menshevik leadership in the Soviet Union, special pressure was put on him. This was one of the first trials to be run according to the new methods adopted by the GPU when confessions and self-accusations took the place of speeches for the defence. Not only did the prisoners accuse themselves of all sorts of crimes but they deliberately sought to arouse hatred for themselves and the ideas which they stood for. Instead of justifying their views they ran down their former ideology and all those who had remained faithful to it abroad.

Efforts were made to force Bukhshtab to admit to having had meetings with Menshevik leaders and to compromise his former comrades. He refused to make public statements even on points of detail, for sometimes such small admissions of true facts were used to support false and fantastic accusations, and anyone who even agreed to appear as a witness was already held to have confessed something and was thus drawn into the huge cobweb of lies. Bukhshtab was one of the few who refused compromise in any way. Such people were usually in the end left alone but isolated. As a result of his refusal to take part in the Menshevik trials Bukhshtab was put in a prison reserved for 'ideological enemies'. Most of these isolators, as they were called, were directly in the charge of the Moscow GPU. There were known to be isolators in Verkhneuralsk, Suzdal, Yaroslavl and Vladimir. Such prisoners, though officially serving their allotted sentence, were not intended ever to come out alive and the great majority were liquidated at the end of the thirties.

In the short intervals between one prison term and another, Bukhshtab lived in the greatest poverty. Although he was an economist he was not, of course, given any work which would have enabled him to live in any of the big cities and earn a reasonable wage. His wife was also a Menshevik and was persecuted in the same way. Early on she was allowed to follow him to his place of deportation but later this was regarded as not in accordance with the 'strictness of the law' and they were sent to different places of exile. As a young man during the Revolution, Bukhshtab, tall and handsome, enjoyed exceptionally good health, but the many years of privations, the hunger strikes which he declared time after time in protest against the persecution of his comrades, and the methods used during his interrogations broke him down physically and he developed tuberculosis. He told me that he had been on hunger strike about twenty times. Usually the strike was unsuccessful or only illusory concessions were made. He would perhaps be moved to another cell or allowed to write letters after being refused such a privilege for a long time for no reason. I was told a lot about Bukhshtab by his fellow exiles when I arrived in 1951 in Kazachinskoye. After he had served his last term in one of the camps in Kazakhstan he and his wife were freed but they were told that they were deprived of the right to live in European Russia. They were sentenced to 'eternal' exile and in order that this eternity should not last too long they were separated from one another by a distance of some 3,000 kilometres. He was sent to the Krasnoyarsk region of Siberia while she was left in Kazakhstan. Both appealed endlessly to the authorities to be allowed to spend the remnant of their lives together: Bukhsh-tab was by then over sixty and the doctors thought that he had only a few months left to live as he was in an advanced state of tuberculosis. There was another reason as well. In Kazakhstan, though she too was old and ill, his wife could practise as a doctor earning close on 600 roubles a month, while Bukhshtab was incapable of doing any work at all. He lived on the money she was able to send him from her small earnings and this was not even enough to buy him the most necessary medicines. Now and then other people exiled in the surrounding villages sent him what they could but Bukhshtab, when he knew of this, refused their assistance – he was very sensitive on this point and preferred to suffer and go hungry rather than accept the help of people who themselves were usually poor and ill. He was also very cautious and suspicious about the source of the money even when there was no reason to be.

Two years later Bukhshtab was at last allowed to leave for Kazakhstan. He got as far as Kazachinskoye, a very small town but the main one of the district, through which all the local exiles had to pass on their way to their next place of residence. On the eve of travelling on further his health got much worse and he was put into the local hospital. It was in the hospital that I came to see him and it was here that our friendship began.

We talked about all sorts of subjects including the situation in Europe, but before we came to this it had become clear to me that an additional misfortune which had befallen this proud old man was that he had become, as it were, spiritually petrified and all the developments since he had ceased to be politically active had passed him by without leaving any impression. The thirties, with the revolution from above which Stalin had brought about, did not exist for him, nor did the war with Hitler and the Terror of the late forties. He was still living the conflict between Bolsheviks and Mensheviks, between Lenin and Martov, and he was convinced that the fate of Russia and perhaps of the whole world socialist movement had been decided by the Bolshevik seizure of power and the collapse of Menshevism. He was sure that at every point from the very beginning the moderates, that is, the Mensheviks, had been right as against the Bolsheviks, and that the cause of all Russia's misfortunes was the October Revolution which had distorted her natural development. As for the Jewish question, he kept to the same position which he had adopted at the beginning of the century. He had never belonged to the Bund or to any other Jewish party; in fact the question did not exist for him for he felt no links with the Jewish people. He stressed that his way of thinking was the same as that of his Russian comrades among whom he had grown up. He was bound up with Russian history and culture and the Russian way of life and thought. What separated him from the Russian nationalists and Orthodox Christians was, he said, his socialist convictions, his Orthodox Marxism, as he put it. For him the Bolsheviks had per-verted Marxism by not taking political and economic processes into account and insisting on 'leaps' which were based only on their own subjective will. As a socialist he was naturally opposed to the per-secution of the Jews such as went on in Tsarist times. He stood for equal rights and above all for giving the Jews the fullest possibility of becoming assimilated. He disapproved of all the efforts to create a Jewish culture or to preserve Jewish national consciousness whether they were made by Bolsheviks or Zionists. He believed that the course of world history doomed small nations to disappear, merging in the large blocs created by economic development. For him, as a Marxist, it was the economic 'basis' which determined the cultural and political 'superstructure', and so there was no point in trying to preserve the independent cultures of small nations. In the end there would be no small nations at all; there would be a united world without any language barriers or national frontiers. If the Jews close in on themselves, he told me, they will stifle for lack of air, whereas living amongst other nations they can reach their fullest development.

I couldn't argue with him too much: he was old, ill, touchy and irritable, but I pointed out that the Nazi massacres of the Jews did not encourage hopes of Jewish assimilation. To this he said: 'These massacres were made possible by your Bolsheviks, who not only taught the Nazis how to stifle democracy but betrayed Western democracy by making an alliance with Hitler in 1939. Besides, the Germans are killers by nature. I know this from 1917. They ought to have been made harmless then. Instead of that Lenin and your Bolsheviks fraternized with them and this too contributed to the rise of Fascism and anti-Semitism.' Bukhshtab, with his extreme hatred of the Bolshevik régime, added that it made demagogic use of 'national culture' as a means of fostering the spread of its ideological popularity. There was clearly no point in continuing this argument.

Bukhshtab had remained faithful to the Second International throughout his thirty-six years of suffering. He was sure that the world workers' movement had also remained faithful to it and that only the schism created by Lenin and the Bolsheviks at the time of the First World War had prevented the victory of 'true socialism' throughout the world. He believed that the Second International had not forgotten the Russian Mensheviks and, in spite of its frequent compromises with the bourgeoisie, which he believed to be necessary and which he said only Bolshevik demagogues could condemn, was doing everything necessary for the progress of socialism. In particular he was impressed with the British Labour Party and its programme of nationalizing industry, and he compared the 'genuine revolution' which it had carried out without any loss of life at all with the doings of the Bolsheviks who had shed oceans of blood and who had ruled despotically from the very beginning, condemning the country to hopeless wretchedness. I objected that the socialist party which he so admired had nevertheless got involved in the Korean War. He replied ironically: 'I thought you were a serious man, and after all, you've been in the West whereas I haven't, and yet you repeat that cheap *Pravda* propaganda like a parrot. Whenever real socialists come to power they help the development of backward nations, they give them the chance to get their share of European culture and they protect them against the feudal elements and the brutal bourgeoisie in the colonial countries. You Bolsheviks no doubt want to drive them out of the colonies in order to get hold of them yourselves, as you're doing in China, Indo-China and Korea. The Korean War is nothing but the result of the policies of Red imperialism. It's a good thing all the same the October Revolution has taught the socialists something, so that they now know what to think of the cheap slogans of the so-called liberators of the colonies.'

Talking of the Middle East, he was strongly in favour of the policy of Great Britain; first because it was hated by the Bolsheviks and secondly because after the war Britain was ruled by a socialist government. Bevin was for him a socialist with great experience who devotedly furthered social justice and was not as much deceived by Vyshinsky (Bukhshtab particularly hated Vyshinsky who had 'betrayed Menshevik ideals for the sake of his career') as were many others. He also thought that Soviet intervention in Middle Eastern affairs was extremely dangerous: the Middle East was a powder keg, an Asiatic Balkans where events threatened to lead to a third world war and through which the Bolsheviks hoped to achieve the subjugation of Turkey and all the Mediterranean bases including North Africa. 'There are no bounds to the appetites of these despots,' he sighed bitterly. 'Everyone who joins hands with them, even for a moment, will regret it to the end of his days. This has been shown by the experience of Beneš and Masaryk.[2] Those who allowed the Bolsheviks to meddle in Middle Eastern politics will also regret it.' He thought that Israel, which had recently been established, would also regret breaking with the British socialists and allowing the Soviets to intervene in the Middle East. I was surprised by his estimate of Israeli policy which I had never heard before from anyone except a Welshman, George Hannah, whom I met in the Tayshet camp in 1950.

2. Bukhshtab expressed his amazement that Beneš, whom he had considered one of the most able democratic politicians in Europe, had not realized that once Soviet troops had set foot on Czechoslovak soil the country was bound to become a Soviet colony. He thought the tragic fate of Beneš and Jan Masaryk was 'historical retribution' for their thoughtlessness.

Bukhshtab's health worsened; he was permanently laid up and the doctor forbade him to have long conversations. I bought food for him in the village and posted his letters to his wife. He wrote to her trying to explain the reason for his delay in joining her, for she knew that he had been allowed to go to Kazakhstan. We exiles tried to think up ways of using some pause in his illness to send him on to her; perhaps something could be done to bring down his temperature and stop his cough, if only for a short period, by using different medicines or getting him warmer clothes. This was at the end of February when in Siberia spring is still far away and there are very cold winds. The Jewish doctor who was looking after him did all he could; he did not think it was possible to save him but he hoped to enable him to join his wife so that at least she should be with him when he died, but he was rapidly getting worse. In the middle of March 1953 I had my last brief talk with him. He said a few words about the death of Stalin: 'This isn't all, this is not the end but it will be easier. The Bolsheviks will start struggling for power again.' He was interrupted by a fit of coughing and added only that he knew he wouldn't get better and that he would never see his wife. A few days later I got news from the hospital that Bukhshtab had died. In the absence of relatives his fellow deportees had to arrange the funeral. We told his neighbours and friends in the small town when the funeral would be held. It was difficult to find people to dig the grave; the ground was still frozen and it was very hard work. We found another Jew, a former communist who had been in camps and prisons since 1937 but was now 'living in freedom' in eternal exile. We dug the grave and knocked together a coffin as best we could. It was four kilometres from the hospital to the cemetery, and the way led through the township. The Jew who had dug the grave hired a horse and cart and we put the coffin on it. There were three of us accompanying it but as we came to the first houses people began to come out and join us. When we were half way to the cemetery I looked back and there was a long procession behind us, men and women, all exiles and all Jews. They told me afterwards they had seen three Jews following a coffin and had simply wished to pay their last respects to the Jew, whoever he was.

We had dug his grave in a corner of the cemetery where, judging from the names on the little planks of wood over the graves, several other Jews had been buried. (There are special Jewish cemeteries only in the main towns in Siberia where there used to be Jewish communities.) When we lowered the coffin into the ground one of those who had come with us, a Lithuanian Jew called Lifshits, came up to me and said: 'We must say the *Kaddish*:[3] there's no one else to say it.'

The few people who knew Bukhshtab asked me to write to his widow and send her what remained of his things. I sent her a small suitcase with his worn-out clothes, his hat and his boots. I found no notes and no letters – over the decades of wandering about between prisons, camps and exile he had made it a rule never to keep anything at all in writing. He had given his few books away to his friends before he went into hospital.

To mark the grave – for it sometimes happened that in winter there was so much snow that it was impossible to find a trace of a grave in the spring – we built a small fence round it and in summer we took some flowers there.

CHAPTER 7

CLERICS

THE ideological struggle against religion began in earnest shortly after the October Revolution and it was not long before administrative measures were introduced as well in the attempt to liquidate all religious faiths as inherently and profoundly counter-revolutionary. After my arrest I met numerous people who had actively tried to abolish religion. Now they were behind barbed wire together with thousands of believers against whom the struggle had been directed and who were doing time for religious activity of one sort or another, though some of them had been arrested for other reasons or on different pretexts. There were other prisoners who came or

3. Part of the daily ritual of the synagogue: specially recited by orphan mourners.

returned to religion only after their arrival in prison, but they usually kept quiet about this, for those who made no secret of their religious beliefs were kept under special observation.

A good example of a 'repentant Bolshevik' was provided by G. Ye. Yevdokimov, whom I met in Norilsk in 1940. On my arrival from the prison on Solovki I was sent to do heavy manual labour. The temperature there in winter often goes down to minus fifty-five, the wind-speed is thirty metres a second, and the working day lasted from pitch-dark to pitch-dark. It was light only from 11 a.m. to 1 p.m., so most of the time we were labouring in the gloom as well as bitter cold. I could not have gone on like this for long, and fortunately I soon had a real stroke of luck. Ilyushenko, my investigator in Moscow, was demoted and sent into a sort of exile as chief of the Third (i.e., Political) Section at Norilsk. As an old friend of mine he was able to have me transferred to a job as an economist in the 'project department'. Conditions there were rather like the ones Solzhenitsyn* describes in *The First Circle*, though for me this circle was neither the first nor the last. Now I lived not in a barrack together with criminals but in a brick building amongst the cream of society.

One evening a friend of mine came in and took me up to the second floor where, he said, someone wanted to talk to me. I was introduced to a middle-aged, tall, strongly-built and fair-haired man who looked like a warrior out of a Russian folk-legend. G. Ye. Yevdokimov was not the man of that name who had been expelled from the Central Committee for factionalist activity, but a namesake of worker origin who had joined the Party before the Revolution and played an important and active role on many 'special assignments' in 1917 and the Civil War. In the mid-twenties he was a member of the Party Control Commission and it was at that time that his doubts began. He knew about the ideas of many Party members who criticized the general line of the Party and proposed various changes and reforms. Such men had been the supporters of the Workers' Opposition or the Democratic Centralists or perhaps of some other group, and discussions about a change of course were still raging at this period. However, Yevdokimov quickly became disillusioned by these arguments because he felt that they did not get down to the really fundamental questions. His religious nature was stirring; he found he disagreed, first with the militant atheism which lay at the basis of Party doctrine, and then with any other sort of atheism, and before long he returned to the Russian Orthodox Church of his boyhood. With an embarrassed smile he showed me a little book. 'This is my ideological platform,' he said. It was a New Testament with a crucifix impressed on the cover.

Unlike the vast majority of us Yevdokimov had been expelled from the Party at his own request. His conscience forced him to resign and become an 'honest non-Party man' and later an ideological opponent of the Party line. Nothing happened to him for several years but then he was denounced by a colleague and arrested. Unfortunately for him there was a shortage of 'terrorists' at that time and so he was given article 58/8 and ten years' deprivation of freedom in 1936. His investigator said that Yevdokimov's religious beliefs were of no concern to him, for freedom of religion was guaranteed by the Constitution. It was however surprising, he went on, that a man like Yevdokimov, who knew many of the founders of the Soviet State, should end up with such fanatical notions, but perhaps the camps would cure him. I doubt it, but I do not know for sure as in 1942 he was moved to another camp and I never heard of him again. I met several other Russian communists who turned towards religion as they grew older, but in this chapter I intend only to write a little about some meetings I had with 'servants of the cult', not simple believers.

The first of these meetings was in 1935 when I was living in a cell in the Butyrki prison with fifty or sixty other prisoners, one of whom was an old man with a big white beard whom everyone called *batyushka* (Little Father). In the circumstances it would have been difficult to talk to him in private but I must admit that I did not try very hard as I considered at that time that there was little we had in common. However, I did sometimes speak to him and learnt that he had served in the Yelokhovsky cathedral, one of the most important churches still open in Moscow. He was accused in particular of preaching about Christian love and mutual help, and had been told that he deserved isolation from the people as he was a harmful element. When he said that his arrest was an example of how the church was being persecuted this remark itself was considered by the investigators to reveal his anti-Soviet attitudes and it even became the basis of the accusation against him.

Luckily for the *batyushka*, this was a time of relative liberalism towards priests (even in the cell he was still wearing his own vestments). He told me himself that persecutions always came in waves and he had been fortunate enough to be arrested in a quiet period when sentences were mild. Indeed, all he got was three years of exile, whereas, for example, a priest I met in the Alexandrovsk Central Prison near Irkutsk after the war was doing twenty-five years for remaining in his parish during the German occupation of the Ukraine and thereby collaborating with the Nazis.

*

In contrast to the Russian Orthodox, the Catholic priests I knew were very defiant and militant in their attitudes, defending their faith with great devotion and even fanaticism. Most of the Lithuanian priests I met in Tayshet and in exile were regarded as politically dangerous and had been sentenced for 'banditry'. They tended to be both intellectual and rather primitive in their approach to life: they knew the fundamentals of their religion and could quote the New Testament endlessly, but they had not personally worked out or come to their own philosophical outlook. They were very courageous and uncompromising, and said that although they were not guilty of the crimes imputed to them they were glad to be arrested as it was their duty to be with their flock and give comfort. Indeed, they did bring comfort to many, by introducing prayer-meetings and even services, which established a new atmosphere in the camp.

One of these priests I remember particularly clearly, although I only saw him once. It was just after the arrival in Tayshet of a new delivery of some 5,000 prisoners (about 100,000 people were sent to Tayshet from the Western regions of the Soviet Union in 1949). It proved difficult to cram this new batch into the available barracks and while they were standing around awaiting distribution I suddenly noticed that one of them, who turned out to be a Lithuanian priest, had climbed on to a large stone and begun to address the prisoners. I went closer to hear what he was saying. After citing a number of passages from the Bible he proceeded to make some outspoken political remarks and advised his listeners to rebel against the authorities' infringements of international and divine law. He mentioned the United Nations, of which, he reminded his listeners, the USSR was a member, and which was supposed to guarantee freedom of thought in its member states. The slavery that was going on here, he said, was a disgrace to humanity and a shame on our times.

Naturally, it was not long before the guards came along and took him to a punishment cell. He had already been sentenced to twenty-five years but we heard that he was returned to Irkutsk to face a fresh investigation, so he may not have been as fortunate as many other Catholic priests who were released and rehabilitated in the mid-fifties and even allowed to return to their parishes.

Earlier, when I was still in Mariinsk, I met a Lutheran pastor who spoke Russian almost as well as German. He had lived and worked in Moscow, and in the early thirties was asked by the German Embassy to minister to their spiritual needs and the needs of other Lutheran citizens in the Russian capital. The pastor, Rüger, agreed, and told me that he was on 'wonderful terms' with everybody, including the GPU. All would have been well, according to him, but for the advent of Hitler, which gradually brought a turnover in the Embassy's staff and before long the arrival in Moscow of a specially appointed German pastor. Rüger, now deprived of his old protectors and friends in the Embassy, was invited by the secret police to inform on the Germans he knew.

He refused and was arrested in 1934, not, of course, for refusing to spy but for being a spy. He was given five years in camp, where I met him in 1935. He had changed amazingly quickly and tried to assimilate with the criminal prisoners in the camp. He exchanged jokes (usually very dubious ones at that), smoked and played cards with them and seemed to be accepted by the criminals, who always spoke of 'Mister Pastor' with wry amusement. I can still remember him sitting in his shirt on the top deck of the plank-beds, his legs dangling down as he had a game of cards with his friends among the bandits and murderers. He blamed his degeneration on the

NKVD and Soviet power and said he was merely adapting to adverse circumstances.

*

Somebody who did preserve his dignity during imprisonment was the Imam of Moscow, whom I got to know well back in 1936. We spent the summer together in the Lubyanka while I was waiting to be called as one of the accused or one of the witnesses at the trial of Zinovyev and others. However, I had reached Moscow much later than expected and was not in fact produced at the trial. Needless to say this delay was not my fault but the fault of the NKVD, which was looking for me in one camp while I was in another. Naturally, given time, it was possible to find a needle even in a haystack as big as Siberia and so in due course I was discovered and taken back to Moscow.

Here I met Shamsutdinov, a Kazan Tartar who, well before the Revolution, had become a mullah and been transferred to Moscow. We quickly became friends and had many interesting conversations because we both spoke fluent Arabic. He had an excellent knowledge of the Koran and I had picked up a good deal of Arabic during my years in the Middle East. It was not long before I realized that he had adapted himself to the Soviet authorities as quickly as he had come to an accommodation with their Tsarist predecessors after his original appointment as Mullah. He had been equally loyal before and after the Revolution, for he considered it to be his duty as head of a Moslem community to accept whatever political authorities were in power. He liked to repeat that all worldly power is both ephemeral and a result of God's will, and so he had even co-operated with the GPU without any particular pangs of conscience.

He was about sixty and had expected to live out his life in peace and comfort under the Soviet régime. He and his large family occupied a big flat, had servants and a car at their disposal and knew no material needs. However, in the second half of the twenties the GPU had begun to urge him to report what he knew not only about foreign diplomats from Moslem countries but also about his own faithful with Soviet passports. He told me that he had tried to do his best for everybody and not had any real difficulties until the end of the decade when he asked for permission to go on a pilgrimage to Mecca. A number of other mullahs submitted similar requests and Shamsutdinov was eventually allowed to visit Mecca with the Mufti of Ufa, the centre for Moslems in the Soviet Union.

On his return Shamsutdinov sensed that he was regarded as less trustworthy than in the past. He was right. Before long he was arrested and accused of encouraging hostile Tartar elements in Moscow to sympathize with Hitler. Article 58/6 (espionage) and then treason to the motherland were brought up and the Imam was threatened with death by shooting. Once he was well and truly intimidated his interrogators arranged a number of confrontations at which some of his followers and several other mullahs, including the Mufti of Ufa, accused him of co-ordinating the actions of anti-Soviet groups in various parts of the country.

One day he returned to the cell in a particularly depressed frame of mind after having been forced to participate in a sort of all-union rally of about forty mullahs from all over the Soviet Union. All of them were under arrest but the meeting took place on the unspoken assumption that they were free and this was a normal meeting. The Mufti of Ufa accused Shamsutdinov of dishonourable conduct and plotting with the Gestapo, the 'minutes' of the meeting were signed by the mullah under pressure from the NKVD (as the GPU was now officially known) and then these minutes were presented to Shamsutdinov again by his interrogators.

It was obvious that before long he would almost certainly be shot, and the only things that seemed to comfort him now were some Oriental sayings, of which I particularly remember one, in Persian: *Inhem mugzaret* – even this will pass. It did. Quite soon he was taken away from our cell and I later heard that he had been shot one night towards the end of 1936.

*

I wish to keep this chapter short and I will mention only one other ecclesiastic, a Rabbi whom I met in 1951 in Tayshet. Another large group of prisoners had just arrived from the Ukraine, and among them I spotted a middle-aged man with a red beard. He looked utterly worn out after his journey, as well he might, for he had only one leg. He had lost the other one fighting in the Red Army against the Germans. He told me that his name was Feldman and that he came from Belaya Tserkov, a small town not far from Kiev with a large Jewish population.

Feldman had had a typical Jewish upbringing and spoke and read Hebrew from his boyhood, when he became an ardent Zionist. In the thirties, when he was a young man, he organized a small group of local Jews to try to preserve their traditional ways of life and thought. His father was a Rabbi and had taught him from the beginning that communism was evil and inherently hostile to Jewish traditions. Young Feldman and his friends were therefore opposed to both Hitler and Stalin, and somehow or other kept in touch with one another during the war. In 1945 numerous Jews returned to Belaya Tserkov and appealed, successfully, for permission to renew their religious activities. They were not given any active help by the authorities but had no difficulty in building a new synagogue on the site of the one destroyed by the Nazis. Feldman was surprised at the amount of financial help given by many individuals and before long the synagogue in Belaya Tserkov, which before the war had been one of the few remaining islands in the USSR where some Jewish culture still remained, again became a meeting-place for many of the Jews living in the area.

In particular, it seemed to be attracting a good number of young Jews, and Feldman told me that their attitudes were quite different from those of most of the Jews there before the war. Now there was a widespread conviction that the Jews must be allowed to live in and build up a country of their own. He said, to my surprise, that his own son, who was then about five or six, used to listen avidly to foreign radio-stations and tell his father what he had learnt in the latest programmes about his own country, Israel. At the end of the forties Feldman had been threatened by the MGB (secret police) and interrogated about his correspondence with relatives in the West. The atmosphere grew steadily worse and before his arrest he was warned that he could easily be sent to a place 'where the polar bears live'. Maybe this is what happened. Before long the Rabbi was sent on to another camp and I never learnt what happened to him, his family and the Jewish community of Belaya Tserkov.

CHAPTER 8

YOUNG REBELS

As the reader may remember, I spent the winter of 1936–37 in Moscow. I had been brought back from Siberia for a further interrogation. Many trials were being prepared and thousands of men were brought to the capital from camps and prisons. Ordinarily it was very difficult to bring people to Moscow from places thousands of miles away – but not for the NKVD. The prisoners wondered how the State could manage its budget when such enormous sums were spent on this. It was enough for any section of the NKVD to want someone in connection with a case for telegrams to fly to Kolyma or Vorkuta in the Far North, to Central Asia or Siberia and, as at the stroke of a magic wand, convoys were immediately arranged – four or five soldiers for each prisoner. There were countless thousands of such cases.

I was at a gathering point for prisoners. In such places it was possible to learn more than anywhere else. Here I realized for sure that the camps were not limited to just a few areas but amounted, throughout the country, to a huge state within the State, living its own life according to its own laws. I met people who had been in camps since the early twenties – Mensheviks, Cadets, anarchists, oppositionists within the Party, as well as recent members of new resistance groups. Not only history and geography could be learned in this way but philosophy as well, and general conclusions could be drawn as nowhere else from this abundance of material.

As I was a prisoner of some experience and was regarded as a quiet fellow with a placid temperament (a very important quality in prison), I was chosen to be the 'elder' of the cell. I had to distribute places, keep order at mealtimes and give the number of the prisoners at roll-call. I also had to receive new prisoners. This usually happened at night-time, and for this reason I soon resigned from my position, for I got no sleep. Normally no new prisoners ('greenhorns' as they were called) were put in with older prisoners; this was a psychological device intended to accentuate the shock of arrest and the first interrogation. The older prisoners were like professors who could teach a 'greenhorn' a thing or two and were therefore normally kept away from him. But on one occasion a 'greenhorn' was put in among us.

I was still an 'elder' at this time. Lying on the bunk next to me was my 'assistant', a respectable citizen much older than myself, an old Menshevik who had somehow survived, Eduard Eduardovich Pontovich.[1] Late at night we lay side by side, talking. He was telling me about his career. Shortly after the Revolution he became a lawyer to the Central Executive Committee of the new régime. He worked directly for President Kalinin and was an assistant to his secretary, Yenukidze. Among his duties had been the drafting of laws. He had so much experience of this under Lenin that, under Stalin, he could formulate a law as easily as write a letter. But he hastened to explain that the laws did not have to go through any parliament; the procedure was much simpler – a note from the Central Committee of the Party, which Pontovich put into legal language and which then became law for 160 million Russians.

He lived quietly in this way until his boss Yenukidze fell in 1935. Pontovich told me that one accusation against Yenukidze was that he employed former countesses and princesses in his library. It was alleged that seventy-five per cent of his entourage were members of the 'former classes' and that others were SRs, Mensheviks and so forth, who had gone unnoticed so long as Yenukidze was in power.

Pontovich, incidentally, was exceptionally well read. He had had a big flat where he had entertained the cream of Soviet literary and artistic society. His chief interest was literature, and he had known most of the pre-war writers – Leonid Andreyev* and Blok, Tsvetayeva and many others who later emigrated such as Merezhkovsky,* Zinaida Gippius,* and so on. He had especially encouraged young writers, and among them was Sergey Yesenin, the lyric poet.

It must have been one or two o'clock in the morning (we only knew approximately, for no one ever told us the time), the hour at which new prisoners usually arrived. Suddenly the door opened, and

1. I mentioned him earlier at the beginning of chapter 6.

a man was pushed in, brutally, so that he would be frightened and not think of turning back. He was a young man with a lot of luggage. It was my job to find him a place, but as the light from the bulb over the door fell on him Pontovich grabbed my shoulder and whispered: 'God, it's Sergey Yesenin!' I calmed him down: the poet had long been in his grave, and Pontovich had been present at the funeral.

But the newcomer did indeed give his surname as Yesenin, though his first name was Yury. This young man (he was twenty-two) turned out to be Yesenin's son by his first wife, a village girl whom he later divorced. He had been brought up with Yesenin's other children by the poet's third or fourth wife, a grand-daughter of Tolstoy. She was better off than his other wives and so she collected his children and brought them up in nicer conditions than they would otherwise have had. It was no wonder that Pontovich had taken him for his father, for he was extraordinarily like him. We learned later that Yury was not himself a writer, although he occasionally made up verses and lived on the reputation of his father. He knew by heart not only all his poems, but even the music to which some of them had been set. He had a fine voice and he often sang them.

We gave him a good place because we felt as though his father had come with him into our cell. Even the ordinary people among the prisoners respected Yury for his father's sake. He stayed among us for several weeks. What amazed us was that a young man who had been so comfortably brought up should be so embittered. We all advised him to be cautious, but he could not control himself and was very outspoken. The source of his bitterness was that although his father had committed suicide, Yury thought that he had been driven to it by others and not by his own internal problems. He could not put it into words beyond saying: 'They hunted my father to death.' Pontovich and some others agreed with him.

He had been brought to our prison from Khabarovsk to be tried for his alleged participation in a terrorist plot. The idea seemed strange. Young and romantic looking, he did not seem in the least like a normal Soviet terrorist.

He had been performing his military service in Khabarovsk as a soldier, and had no idea that there was anything against him. All he thought about was his soldiering, which he found interesting and exciting. When he was arrested he thought at first that he had offended some officer or broken some rule of military discipline, and he could not believe us when we explained to him that for such things people were not brought all the way to Moscow.

Before long we understood Yury's case, and so did he, in a most tragic way. In the early thirties he had been one of a circle of young people – children of old intellectuals or of highly placed officials – who had been schoolfellows or whose parents were friends or who simply liked to talk together. Some time in 1935, after the assassination of Kirov, one of them – the son of an old Bolshevik, and now a public prosecutor – encouraged these boys to express their discontent with some aspects of the Soviet régime.

A typical student-reformer conversation ensued. They declared the situation was becoming impossible, that the Government was too repressive, that the people could not develop, that the country was going to the dogs. One boy went so far as to remind the others that decent young people ought to take things into their own hands. Yury, who had not spoken much but was essentially in agreement, commented that it would not be difficult to bring about a *coup d'état*: it just depended on a few people, perhaps even on one man, and that if, for instance, the Kremlin was blown up all these questions would be solved. Another boy, a member of a technical institute, said that blowing up the Kremlin was not so difficult either, and that he personally had the technical knowledge necessary for such a job. When everyone had had his say the meeting ended as usual in dancing and drinking, and they did not mention the subject again. Indeed, they forgot all about it.

But, as Yury found out at the very first interrogation, it had not been forgotten in another place. One or two boys who had been present at the gathering happened to be arrested on other charges, and the meeting was recounted and put down in the NKVD records as a meeting of terrorists. When we heard this we realized how serious his position was: once the case had been taken over by the department which dealt with terrorism he was in great danger, not merely of the maximum prison sentence, but of losing his life.

Unfortunately Yury himself was by then so frightened that he did not confide in us and thereby did himself a bad service. It was only several weeks later that he came back from being questioned and finally told Eduard Eduardovich and myself all that had happened. We learnt that Yury was to appear at the trial, not only as one of the participants in a plot to blow up the Kremlin and kill the leaders, but also as a principal witness.

The interrogators had approached him with great tact and managed to deceive him completely. They spoke to him of the great honour in which his father was held and said that neither the government nor the NKVD wanted to see the son of Yesenin in prison or a camp. They even convinced him that they had brought him back from the Far East only to help him to get out of this affair. These talks were conducted to the accompaniment of good meals and cigarettes, and they made a great impression on him. That was why he had told us nothing. The interrogators had made him feel that he had no connection with his fellow prisoners and would shortly be released.

But they had made just one condition – that he should tell his story in detail and if necessary confirm it when confronted with the accused. For several days the silly boy did what he was told. He was not asked to sign anything, but the other members of the group were brought in one by one; some confessed and Yury confirmed their statements, others denied the charges and Yury argued with them. Then, suddenly, the interrogators changed their tone and he was asked to sign the accusation against himself. So far he had only been a witness but, when it came to formulating the charges, he became one of the accused.

Now he was almost in tears and begged us for advice. When he had reminded the interrogators of their promises to him they merely laughed and asked him how could they, the representatives of State Security, overlook his crime, a grave crime against Security, against the leaders – how could he even think of such a thing? No, he would be punished. But perhaps, as Yesenin's son, he might get away with only a five years' term in prison.

We did not believe this. In 1937 'terrorists' were repressed with extreme severity, even when their crimes were only words, not deeds; they were tried under paragraph 58 of the Criminal Code and as a rule shot, and only in rare cases sentenced to ten years. We realized that he was being tried not merely as a member of the conspiracy but as its leader, and was therefore likely to get the maximum sentence. It was difficult to advise him. He had already tried to withdraw his statements, saying that he had been tricked or forced into making them, but we knew this would be of no avail. A few days later he was removed from our cell and, so far as we could discover, all the accused lost their lives, though there may have been a couple of exceptions. Had he been condemned only to a term in camp, someone would surely have heard of his existence later, especially in view of the great interest in his father's work. Far from trying to save Yesenin's son, the apparatus must have done its best to finish him off.

*

I can still remember one morning a little later in 1937 in the same prison in Moscow. I had slept badly but just before dawn I had a short, vivid, blissful dream. It seemed to be a mysterious answer to the worries which had kept me awake.

Most of my cellmates were held under Article 58/8 on charges of 'terrorism', which was punishable by death. Not one of them admitted his guilt and I had learned enough since my own arrest to realize that they were probably telling the truth. Had the Government any grounds for behaving as though it was threatened by a country-wide terrorist conspiracy?

In my dream, the doors of the prison were held wide open by two young men who were dressed as students. The prisoners were filing out. Each one handed his charge sheet to the young men, who tore them up, laughing and saying: 'There aren't any terrorists. Go home. Go back to your wives and families. Go in peace.'

Every morning the cell was like an office in which dreams are filed, sorted and examined for omens. Dreams put a prisoner in touch with the outside world in a way which no isolation could prevent, and he tended to talk about them at great length. But on this occasion there was no time to discuss mine because almost at once two new prisoners were pushed in. The extraordinary thing was that one of them, a young, slender, determined-looking man who turned out to be a student, was like one of the two students in my dream.

His name was Dmitry Ivanov. His companion, Alexander Dubinsky, was much older, with strong features and intelligent brown eyes half-hidden behind bulging spectacles. Despite the difference in their ages they were friends, in part because of the Leningrad 'territorial link' which, Dubinsky said, bound them closer together than any shackles could.

Both had been transferred to the Butyrki from another prison. Asked what he was accused of, Ivanov staggered us by saying – firmly and with conviction – 'I am a terrorist'. We had never heard such an admission before.

Deeply impressed, we gave them better places than they were entitled to as newcomers, and prepared to listen to their story. Ivanov, however, after his first dramatic statement, sank into a gloomy silence which lasted for days. It was Dubinsky who spoke. He was a sociable character, with a strong sense of humour – a godsend to a cell full of discouraged prisoners. He and I had many interests in common and we soon became friends.

Born in St Petersburg, he had taken part in the 1905 revolution, emigrated to Switzerland, where he met Lenin, Zinovyev and most of the other émigré leaders, and followed Lenin back to Russia in 1917, travelling, like him, on a German train.

I was later to meet some Mensheviks who regarded Lenin's defeatism during the war merely as part of his manoeuvring for power in Russia, and who accused him of making a deal with German imperialism. But Dubinsky was convinced that Lenin had only had the interests of the world revolution at heart and was right in 'making use of the differences between the imperialists'. He also told me that Fritz Platten, the Social Democrat who had started the Swiss-German negotiations for Lenin's repatriation, was now out of favour with the Stalin régime. I learned later that Platten was in fact arrested in 1939 and died in a concentration camp.

Dubinsky took a prominent part in the October Revolution and the Civil War, and was one of the founders of the Marx-Engels-Lenin Institute, but his closest ties were with the leaders of the so-called 'Leningrad Opposition' – Yevdokimov,* Bakayev,* Gertik* and Safarov* as well as Zinovyev and Kamenev.

These were men who regarded themselves as the very heart of the Party but who, Dubinsky believed, had suffered a crucial defeat at the very outset. Before and for some time after the Bolshevik seizure of power in October 1917 they favoured a coalition of Bolsheviks, Mensheviks, Anarchists and other Left-Wing parties, in preference to an exclusively Bolshevik government – and he still thought that such a united front would have averted many disasters. A rapprochement would have been possible with Western socialism, Russia would have been less isolated from the world outside and fewer sacrifices would have been required of her people.

He recalled a conversation he once had with Kamenev who had just been addressing a meeting at a factory. Cold, hungry, miserably lodged and clothed, the workers were demoralized and production had gone down. Alone with Dubinsky, Kamenev admitted his own disappointment: 'If only they had listened to us! We wouldn't be facing the hostility of the whole world. We wouldn't be placing this intolerable burden on the people.' Dubinsky reminded him that, as members of a coalition, the Bolsheviks might have been outvoted and lost power. 'So what?' Kamenev grinned. 'We would have been in opposition for a time and returned to power if the people supported us. But it's no good crying over spilt milk. There's no way back and now we've got to go through with it.'

Dubinsky spoke of his friends' misgivings when NEP was introduced: if Russia was not ripe for socialism, why had the dictatorship of the proletariat and a single-party régime been established at such great cost? He also mentioned their growing bitterness at the plight and repression of the workers even in the twenties and the denial of the right to criticism within the Party. By the time they realized their need for unity among themselves and for active struggle against Stalin it was too late. Power had passed from the Party as a movement into the hands of *apparatchiks*[2] appointed and taking

2. Permanent salaried functionaries of the Communist Party, etc.

their orders from above, and Stalin's absolutism had in practice become invincible. No one else seemed to have the personality to become leader. Trotsky had never grasped the importance of Stalin's use of that part of the Lenin tradition that lays stress on organization and the penetration of the masses by Party cells. Now it was too late. Even when Trotsky was in exile and might have unified millions of workers in the West he did not even try to adapt his doctrines and bring about this unity but created more and more splits and followed an even more sectarian line than before. The liquidation of the revolutionary Russian workers went on with hardly a word of protest from the Western working class.

Like many other members of the Opposition, Dubinsky was exiled in the mid-twenties and, when he returned to Leningrad some five years later, buried himself in his work, secretly disaffected but outwardly supporting the official policy. He realized later that by this attitude the remnants of the Opposition had lost whatever chances they might still have had in the early thirties: by taking part in the ruthless collectivization of the land they finally discredited themselves with the masses and became an easy prey. No wonder so many people were delighted at the harsh sentences passed on most of the Old Bolsheviks. One sometimes heard a prisoner say that he would now willingly accept whatever fate was in store for him – it was enough for him to have lived to see this day. What puzzled Dubinsky, though, was why Stalin had decided – as he evidently had – physically to exterminate them now, when his power was at last so firmly established.

For several days we were not called out for interrogation and life in the cell seemed to be at a standstill. Very occasionally, Ivanov joined in our conversation. Dubinsky laughed at his despondency, trying to shake him out of it, but admitted that both his and Ivanov's situation could hardly be worse. Like the prisoners in Anatole France's novel about the French Revolution, *Les Dieux ont soif*, their only hope – and a very slender one at that – was 'to be forgotten' for as long as possible. If the investigation could be made to drag on for several months they might get away with only life imprisonment. The great thing was to 'keep out of the mincing machine while it's working full time'.

That the machine was working busily was proved by the arrival of more 'terrorists', all of them newly-arrested workers and communists.

One day a very young, dishevelled man was dragged in, resisting violently; he started hammering on the door as soon as it closed. When he finally gave up and turned to us, we saw a ragged, exhausted but exceptionally handsome boy with broad shoulders and a resolute face. Instead of trying to negotiate a 'good place' near the window, he looked round as though choosing his company and walked straight up to Dubinsky and Ivanov. 'Article 58/8?' he asked them. 'I thought so.' He sat down on Ivanov's bed, and began to curse as I had rarely heard anyone curse before.

The terrifying thing was that he cursed the Government, the leaders and even Stalin himself by name. It was dangerous for all who listened. Ivanov reminded him that he might be overheard by spies.

'Let them listen,' said the boy. 'What have I got to lose?' He told us that he too had belonged to the Opposition – 'and don't we see just how right we were!' – but that now it was not only the end of the Opposition: what the authorities were trying to destroy was 'every trace of life and thought in the country.' It was the end of the whole workers' movement at home and abroad. 'For centuries to come, Europe will curse the Russian revolutionaries,' he ranted. 'You'll see, the West will move in, and the workers of the world will rejoice to see this scum wiped off the face of the earth.'

We listened, too astonished to say anything. Then the door opened, the boy was removed and we never heard of him again.

The reaction of the prisoners was characteristic. Some remained silent. Others whispered: 'Poor chap! What he must have been through!' But nearly all said loudly: 'There's a really dangerous counter-revolutionary for you.' A former lawyer even made a speech, justifying the Government's repressive measures by its need to 'defend itself against such desperate criminals.' Had the unfortunate stranger been tried, not by a special court but by the inmates of this cell, all of them accused of counter-revolutionary activity, they would undoubtedly have condemned him to be shot. In other words, they might well have judged him more severely than the court.

In reality, nearly everyone sympathized with the young man but few dared to commit themselves for fear that he had been put among us as an *agent provocateur*. As time went by, I became increasingly convinced that he was not.

Physical torture was rarely used before the second half of 1937, but from then until 1939, during the war and in the later forties, nine prisoners out of ten were tortured in one way or another. As a result, most people signed confessions, implicating hundreds of other innocents. Of those who could not bring themselves to do this, a few chose an equally certain but sometimes quicker way to death. Instead of confessing to imaginary crimes they said what they really thought. Some of them would talk for days on end and insist on the interrogators putting it all down – they wanted to get everything off their chest. After this, of course, they cared nothing about spies. They welcomed the audience of their fellow-prisoners, a few of whom might survive and remember their testimony. The outburst we had heard was only the first of many I was to hear. It may have been the impression it made on Ivanov that finally broke down his reserve.

Like his friend, he came from Leningrad. Both his parents were communists. His father had been killed in the Civil War.

The day of Lenin's death, he told us, had been the saddest day in his life. Immediately after it he joined the Komsomol (the age of admission was lower than it is now) and gave himself, heart and soul, to political work.

The programme of the Komsomol (later it was altered by Stalin) described the October upheaval as the beginning of world revolution and in Leningrad, where the international tradition was particularly strong, many young people lived in expectation of an imminent response from London, Berlin, Paris and perhaps New York.

Trotsky had said that the Russian workers had seized power with comparative ease, but their further journey was along a country dirt-track full of pot-holes; in England, on the other hand, the workers had first to overcome a régime that was more formidable, because it was modern and sophisticated, but would afterwards travel on a macadamized highway towards communism. It was difficult to see how Russia, with her backward economy and hostile peasant masses, was to achieve socialism, but her Revolution would be tested by its success abroad: the liberation of the western proletariat would be *its* victory.

These were the ideas preached by the Leningrad Party leaders. Their defeat at the Fourteenth Party Congress in 1925 was a bitter surprise for Ivanov and his friends. It was immediately followed by repressions. A delegation arrived from Moscow. Moscow nominees replaced the local heads of the Komsomol. Public meetings were held which confused the rank and file but did not convert them to the official line. Individual members could still meet in private. They believed they were the victims of the temporary victory of a clique headed by Stalin and Bukharin, and that genuine Leninists would soon come back to power.

The resistance of the opposition groups in 1927 filled them with optimism, and they took part in the anti-Stalin demonstration in November, but its defeat soon marked the end of their own hopes.

The Government now concentrated on suppressing the independent tradition of the Leningrad Komsomol once and for all. Leaders were corrupted or broken down by the GPU. Even after the organization had been brought to heel more and more of its former members lost their jobs or were imprisoned or exiled between 1928 and 1930.

Yet secret meetings were still held. Ivanov's friends had not changed their minds, though they realized that no direct action was possible and kept their ideas to themselves, biding their time and pretending, like so many others, to agree with the Party line.

'So you accept the accusation of hypocrisy made against the Opposition?' I asked.

'It should be made against the Party,' Ivanov said. 'Hypocrisy is built into it.' Long before 1934, he claimed, the authorities knew that not only the survivors of the Opposition but ever wider circles of outwardly orthodox communists were disaffected. 'This is why, in spite of his apparent triumph, we could still believe that Stalin's downfall was only a matter of time. The question was – who would shoot first?'

So it was a question of shooting and terrorism? Was it possible that the charge of involvement in the murder of Kirov, made against the Leningrad Komsomol, was true after all?

'You can take it from me, it was not,' said Ivanov.

I believed him at the time, and his statement was later confirmed by many prisoners I met who had been members of either the Opposition or the Security Forces used to crush it. Many hinted that the assassin, Nikolayev, had been backed by the NKVD in Leningrad and perhaps in Moscow (though not by Stalin himself – this I only heard abroad after my release), but no one believed the Komsomol had had anything to do with it.

The news of Kirov's death, Ivanov said, came like a bolt from the blue to his friends in the Leningrad Komsomol. Immediately, its acting Secretary was arrested, as were nearly all those who had served on its Executive Committee in the twenties. Ivanov was picked up on the night of Kirov's funeral.

That day long lists had been published of summary executions carried out under the Decree against 'Terrorists', issued on the 1st of December (the day of the murder).

Ivanov was accused of being connected with the so-called Kotolynov 'terrorist' group. Its sixteen or so members were subsequently shot. Some thirty of their friends, Ivanov among them, were present at their trial but for some reason, at the last moment, their cases were held over for further investigation.

The death sentences had been published before my arrest, but not the proceedings – nor were they likely to be, judging from Ivanov's description of the attitude of the accused: they had admitted their hatred of the régime, said it was completely justified, and pleaded guilty, 'but in the best pre-revolutionary tradition'. So moving was his account of it that even today I feel almost as though I myself had been present at the trial.

The most impressive speech was made by Volodya Levin. He started by saying that he was not going to answer the accusations in detail. 'I know that this statement is not only the last I shall make at this trial, but the last in my life.' He knew he was condemned in advance, as were countless others who would have no chance to make their protest heard. 'Only here, behind closed doors, in front of these few people whom you trust, can the truth be said.' He would speak for all the others – the Komsomol, the old Bolsheviks, and the Russian workers.

Continually interrupted by the judge, who kept insisting that his remarks were irrelevant, Levin spoke of the wrongs, the violence and the injustices committed by the régime. The country was on the verge of economic ruin. The peasants were pauperized and the workers poorer than under the Tsars. 'And we, who assumed power in their name, are forbidden even to criticize what is going on.'

For ten years the members of the Opposition who were in the Komsomol had been hunted as enemies of the Revolution. As children they had taken part in it, their fathers had died for it and they had been bred and brought up in its traditions. But they had long since come to the conclusion that its ideals had been betrayed, that material and spiritual disaster threatened Russia and perhaps the world, and that they must do something soon to avert it.

Levin had been asked for information about plots, terrorist assassination attempts and hidden stocks of arms. He had none to give. But he had weighed up the life of one man against the lives of millions whose misfortunes he had caused. . . .

The moment Levin spoke of Stalin, he was hustled out of the court room.

The statements of the other members of the group were no different in substance from his. They denied their participation in an organized plot and in Kirov's murder (of which no shred of evidence had been offered by the prosecution), but they all admitted their hatred of Stalin's methods and the NKVD.

This, of course, was more than enough to condemn them and, according to Ivanov, also to seal the ultimate fate of those like himself who were present at the trial but had so far been spared. The trial had thrown a dramatic light on the state of mind of an unknown number of young people and their sympathizers both in the Party and outside it. Since then, each new wave of arrests must have brought new evidence. 'Our misfortune,' said Ivanov, 'is that we are so many.' Besides, the situation was continually being worsened by the very fact of the arrests and their effect on the population. Mass repression could only harden mass resentment and, with it, the Party's fear of the masses, making it more and more difficult for the policy of Terror to be relaxed.

*

As the Terror continued, I asked myself again and again what its true explanation was. I came to a strange conclusion.

The history of the twenties and early thirties is the history of continual political conspiracy within the Party. As the Party changed from a movement into an executive machine, group after group crystallized as part of an ever more helpless opposition. Its leaders were never in a position to appeal for help outside the Party either abroad or at home.

Early Bolshevik intransigence had isolated them from the workers' leaders in the West. It had led not to world revolution but to Russia's being cordoned off from the proletariat of the world and her own workers left to the mercy of Stalin. His opponents could count on none of the international support enjoyed by the revolutionaries under Tsarism. By the early thirties his prestige abroad was unassailable – a hero to the Left, he was a factor of stability in the eyes of the Right, who recognized him as the destroyer of 'October'. At the same time, the rise of Fascism and Nazism made it more difficult than ever for Russian communists to think of calling for foreign help.

Most important of all, they were by then fatally compromised with the masses at home – not by their opposition to Stalin but by their support of his collectivization of the land with all its attendant horrors. Any appeal they might have made to the population would have been rejected as coming from a discredited source.

The only weapon left to them was terrorism – the assassination of Stalin and his close supporters. There were many psychological reasons against this. Used against the Tsarist régime, it had been condemned by the Bolsheviks as an individual (not a mass) weapon and as wasteful, difficult to control and politically ineffective. Their whole training and tradition were against it. This is perhaps the most important clue to an understanding of their defeat.

Unfortunately Stalin thought them capable of assassination. Believing that this, not Nazism, was his only real danger and regarding his opponents as mistaken in not using it, he acted on the assumption that they might at any moment resort to it. Thus the Terror was launched as a 'prophylactic measure' against terrorism.

Once it had been launched, the Government could not draw back. It knew that the greater the massacres, the greater the hatred which could only be driven underground. It was there, in the privacy of people's lives, thoughts and unconscious minds, that the Government pursued terrorism, ever more convinced because of its own crimes that the enemy must be lurking somewhere near, especially amongst those who had taken an active part in the upheaval of 1917 and sincerely believed in communism. Yet at the time all this was altogether incomprehensible to most of the victims, onlookers and even interrogators, as was clear from many of the talks between them and the accused.

Never for a moment, however, did Stalin himself believe that his victims could forgive him or his instruments. This is why he used as his accomplices those he already meant to destroy, why those who had been victimized in the thirties but survived were again arrested in the forties, and why every period of Terror ended in the sacrifice (as a libation) of a part of the NKVD.

Like his communist opponents, Stalin had made a thorough study of history. If the Bolsheviks had learned from it the ruthlessness needed to make the Revolution final, he had learned from it the even greater ruthlessness and subtlety needed to protect a tyranny. Thus the explosion of popular hatred which, on past evidence, appeared inevitable, never came about. After each apocalyptic yet carefully measured peak, the Terror was relaxed, though it was never given up entirely.

From about 1933 to 1953 its aim – since not *all* the potential 'enemies' could be exterminated – was to prevent, rather than to punish, every least sign of political initiative, whether in action or in thought, among Stalin's subjects. Only after his death, and very timidly even then, could an attempt be made to cure the paralysis induced by the 'prophylaxis'. In making use of the apparatus of repression and various methods of mass or selective terror the Soviet rulers still take historical experience fully into account. It is only by being aware of this difference between them and earlier despots that we can make a correct analysis of our time and estimate future prospects.

*

It is sometimes said in Stalin's defence that the Terror in the 1930s was the price of industrializing the Soviet Union. However, in the victims of the Terror the country lost the very men responsible for its great industrial achievements of the twenties and early thirties. The main implementors of the Five-Year Plans were 'Opposition-ists', who built roads, railways and power-plants, giving their every ounce of energy to their work, whether they agreed wholeheartedly with Stalin or not. At the same time, of course, they were strength-ening Stalin's instruments of internal oppression to which they shortly fell victim. There were many such people on the staff of Stalin's fellow Georgian and loyal personal friend, Ordzhonikidze,* appointed Commissar of Heavy Industry in 1932 and today described by the Soviet encyclopedia as 'an outstanding organizer of Soviet industry'. All of them were liquidated after his death.

I had known a young Georgian protégé of both Ordzhonikidze and Stalin since the late 1920s when we met at a session of the Executive of the Komintern.

Tall and well-built, exceptionally intelligent and energetic, 'Besso' Lominadze had made a brilliant career in the Komsomol. Although trained by some of its more independent early leaders, he had con-sistently supported Stalin against all opposition and had risen to be not only a member of the Central Committee of the Communist Youth International but the Soviet representative in its Executive Committee. By 1929 he was helping Manuilsky and Pyatnitsky to shape the policy of the Komintern. He qualified for this by his work two years earlier in China.

Attacked by Trotsky for his inadequate support of the Chinese communists, Stalin had sent Heinz Neumann, with Besso Lominadze as his assistant, to organize a rising in Canton. Ill-prepared, the rebellion ended in a blood-bath and a long-term defeat of the Chinese workers' movement by Chiang Kai-shek. A reckless adventure, the incident could not be allowed to go down in history as such. Stalin claimed it as a moral victory, and Lominadze – one of the few leaders who returned – was rewarded as a hero accordingly.

I saw a good deal of him. An orthodox Stalinist, he had only one difficulty. Temperamentally, he favoured a more dynamic approach to world revolution than did the Komintern. If so militant a step as the collectivization of the land was being undertaken at home, surely, he thought, a more active, openly subversive policy ought to accompany it abroad.

When, by 1930, he resigned himself to seeing revolution in the West indefinitely postponed, he began to doubt the wisdom of the methods used to collectivize and felt increasingly irked by the bureaucracy and lack of freedom of speech in the Party. When I saw him, with another of his friends, in 1931, he was boldly critical of Stalin's leadership. Now that opposition from both Left and Right had been suppressed, he thought the next logical step was a radical reform of the Party and its personnel.

'What about the General Secretary?' asked his friend.

'If there is a spring cleaning, every piece of furniture has to be moved, including the biggest one.'

'But who could replace him?'

'That's up to the Congress.' It was time for younger men to take a share of the responsibility – men who had some practical experience but had been less involved in the struggle between the factions.

Needless to say, this was extremely risky talk. It even occurred to me that Lominadze saw himself as a suitable successor to Stalin. Two years later I realized I had been right. The Central Committee published a resolution condemning a so-called 'Lominadze group' which had openly demanded Stalin's removal. But at the time I dismissed the idea – it seemed impossible seriously to suspect him of so dangerous an ambition.

Whether he had a charmed life or it was true, as rumour had it, that 'Stalin loved him like a son', Besso was not arrested for his views – instead he was appointed Party Secretary at the huge new power station in Magnitogorsk. Experience of this sort was then regarded as preparation for high political office.

At the Seventeenth Congress Lominadze, like so many of Stalin's critics, voted for his re-election, and for the next couple of months wrote and spoke in support of the Party line.

By then I had lost touch with him and I heard the rest of his story only in the summer of 1935. It was told me, at the Mariinsk camp, by an old and intimate friend of his whom I will call Mironov, who had been with him in the Komsomol and, as his second in command, at Magnitogorsk.

For two years Besso had worked with his usual energy, though without the fiery enthusiasm of their days in the Komsomol.

In December 1934 came the news of Kirov's murder and the mass arrests and executions in Leningrad and Moscow. Lominadze became intensely nervous and depressed. He would come to see Mironov late at night. They listened to the news. Sometimes he insisted on their going out and walking about the empty streets in the bitter cold. He talked – endlessly – about the Party and the men whom 'circumstances had brought to power'. They were more determined and ruthless than anyone who did not know them could imagine, and Stalin was capable of pursuing his ends with all the vengefulness of an Oriental tyrant as well as with the trained single-mindedness of a Bolshevik.

As Party Secretary, Besso had received and communicated to the local members the 'secret letter' from the Central Committee issued after Kirov's death. It had poisoned the atmosphere with its talk of 'two-faced men' and its call for vigilance. Everyone felt unsafe. Everyone was in duty bound to suspect his neighbour.

After the trial of the Kotolynov group in January 1935, Lominadze was urgently summoned to Moscow, and left without even having time to say goodbye to his family. He returned a week later. Mironov saw him the same night, looking mortally weary and distressed.

The summons had been a telegram from Ordzhonikidze, and it was from him that Besso had learned the extent of the disaster. Stalin, it appeared, was full of self-reproach – it was *he* who had lacked the necessary 'vigilance'! He had been 'too trusting', but now he would make up for it. It was not enough that the 'chips should fly', as he had once promised they would; the whole forest of discontent must be felled and uprooted.

Ordzhonikidze personally still seemed to be in Stalin's favour and so was Lominadze, he believed. But this meant only that their danger was less immediate. All those who had ever held responsibility must tremble for their lives, and not only they – it was impossible to foresee how far Stalin would go. Ordzhonikidze – so Besso told his friend – could see no way out.

Before leaving Moscow, Besso had a brief audience with Stalin himself, but his reception was cool.

Now he was filled with despair. His friend asked him if there was really nothing to be done, or at least attempted. After a long silence he replied: 'There may be just one hope. There are *thousands* of us willing to try. Not by marching, demonstrating or shouting slogans, but by dying.'

Bewildered, Mironov asked him what he meant.

'Exactly what I said. A hundred thousand suicides among prominent Party members might possibly make Stalin reflect.'

Many people had already been arrested in Magnitogorsk. The charges were not known. Lominadze was not told of the arrests in advance. It was no longer the custom, it seemed, for the Party Secretary to be consulted or even warned. The NKVD were trusted to act at their own discretion. Everyone else was suspect.

One day Besso was rung up from Chelyabinsk, the administrative centre of the region, where the Party Secretary, still believed to be in good standing, was a friend of his. Besso told Mironov he had to go to Chelyabinsk at once, ordered his car to be brought round, but dismissed the chauffeur, saying he would drive himself. At the last moment he borrowed the chauffeur's revolver on the pretext that he might be coming back alone late at night.

Worried about him, several of his friends followed him in another car. Halfway to Chelyabinsk they found him. He had stopped, got out, walked into a field and shot himself.

Two days later *Pravda* published an obituary hinting at the reasons for the suicide. The same hints were dropped by the officials who made speeches at the funeral. It was said that Lominadze had become ideologically 'confused' and had taken an easy way out, unworthy of a Bolshevik. A wave of arrests swept Magnitogorsk, Chelyabinsk and other industrial towns. Everyone who was known to have had the slightest connection with Lominadze was picked up.

The reasons for the suicide were obviously understood: it was interpreted as an act of protest and, as such, a political crime.

In the course of his interrogation Mironov was told that 'it was a pity the conspirators weren't arrested in time'. He gathered that Lominadze's arrest had been imminent; the telephone call from Chelyabinsk might have been a warning and perhaps a signal. On the whole, as anyone could turn out to be a 'double-dealer' it was thought best not to inform a friend of his impending arrest in case it came out under subsequent interrogation that one hitherto un-discovered 'double-dealer' had warned another.

I asked Mironov if other suicides had followed. He said he knew of several and believed that others had been prevented only by the speedy arrests of the people concerned.

I was to hear of many more in 1936 and 1937, though the papers spoke only of those which could not be concealed. The best known were those of the Chairman of the Supreme Soviet of Byelorussia, Chervyakov, the Chairman of the Ukrainian Council of People's Commissars, Lyubchenko, General Gamarnik, Tomsky, the Chair-man of the Council of Trade Unions, and 'Sergo' Ordzhonikidze.

*

If ever there was an unpopular and dirty war it was the 1939–1940 war with Finland; it was one of Stalin's greatest crimes as well as a gigantic miscalculation. His attempt to justify it on the grounds that it was necessary to ensure the safety of Leningrad was not accepted in the Soviet Union; nor was his line that the campaign was merely punitive and did not affect Russia's neutrality in the Second World War.

In 1944 Roosevelt said that totalitarian régimes had a great advantage in the ease with which they could manipulate public opinion. None the less, however total the control of propaganda may be and however clever its devices, it needs time to build up and become effective. The propaganda concerning Finland had a most unpropitious starting point. The Red Army's entry into Poland, described by Molotov as the peaceful liberation of the Byelorussians and Ukrainians there, as well as the pressure on the Baltic States, were fresh in everyone's mind. The propaganda line then was that Stalin was keeping Russia at peace while, like the walls of Jericho, the frontiers of neighbouring countries fell before his trumpet blast. A little while later the people were told that Russia was at war because the Finns had started shelling Russian positions. The propagandists may have thought the people would by now swallow anything, but no one believed *this*. The day after war broke out a *Pravda* article ended with the words, 'See you in Helsinki'. The country was assured that the war would end with lightning speed. Hitler had taken a fortnight over Poland, so Stalin would surely need less than that for Finland.

The fact that the Red Army met with little success was due to a number of causes: at first only the Leningrad area was mobilized; since the Tukhachevsky trial the army had been leaderless and short of experts; but perhaps the most important cause was the disapproval with which the war was regarded. Such feeling as there might have been for the reconquest of a country which had once belonged to Russia was outweighed, particularly among Party members, by the recollection that Finland had been the first country to be granted independence by Lenin. This also served as a reminder of the differences between his policy and that of Stalin, though, with Stalin in power, no one dared to mention annexation. These were the reasons on the Russian side for the lack of success of the Red Army.

On the other side, the courage of the Finns was an important factor; during the hate campaign against them the press had said that the Finns boasted that each of them was ready to take on a hundred Russians. As the months dragged on people remembered this and began to feel that the Finns were making good their threat.

The slowness of the advance had a deeply depressing effect and Stalin's over-estimation of Soviet military strength discredited the Government to an extent which it is hard to convey. Yet few people thought that the war could be won more quickly if very large forces were used, and certainly the Generals I met in the Norilsk camp were of the opinion that the terrain was such that if vast forces were deployed the only result would be enormous losses. Even as it was, great losses were sustained in the attempt to break through the Mannerheim line, and when an attempt was made to outflank it large units were encircled and captured.

In the spring of 1940, when the war had ended and communications between Finland and Russia were reopened, new prisoners were expected in our camp. We waited tensely to find out who they would be. They came by river up to Dudinka on the Yenisey and from there travelled in open trucks on the narrow-gauge railway to Norilsk. Such was the curiosity they aroused that, in spite of the guards, recce parties got as near as they could to the railway line and called out to the new arrivals. One such scout hid in some bushes close to the track and as the trucks passed by shouted 'Who are you?' Receiving no reply he assumed that the men were too frightened to answer. When a second echelon drew near he tried again, and coming out of the bushes stood close to the rails. Thinking the men were probably prisoners of war he called out, 'Are you Poles? Are you Finns?' Finally a voice arose above the noise of the wheels crying, 'We're not bleeding foreigners, we're Russians!'

And indeed the convoy consisted of Russian soldiers who had been captured by the Finns and released by them under the treaty. The news spread round the camp like wildfire and though the new prisoners were kept strictly isolated it was not long before we knew that all the Soviet POWs, some thirty thousand of them, had been arrested the moment they were returned by the Finns. The officers had been shot (I do not know whether there were any exceptions), while the other ranks were sentenced to five or eight years in camp, and shipped off immediately without even being allowed to see their families.

Even we, who had known the great purges of the thirties, were utterly horrified that Stalin was working off his frustration at the failure of the war on these poor people, many of whom were not even in uniform but dressed in their ordinary clothes. Later I was told that in the West this treatment of men who had become prisoners was attributed to a Tsarist tradition, but I do not think this can be so.

When Russia was at war with Germany this heartless attitude proved very harmful, and later I met many demobilized soldiers who told me that because they had been captured they hesitated before coming home after their release. Many others stayed in the West for good. Before going to the front they had been indoctrinated with the fantastic lie that Red soldiers were never captured alive and that if this looked like being their fate they must keep the last bullet for themselves (a line particularly stressed in the case of officers). This crazy, costly fiction was kept alive until Stalin's death. It is to Sholokhov's credit that in his *Fate of a Man* (1957) he pointed out that a captured soldier does not necessarily lose his honour.

Our POWs from Finland were used to build a foundry in terrible conditions of cold and hunger, and were kept docile by further lies. They were assured that since they were 'clearly not criminals' they would be released as soon as their task was done. In fact, those who did not die as a result of the hardships they endured sweated out their five or eight years to the end. During all this time they were not allowed to get in touch with their families, who believed that they were dead. This treatment may seem surprising since, if the aim was to terrorize other soldiers into refusing to be captured, it would seem natural to have used the fate of the soldiers who had been taken prisoner by the Finns as an example. Yet apparent illogicality has always been part of the system of terror.

For instance, the names of those who were shot by Stalin were kept secret. Naturally, when the relations of a prisoner stopped receiving letters from him they made enquiries. I personally know the wife of a member of the Central Committee of the CPSU who for seventeen years was assured that her husband was alive until, in 1956, she learned that he had been shot in 1938.

Uncertainty undoubtedly added to the Terror, but I think the main cause of the use of secrecy lay within the machine itself after mass murder had reached gigantic proportions. It was one thing to learn that Bukharin, Zinovyev or some hundred others had been killed; this was frightening enough, but even the NKVD chiefs were afraid that if the total figure of those murdered was known it would be something which the country would not submissively accept. And so even the top strata of the Party were kept in ignorance of the massacres. There was also another consideration which, from Stalin's point of view, made concealment valuable: as long as people had, or thought they had, a relation alive in a camp they kept quiet so as not to harm him, whereas if they were sure he was dead this brake no longer functioned.

I have met people who would have been capable of any form of resistance up to sheer revolt, but who never moved a finger because they had someone in camp who *might* still be alive. I know too the ideas that occurred to my wife when she thought I was probably dead. It was the lingering doubt as to whether the prisoner might not still be alive that paralysed his relatives.

*

During my time in the 'stone sack',[3] which followed my re-arrest in the Norilsk camp on the outbreak of the war with Germany, I got to know one of the young POWs very well. His story will serve to illustrate the situation of many of his contemporaries.

The cell we were in was on one side of a corridor about a yard wide; practically all those in it were due to be shot. When the sentence had actually been confirmed the man was transferred to a cell on the opposite side of the passage from which he knew that at any moment he might be taken out and executed. Only one or two of my companions escaped death; Seryozha was not one of the lucky ones. He was twenty-one, a tall, handsome boy with brown hair. His father had been a pianist, a Russian of Finnish origin, and his mother was Russian; Seryozha had had a purely Soviet up-bringing. He had no recollection of pre-Stalin times, was proud of his country and believed that it was far ahead of the rest of the world; not that he had read much Marxist literature or participated in study circles – his interests were almost entirely devoted to music. He played the violin and had even given recitals. He told me that the year from Spring 1938 to Spring 1939 had been the most wonderful of his life. He was in love, in an idealistic way, and went to the opera and to concerts – in short, he was young and happy. In 1939 he was called up to do his military service and, since he was strong and also well-educated, he did well in the army. In spite of this he was looking forward to being demobilized, returning to his music and getting married.

His father died while he was with the army; this was a great sorrow to him, but he was stationed near the Finnish frontier, not

3. This was a cellar. Prisoners committed to it were not allowed any exercise and often terrible punishments were inflicted on them.

too far from his home for him to be able to see his mother whenever
he had leave.

When the Finnish war broke out his unit went into action
immediately and suffered heavy losses. He told me how brave the
Finns were and how the whole people resisted. 'There were partisans
everywhere – girls, old women, even children. Bullets came from
every tree and rock: it was a real people's war.'

The Soviet troops had been assured by their officers that the war
was going to be a picnic; they were of course quickly disillusioned
and morale fell. Seryozha was slightly wounded and spent some
time in hospital; as soon as he was convalescent he asked to go back
to the front.

Instead of that he was summoned one day to the Komsomol cell
for a talk with some Komsomol VIPs. After praising him for his
courage they told him that a Finnish Government headed by
Kuusinen had been set up in Terioki. It would establish a Finnish
people's régime and was appealing to young Finns to join a special
Finnish Unit which would fight alongside the Red Army for the
liberation of their country. At first Seryozha was pleased to know
that there were Finns who favoured this and thought it a good idea
that such a unit should be formed; then he realized what the conversation was leading up to and this, he said, 'just knocked me
sideways'. The proposal was that he, who knew only a few words of
Finnish, and who had always considered himself to be a Russian,
should join this unit 'as a Finn'. He replied that while he was ready
for any duty, however dangerous, his place was with the Red
Army, for he was not a Finn. The Komsomol leader argued with
him but failed to convince him and in the end let him go.

At this point Seryozha asked me whether I understood why he had
been asked to join the Finnish unit. I had no difficulty in replying to
this question. Since no Finnish volunteers could be found, Finns
were to be 'made by order' (as, later on, Poles and people of other
nationalities were manufactured if and when the need arose).

When Seryozha was again invited to volunteer he refused outright and even signed a paper to that effect. At the same time he
again professed his loyalty and declared his readiness to serve in any
capacity in the Red Army.

He was summoned a third time and on this occasion he was interviewed by a General who told him:

'I have come here to inform you that your refusal to serve with the Finnish unit is a breach of army discipline and in time of war will be considered as a counter-revolutionary act.'

Completely bewildered, Seryozha explained that he believed that mobilizing phoney Finns was against the interests of the Red Army. Surely, he said, a national unit should be national? Before he had finished speaking he was disarmed, put under arrest and told he would be courtmartialled.

In fact, he was tried for disobeying orders; the charge of course made no mention of the 'Finnish' unit.

The judge gave him a last chance to 'obey orders'. Seryozha knew that the alternative was death, but he said that since the order was against his conscience as a member of the Komsomol he had to refuse. He was an honest boy, lying was unthinkable to him and besides this he felt that by pretending to be a Finn he would be deceiving not only the Finns but also his Russian comrades.

He was condemned to be shot but at the last moment the sentence was commuted to fifteen years in a labour camp and he was sent to Norilsk. He did not appeal; he was too shocked and disillusioned. The fact that he did not do so was fatal to him for it convinced the authorities that his unbroken spirit made him a dangerous person who must be liquidated.

That he lived to arrive in our cell was surprising enough, for at his trial it was explained to him that since he had been discharged from his own unit in order to join the 'Finnish' unit, the fact that he refused to do so meant he was guilty of desertion! From the moment of his arrival in camp he was ceaselessly watched and constantly provoked by agents and, being inexperienced, he did not know how to avoid falling into the traps they set for him.

He had no doubt at all that he was going to be shot. He was ill with scurvy and, being young and tall, suffered even more than we did from hunger; yet he was always considerate and a model of unselfishness. What tormented him till the end was the contrast between the principles of truth and honour in which he had been trained by the régime and its glaring failure to put them into practice. Until all this had happened to him he had not given much thought to the meaning of life; now, during the weeks he spent with us awaiting his transfer to the death cell across the passage, he never ceased to think about it. He felt that since he was to be put to death at the age of twenty-one he had a duty not to waste even a moment. All of us had periodic outbursts of desperation but they were rare with him; he did not even give way to personal regrets or nostalgia for those he loved, but spent his time meditating on good and evil, truth and lies, and moral and educational problems. He would listen to the stories of other prisoners and later come and ask me why I thought such an innocent man as so and so should be faced with imminent and inescapable death, while base men whom he had met when he was still free were prospering. He had some strange ideas. For instance, he found that certain musical themes were associated in his mind with a particular train of thought; so according to what he was thinking about he would hear in his mind a Beethoven Sonata, a Fugue by Bach or a song by Schubert. One day an old Party member told him that he should not be so self-absorbed and ought to be thinking of the collective. Seryozha's reply put an end to the conversation. He said: 'But it isn't the collective who'll cross the passage for me [to the death cell]. I'll have to do it myself.'

He left us to cross the passage and was one of the first to be shot. The jailors came to the death cell at night (later the prisoners were gagged but at this time they were still able to say something as they left), and on the night when the double doors were opened and he was led away we heard his voice, but we could not make out what he said.

In a passage in her *Letters from Prison* Rosa Luxemburg describes a scene she saw from her cell window when she was in jail in Germany during the First World War; she says that for her it epitomized the whole war. A soldier was driving a wagon which was so heavily laden that it was beyond the power of the two oxen harnessed to it, to move it. The soldier flogged them with a metal-tipped whip until their proverbially tough flanks were torn and blood flowed down them.

For me, in a similar manner, the destiny of the whole Russian people in the Second World War was summed up in Seryozha's fate. I had seen his spirit bleed, the spirit of a man whose honour had condemned him to death, and it seemed to me that it was a symbol both of the terrible perversions of power and of the terrible misfortunes of the people.

CHAPTER 9

THE WAR YEARS

THE few surviving old Party members who had some political understanding looked on the Nazi-Soviet pact and the partition of Poland as a betrayal in complete contradiction to the Party line, but it must be admitted that there were people, chiefly Russian nationalists, who approved of the new policy and judged it to be a return to sanity in international affairs. They thought that Russia and Germany made the strongest combination in Europe and perhaps the world (not much notice of the United States was taken at that time), and believed that together they could break Great Britain once and for all.

The word 'Fascist' vanished from the papers (Ehrenburg says that it was even struck out of one of his reports); instead, the Nazis were respectfully referred to as the NSDAP, while their enemies were described as 'the Anglo-French capitalists [or: plutocrats] who had unleashed the war'.

There was talk of economic and cultural exchanges between Russia and Germany; Wagner's *Ring* was put on at the Bolshoi. Some elderly people who remembered the days when German culture was greatly esteemed in Russia were delighted and looked forward to a future of close collaboration. It is only fair to say in this context that nothing was then known about Hitler's atrocities against the Jews,[1] and also that the majority of intellectuals *were* profoundly indignant. The warm feelings they used to have for

1. Even after Russia and Germany were at war no mention of the extermination of the Jews was permitted. This may have been due in part to the fear of fanning Russian anti-Semitism.

France now revived, as was later demonstrated. For instance, I shall never forget the scene in the camp at Norilsk when the radio announced the fall of Paris. I was in the special barracks where most of the prisoners were distinguished specialists, engineers, scientists or professors, nearly all of them apolitical, 'old style' men; on hearing the news many of them burst into tears.

About the time of the pact, mass arrests stopped and some charges were dropped; none the less investigations went on and every man felt that a sword still hung over his head. Earlier excesses were now ascribed to NKVD officials who had supposedly exceeded their orders, and also to the fact that the informers, whom Yezhov had placed everywhere, had given false testimony. Stalin's personal responsibility was not admitted. This myth was accepted by the masses and encouraged by the authorities. In fact, it made life more tolerable for the victims and their families if they could believe that at the head of the State was a man who did not know about the arrests, the tortures and the shootings. As a result of this deception many people died with the words 'Long Live Stalin' on their lips, and a Red Army leader such as Yakir* could appeal to Stalin in terms which showed that he felt certain that Stalin was not responsible for the purges. (As if to spite him for this naïve belief the decision to liquidate him was taken and signed by Stalin, Molotov and Kaganovich.)

During the lull in persecution, which was later found to be one of Stalin's devilish tricks, we estimated that perhaps ten per cent of all the prisoners were released; but the reversal of their sentences was used as proof that the remaining ninety per cent of the sentences were just, and twenty years later it was admitted that at this very moment new lists of chance survivors among those arrested in 1937 were drawn up and that these people were liquidated in such strict secrecy that even top Party members were unaware of their fate.

It was at this time that the decision to kill Trotsky at any cost was taken. In theory his liquidation could have been justified by the fact that he had previously been condemned to death, but Stalin refused to admit his responsibility for this murder. On the contrary, he sent *agents provocateurs* to people in the camps to provoke such an accusation or an expression of regret at Trotsky's death. In the investigation which ended in my second death sentence (1941) an agent's report was used as incriminating evidence. In this he said, 'On the 21st of August *Pravda* announced the assassination of Trotsky. I asked Berger: "What do you think of it?" He did not reply.' I enquired of my interrogator, 'What was wrong with that?' He replied, 'Why didn't you say, "A dog deserves a dog's death"?' So it seemed that either to say that Stalin was responsible for Trotsky's death, or to regret it, or even to make no comment at all proved that one was 'an enemy of the people'.

As Hitler extended his possessions the Russian people became increasingly hostile to Germany, though there were members of the upper strata who looked upon Nazi victories as 'those of our allies' and held that there was some secret understanding by which eventually these conquests would prove to be to the advantage of the Soviet Union. The press, of course, heralded them triumphantly. All the same, it seems likely that as early as the spring of 1941 Stalin, who must have known of Hitler's preparations, realized that war with Germany was inevitable. His aim henceforth would be to gain time; on the one hand for American intervention to become effective, and, on the other, to complete his own preparations. In this struggle for time he had recourse to various desperate devices, and not without success. He had already extended his frontiers in the West; now he reached an agreement with Japan to secure his rear, and also made sure of Turkey's neutrality. This meant that the safety of the East and the South was ensured and that an invasion on two or three sides, so much dreaded by the General Staff, could be avoided.

Another motive for trying to delay the outbreak of war was the need to bring in the harvest; both he and Hitler realized the importance to Russia of saving the harvest, and that Stalin should have imagined he might be able to stave off hostilities till the late autumn is yet another illustration of his conceit.

In the camps the prisoners followed events tensely; almost all of them hoped that war between Russia and Germany would break out. Their despair and sense of helplessness made them long for *something* to happen; they believed that Stalin in his hour of need would turn to them, thinking, and rightly so, that he would find them loyal, and they were convinced that in the end the Soviet Union would be victorious. There were of course some defeatists, especially among the criminals and 'former people'.

On the 21st of June, just before Germany attacked, I talked to an engineer friend of mine who had been transferred to another block but with whom I was able to exchange a few words through the barbed wire when the guards were not in the vicinity. He said he thought that Hitler was bound to make a move before the end of June: either a landing in England if the Rudolf Hess mission failed, or an attack on Russia. (Hess's mission was taken very seriously and Stalin certainly believed that negotiations were going on.) At that time I thought Hitler was more likely to be defeated if he first attacked England, and said so. The engineer replied, 'Of course, you are right. All the same, my inmost feeling is, "God grant that it may be Russia".' Next day his wish was fulfilled.

Hitler's successes had been so spectacular that no one could seriously expect a quick victory for Russia. Many people thought that the Soviet Union would fly into pieces at the first impact and that the Germans would reach the Volga or even the Urals, but nearly everybody believed that this would not be the end. Stalin might indeed fall at the first blow, but it was confidently hoped that in time resistance would be organized by genuine communists and that Russia would hold out and eventually counter-attack successfully from the East.

It was anticipated that the non-Russian republics would fall away and become Hitler's satellites, but so long as the Russian nucleus remained intact most prisoners believed that, in the end, all Soviet territory would be won back.

When the blow came and Russia did not fall apart, even the worst pessimists ceased to predict disaster and, on the historical parallels of the Napoleonic and Civil Wars, it was expected that only the first year would be dangerous.

Although the radio amplifiers in the camp were disconnected before the end of Molotov's speech on the day war broke out and were not reconnected until the capitulation of von Paulus, we were rarely without news. For instance, on the first day of the war I listened to the BBC, for there was a foreign radio-set belonging to some hired labourers who were working on a large building site within the camp.[2]

What happened in the camp on the outbreak of war was by no means the relaxation that the prisoners had hoped for. All camp commanders were summoned to a meeting and received special instructions as a result of which they started a new Terror. The prisons inside the camps became even more overcrowded. On the Sunday when the German air-raids began a huge wave of arrests took place. The lists of the victims had been prepared as part of the mobilization process. They were aimed largely at the national minorities. As a start practically all the Germans were deported, and it was only later that the German section of the Komintern was able to get some of its members back.

One case I know of personally is particularly interesting. The man involved was a German who had been in Russia since the early thirties and with whom I had been quite friendly. He was a direct, straightforward fellow who had evaded the 1937 purge in which many Germans were killed. In the summer of 1941 he held a highly responsible job; in spite of this his wife had had to get him out of prison five times by ringing up the German section of the Komintern, which then brought pressure to bear on the Russian section. Each time he was re-arrested he protested that he had only just been released, but he was told, 'Well, they'll have to release you again then.' I heard this from his wife, Popova. The man was sent to Ulbricht in about 1949 and later became one of the chiefs of the East German Secret Police.

*

All those already in camps who were regarded as potentially dangerous either to the maintenance of order in the camp or to the security of the country in wartime were arrested. The head of the

2. It was only later that such sets were ordered to be handed in. After the war had ended I often heard both the BBC and the 'Voice of America'. Foreign language broadcasts were not jammed at that time and in the Arctic region we could hear London better than Moscow. Thus we listened to Churchill's speeches on V-Day and at Fulton, and of course it was enough for one prisoner to hear the news for everyone to know about it within a very short time.

'operational' department of the NKVD in our camp, a Major from Moscow, told me later that he had been sent there to carry out these new and very harsh directives. When he arrived he asked to be shown the files of secret denunciations. He then made a list of those who had the thickest files and ordered these people to be arrested forthwith.

My file, Case No. 5, was a particularly thick one. So, on the 17th of July, twenty-six days after the outbreak of war, some NKVD men came to fetch me from the barracks in which I was kept, and at three in the morning I was brought to the Office of the 'Operational Cheka'. This was a new term, invented at the beginning of the war in order to inspire terror; the word Cheka in itself aroused horrible memories and 'Operational' made it sound even more frightening.

From the moment the NKVD men appeared I realized that I was being arrested under a special directive issued at the beginning of the war, and I thought that my death sentence had probably already been decided on. But after I had been in the Cheka Office for a quarter of an hour I started to harbour a tiny hope. I began by protesting that it was ridiculous that I, who was already a prisoner, should be arrested once more since there was not and could not be any further incriminating evidence against me, and that, so far as the war was concerned, my attitude was perfectly sound. It was then that the inexperienced Lieutenant who had carried out the search and who was supposed to interrogate me let slip these words: 'Well, even if there isn't any evidence, we'll have to take prophylactic action'. This was enough to make me realize that the 'Operchekist' department had not deferred my arrest until they had found something on which they could charge me. Evidently they intended to get the necessary evidence by bringing such pressure to bear on me that I would end by incriminating myself.

By now I had been a prisoner for six years; I had been through three investigations in Moscow and I had heard the stories of hundreds of prisoners. I told myself that nothing worse could happen to me than being shot, that it looked as though this was to be my fate anyway, but that I might as well grab at any chance which challenging the Cheka offered me. I therefore went straight into the attack;

I declared that the action taken against me was illegal, a breach of NKVD regulations, and that since I had no other means of protesting I would refuse to write down my part in the investigation or to sign any paper connected with it. All I would do was write and sign a statement that I refused to give evidence or take any active part in the investigation. At the time this offer was declined. To emphasize my protest I would go on hunger strike.

When the Lieutenant heard these words he let out a roar and went to fetch his superior. Polikarpov, the newly arrived Major from Moscow, came in in a fury. This seemed to me a good sign, for experience had taught me that when a prisoner is treated with civility and offered a cigarette he is in a very bad position, for it means that the NKVD have all the proof they require and need nothing further from him.

It was when they lacked evidence and had to get something by exerting pressure that they went quite wild, partly because that was how they felt, as anyone might, and partly as a means of terrorizing the prisoner into making a confession.

So now Polikarpov's rage reassured me; it made me feel that I had made a correct analysis of the situation and taken the right decision. He said at once that he personally would be in charge of my investigation, and in the days that followed he kept so strictly to this plan that if one of his assistants came into the room he stopped the interrogation. In explanation he told me that, according to my file, I was a dangerous agitator and he did not want other people to hear what I had to say. As I refused to co-operate in the interrogation Polikarpov himself was obliged to write down both the questions and the answers.

Every night, between eleven and twelve, I was taken from my cell for questioning and did not return until morning. When I went on hunger strike I was not, as is usual, put into solitary confinement. This, I was told, was because the investigator refused to recognize that I was hunger striking, preferring to regard my behaviour as sabotage. Ostentatiously he went on with the interrogation. In fact, carrying on my hunger strike in an overcrowded cell and being obliged to watch other people eat made my trial all the harder. After five or six days I was so weak that I had to be carried to the

Cheka Office. When I got there I always began by saying: 'If you want to talk, by all means let us talk, but I'm not going to sign anything.'

Night after night our battle went on. At one moment, I think it was round about the twelfth to the fifteenth day, I made Polikarpov an offer. I said that though I would not sign any minutes I was prepared to write a detailed 'explanation' of the reasons for my hunger strike. He seized on this, stopped asking me questions, thrust a piece of paper in front of me and said I was to begin at once. As I wrote, he sat behind his desk watching me and as I finished each page he took it from me, read it, and did not return it.

Rarely have I had to write in such an atmosphere, with somebody analysing each word as I penned it. Since this was not a formal part of my investigation but an 'explanatory note' on my hunger strike I considered that I could write what I liked. I therefore made a declaration of my principles. In doing this I tried to stay within the framework of a Party member who had been wrongly arrested, but within this framework I was very forthright. I said that it was a great tragedy that at the moment when Hitler was attacking Russia people like myself should be in prison, and that the proper course would be to annul all political sentences and permit able-bodied young prisoners to join the army or serve the Soviet Union in other useful capacities. I myself was thirty-six at the time and anxious to play my part in the defence of the country.

I went on to criticize the 'third degree' methods used by the NKVD to extract confessions. I remember my exact words, because when he came to this passage Polikarpov read it aloud. 'The methods used to force confessions are wrong not only because of what they may do to the prisoner, but because of their corrupting effect on those who use them. The hand used to strike a defenceless victim will, when it comes to facing an enemy armed to the teeth, no longer be capable of using a rifle efficiently.'

When he had finished reading this sentence Polikarpov shouted 'STOP!' He was an unsophisticated man, a sadist who had often beaten up prisoners and then shot them, and now he walked up and down the room in a state of great excitement. It was then about three in the morning and the sun had risen out of the white polar night. What follows gives the gist of our discussion, which I clearly recall, though after the years that have passed since then some words may have slipped my memory.

'Let's sort this out,' he said. 'You're a Party member; suppose you've been put in charge of a partisan unit. You have been ambushed by Fascists, you're encircled by them, and it's vital for you to know where the enemy is and what he's planning to do. To get this information you need to catch a "tongue" [informer], and when one has been caught you know that the lives not only of your men, but also of all the men and women in the neighbouring villages who have helped you, depend on whether or not he talks. You only have a few hours left. Can you imagine this?'

'Yes,' I said, 'I can imagine it.'

'The minutes are ticking away. The man refuses to speak. You have a choice between sparing the reptile or sacrificing many lives. Which would you do?'

I did not reply. 'I order you to tell me,' he shouted. I still kept silent. Then he came up to me with clenched fists. 'If you don't answer me I'll . . .'

'All right,' I said. 'If the situation was exactly as you describe, if the unit was encircled and there was only a short time left, then I would strike the man.'

Polikarpov laughed. 'Well then, what's all this fuss about and what are you writing all this for?' The interrogation ended at that point. He felt that he had justified himself; the fact never even occurred to him that in our camp there was no analogous situation. Later he read the pages in which I demanded the end of persecutions and the release of political prisoners and he said to me:

'Suppose we let you go. Would you be satisfied?'

'No,' I answered. 'I should demand to be reinstated in the Party.'

'And would you stop at that?'

'Of course not. I should demand a revision of my case and the restitution of all my rights.'

'And what would you do after that?'

'I should demand that all the other people who have been treated like me should be released as well.'

'And what would they do then?'

'Go to the front or do other war work, and no questions asked till after the war is over.'

'And when peace has come? People aren't angels, you know!' He flapped his arms to imitate wings. 'Do you think they would have forgotten they had been arrested, imprisoned and beaten up?'

'I doubt it. And after the war, but not till then, things will need to be sorted out and it will have to be determined who was to blame for having these people arrested, imprisoned and beaten up.'

'So, you'll insist that *we* should be put in prison?'

'If it turns out that that is what you deserve.'

'You needn't think we are fools.'

And that was how the conversation ended.

I was not surprised by this conversation. Polikarpov had lived through the great purges of the thirties. 'It runs into four figures,' he once told me, 'the number of men I've shot myself.' What kind of a man was Polikarpov? What had his life been like? So as to try to gain my confidence, he had in the early days of my investigation told me a lot about himself. He had started life as a worker in the Donbas, and did not join the Party during the Civil War. In 1924 he was drafted into the NKVD, first as a private; then he was sent off to some special courses and became an interrogator. He appeared to be a good father and husband and through all the years had kept to a certain degree of austerity in his personal life. For instance, he ate only black bread in my presence, and I believe this was his custom.

When my 'explanation' was completed – it ended with the words 'Long live democratic socialism!' – it ran to twenty-three pages. Polikarpov said, 'Sign it.' I signed my full name. When I had done this he remarked, 'You have signed your death warrant.'

I replied, 'If what I've written is cause for a death warrant I still won't alter one single letter of the text.'

On the fifty-sixth day of my hunger strike Polikarpov said to me,

'You won't give us the information we want, and you won't sign the minutes. I am stopping the interrogation, so now will you stop your hunger strike?' I agreed.

After this I was not summoned for interrogation again for several months, but I was refused all medical attention and consigned to the 'stone sack'.

On the 27th of January 1942, the seventh anniversary of my arrest, Polikarpov summoned me for a talk. I feared that having tricked me out of my hunger strike he intended to begin the interrogation all over again, but when he saw me he said: 'I don't need any evidence from you. I have plenty. I don't intend to renew the investigation. I've wasted enough time on you already.' He actually reckoned up the number of hours he had spent with me to no avail. 'But do you remember that you promised me a written statement?'

'Yes,' I said. 'But you refused it.'

'Now I've changed my mind and I'm doing you a favour; I will accept your written statement.' To this he added a lot of compliments, saying that he knew I was a man of my word.

He gave me a piece of paper and I began to write, but after a few moments I threw away the pen and exclaimed, 'I won't write, and I won't sign, and I'll tell you why. I was going to do this, but when I saw that devilish smile on your face as I picked up the pen I realized that my life was at stake.'

Of course he cursed me and shouted that he had treated me too well. I could not refrain from querying this, at which he bellowed that he could easily have shot me or starved me to death. But I did not sign and as it turned out this saved my life.

It was only later that I learned why Polikarpov was so determined to get my signature on a statement of my case. Some years before, a decree had been passed making it illegal to put anyone to death without trial. Later, I think it was in December 1941, a new law was passed, and death sentences under Article 58 could be passed *in absentia*, but sentences passed by the local *troyka* in the absence of the prisoner had to be confirmed in Moscow. Polikarpov had sentenced me to death, but unless he got my signature on the report of my interrogation it would look as though he had sentenced me *in absentia*, and this meant that he would have had to send my case back to Moscow for checking.

I spent nearly all the next year in hospital from which I was removed at intervals to the 'stone sack', although the other prisoners protested against the presence of a dying man in their cell.

I could not make out what was happening for normally I should either have been shot or returned to the ordinary part of the camp. When sentences had been confirmed in Moscow the executions were usually held over for a few days and then, one night, the men were led out and shot; but if the sentence was not confirmed the prisoners were soon removed from the 'stone sack'. In my case I remained under an unconfirmed sentence of death from July 1941 to August 1943.

It was after Stalingrad that my new interrogation began. Polikarpov had gone, and was replaced by a very civil and considerate Georgian called Getsayev. He began by telling me that he was now in charge of my case; that he could not release me, because I had previously refused to co-operate, but that he wished to assure me that in no circumstances would I incur a death sentence so that there was no longer any reason for me to refuse to take part in the investigation. I knew that things had changed a great deal and that many people who had been condemned to death had been reprieved, so I said I would agree to take part in the investigation on one condition: I wanted to see the whole of my dossier.

Getsayev then broke off the interview, but the next time he called me he had my file, and told me he would lend it to me and that after I read it we would have another talk. I read this secret material with great interest. In the first paper it was stressed that I had lived abroad and it was suggested that I had been sent to Russia as a spy. Then it was stated that thanks to my 'exceptional gifts' I had got into the Komintern and that I had continued to conduct propaganda in the camp and got together a group of foreigners; these were named. It was also asserted that I had tried to promote a revolt. For all these reasons it was proposed to sentence me to death. The document was signed by Polikarpov and the local procurator. The next document was the death sentence, which said that for the reasons already stated '. . . Berger had been sentenced to death, without confiscation of property, since he had none.' It was signed by the local *troyka*; to these names were added the signatures of the Krasnoyarsk regional authorities confirming the sentence.

Next I came upon a document from Moscow saying that Case No. 5 was to be returned to the Operchekist department at Norilsk for further investigation. The death sentence had not been confirmed and there was to be a new interrogation. Two reasons were given for refusing confirmation: the first was that nowhere in the dossier did the signature of the accused Berger appear; the second was that no sufficient explanation had been given of the accused's persistence in his fifty-six day hunger strike.

I can only guess why the absence of my signature saved my life. No doubt the authorities suspected that the thousands of people who were employed by the local security forces killed their prisoners when there was the least reason to do so, and assumed that where a signature was missing something odd must be going on. It was not necessarily because of any sense of justice that enquiries were started, and they probably arose merely from the desire to exert control over the local security officials. The man who had to sign the death warrant simply saw that it was not in order; it did not matter to him whether the prisoner was innocent or guilty – what did matter was that the interrogator had not filled in the form correctly. He ought to be rapped over the knuckles; as for the prisoner, he was always at hand to be investigated again.

I now realized that if I had signed the statement which Polikarpov had asked me for I would have been shot shortly afterwards. The absence of my signature had caused my case to fall off the conveyor belt; so, while thousands of death sentences were being confirmed, mine remained in a pending tray. It stayed there for two years and by then things had changed. This is the rational explanation of my escape.

People have asked me what it feels like to be under sentence of death for so long. In fact, because a man cannot live in a constant state of extreme tension, after the first few months one gets accustomed to it. This is also true of long prison sentences. When a new prisoner arrived with a term of ten, fifteen or twenty-five years he was still completely shattered and when old prisoners said to him, 'It's the first year that's the worst', he would think they were joking. Later, he realized it was true.

Yet even if those of us in the death cell could forget our bleak prospects for a while, things regularly happened to intensify our apprehension. Every time men were led out to be shot our state of tension was indescribable. There was the screech of the locks in the

night, the slamming of doors, and the knowledge that our neighbours were going to die, and however often this happened, to those
under sentence of death it was like falling into an abyss – something
a little like the sensation one has when one is a passenger on a plane
that falls into a deep air pocket.

*

After the annexation of Estonia, Latvia and Lithuania in 1940 all the
Baltic officers were given ranks in the Soviet Army. There were even
generals who commanded their own Baltic units. This did not last
long, for rumours about disloyalty began to circulate and there were
said to have been some desertions. The Germans had certainly
organized a Fifth Column in the Baltic States, as was proved when
they reached Riga, where snipers had shot at the Red Army from
windows, and where there were Nazis in key organizations such as
the radio.

Shortly after the beginning of the war the Baltic officers were
instructed to entrain for a training course in Moscow. When they
heard this news those who were in contact with German espionage
organizations went into hiding, but those who were loyal obeyed
the order without hesitation. Among these was the General of
Artillery, Brede, an Estonian who had studied at the Sorbonne,
spoke excellent French and German, and was politically very
experienced. He had served in the Russian Tsarist army and, in
1918, had helped to establish the independent state of Estonia. Later
he had held posts in many of its cabinets as a supporter of the liberal
General Laidoner.*

And here, to explain what follows, I must mention that in 1924
there had been a communist plot, led by Jaan Anvelt, to seize
power in Estonia. The Komintern had worked out a plan by which,
on a certain night, all strategic points were to be seized and union
with Soviet Russia proclaimed. However, Estonian counter-
espionage got to hear of the plot, prevented it from succeeding and
passed harsh sentences on the rebels, some of whom were shot while
others were sentenced to long terms of imprisonment. A few,
including Anvelt, escaped to Russia.

I got to know him in February 1925, when we were both participating in a session of the enlarged Executive Committee of the Komintern. He was put into my room at the Lux Hotel, a building often used at that time for foreign delegates of the Communist International. Anvelt had a bandage round his head – a sign of a wound he had received during the fighting in Tallinn. During the days we spent together we discussed many ideological and practical questions; he was a well-educated man who had read a great deal of Marxist literature without becoming indoctrinated. He told me that prior to the uprising he had been assured that help would be forthcoming from Russian troops, who were to move from Leningrad to the Estonian capital as soon as the formation of a Soviet government in Tallinn was announced. More than fifteen years later it was strange to find myself in captivity in Norilsk together with people against whom the rising of the Estonian communists had been directed in 1924. By that time Anvelt himself had of course disappeared in the purges.

In 1940, when the Estonian Republic was joined to the USSR, the generals, including Brede, professed their loyalty to the Soviet régime. It was in the middle of June 1941 that over a thousand officers (including 250 Estonians and about 400 Latvians and 400 Lithuanians), almost the whole officer corps except for those in hiding, arrived in Moscow. There they were disarmed, arrested, transported to Siberia by train and put on a river steamer to Norilsk, where they were informed that they were about to be put on trial. Naturally they were indignant. Some wrote to the Army Council declaring that they were loyal and willing to serve in any unit. No attention was paid to their protestations.

A few of the men involved were in the 'stone sack' with me. The NKVD would have preferred to keep the Balts in isolation but the large number of prisoners made this impossible and so their tragedy was enacted before our eyes. Many of them hoped till the last that there would be some intervention from abroad on their behalf, for even in camp we had heard that the Atlantic Charter had been signed not only by Roosevelt and Churchill but also by Stalin, and we had been assured that the world was now to be liberated from fear and want. The Balts, some of whom had relations in America and England, tried to smuggle out messages to them. They were unsuccessful and the mood in the 'stone sack' became one of desperation. Every fortnight a batch of officers was shot.

They were led out of the 'stone sack' one by one and then the 'trial' was held in the passage outside. An NKVD officer read out the accusation and stated under which article of the law it fell. The officers were charged either with having had links with a Fifth Column, or with having made anti-Soviet statements, or with misdeeds perpetrated long ago. Brede, for instance, and other Estonian generals were accused of having taken part in the repression of the communist *putsch* in Tallinn about twenty years earlier. The officers were allowed to speak for five or ten minutes in their own defence, then they were sentenced to death, and lastly, when the sentence had been confirmed in Moscow, which did not take long, they were shot.

Some 400 officers were killed in this way, from General Brede down to young lieutenants. The selection appeared to have little relation to their political views. Brede, for instance, whom I knew, was a Liberal and a resolute anti-Nazi. He was shot, but a close friend of his was sentenced to only eight years, ultimately released and went back to Tallinn where he was given a responsible post. It appears that there was an order to shoot a certain number of Balts; when the figure was reached the rest were spared. The massacre made a terrible impression in the camp.

Observing the survivors, I was very interested by the different characteristics of the three nationalities. The Lithuanians in general knew no Russian and were intensely nationalistic; all the same they adapted themselves well to camp conditions, organized work brigades, worked very hard and even over-fulfilled their norms. Most of them were physically strong and came to be regarded as excellent and conscientious workers. The majority came from rather rich peasant families, had been to secondary school and had then joined the Lithuanian Army to do their national service. There were also a few intellectuals among them.

The Latvians were of two sorts: one lot behaved very much like the Lithuanians, the other continually protested against their arrest, reproached the authorities with having broken all their own laws, and refused to speak Russian.

As for the Estonians, they seemed to have made up their minds that since Estonia no longer existed, an Estonian officer had no business to go on living. They refused to work, went on hunger strikes, committed suicide individually or resorted to terrible group killings. Within a few years only a handful of Estonian officers were still alive.

The purge of the officers was not the only one that the Balts were to suffer, for in the last months before the German invasion the Soviet authorities deported hundreds of thousands of Balts to remote regions of Siberia, where many of them died.

After Stalin's death most of the surviving intellectuals, Members of Parliament, journalists and writers were sent home, among them people who had taken part in politics and were known to have made anti-Soviet statements. However, when I was freed in 1956 some were still being held, though many of these were repatriated in 1957 and 1958.

While in camp I met many members of the (Catholic) Lithuanian and (Protestant) Latvian clergy. I found they had many traits in common; in particular their honesty and capacity for hard work. I also made friends with some young people, still in their teens, who had suddenly found themselves uprooted and dispossessed. They felt the loss of their countries' independence very deeply, for they believed that they had created something new and valuable by building up their states, the revival of their languages, and the restoration of forms of government closely linked with their traditions. The contribution their compatriots had made during the short period of independence to culture, science, art and sport filled them with pride. They were convinced that their reunion with Russia was a backward step. Most of the men who died in Siberia were, however, not intrinsically anti-Russian. They were peasants who regarded the Baltic Barons as their chief enemies – they described them as cruel and arrogant – and they loathed the Germans. Many of them had links with Russia and had regarded the Russians as friends until the Soviet occupation, after which they said that almost everyone became anti-Russian.

They were all very bitter about the failure of the West to intervene on their behalf and in particular were disgusted that Britain had not even tried to obtain some cultural independence for them after the seizure of their countries by the Soviet Union. They suffered keenly as a result of their separation from the West, from which they had taken their educational system and much of their culture, and they found it impossible to integrate themselves into the family of Soviet peoples. They respected Russian culture but thought it was alien to them, for they felt that their cultural links were with France and America. Nor did they think it right that they should be placed on the same footing as other minorities such as the Turkmenians and the Uzbeks.

The closest friend I made among the Balts was an army doctor who had been at the head of the Estonian Army Health Service. When I first met Dr M. he was a tall, handsome man in his fifties. He was a great humanist and belonged to no political party but was a liberal in the English style. He had great respect for the British constitution and social structure. He would often ask me why, in contrast to what happened elsewhere, every recent development in Russia was so morbid and complex. I tried to explain the history of the Revolution and of the Party to him, telling him what I thought had been right and where I believed that things had gone wrong. He listened attentively and asked businesslike questions, but I certainly failed to convince him. Whether as a result of our conversations or of his natural pessimism, he formed the impression that the destiny of Russia and of the countries now linked to it, such as his own, was fated to be far more complicated and tragic than those of other nations, whose development would, he expected, be smooth and straightforward.

The doctor had studied under a famous French heart specialist, had a thorough knowledge of French, Russian and German nineteenth and twentieth century literature and was a member of the intelligentsia in the best sense of that word. He was also a man of exceptional kindness.

His prestige both as a man and as a doctor was very high and not only his fellow prisoners but the free salaried workers often came to him for help, which he gave unstintingly and with great efficiency. He had a sense of mission about his work and was always fighting the authorities to obtain more medical supplies for use among the prisoners. He felt keenly the sufferings which they endured and was very unhappy when he had no means of alleviating their pain.

Our first contact arose from the fact that before my arrest I had known some friends of his. In the end we talked for hours not only about mutual friends and the camp but also about everything to do with the Soviet Union. He bore no hatred of the Russians or even of those NKVD men who carried out the harshest measures of punishment, for he was a devout Protestant who looked upon his own destiny and those of others from an all-forgiving point of view rooted in his Christian faith.

He told me that among all the fellow-prisoners with whom he had talked I was the only one who had a basically optimistic attitude. Seeing the immense number of deaths that took place at Norilsk, not only those due to executions but also those caused by the terrible climate of the Far North, over-work, sickness, hunger and so on, the doctor believed that the majority of us, including himself, would die there.

I argued that many of us would survive and that these would one day go back to their homes and families. I believed this; but, in any case, I felt justified in making my prophecy, for those who died would be in no position to contradict me, and those who survived, as I was later able to confirm, remained very grateful to me because in the hardest periods I had foretold that there would be a way out and a chance of happiness in years to come. I based my hopeful views on quite practical considerations, for I really believed that if a man could keep his self-control and had the physique to stand up to the conditions of the camp, there was a good chance that he would live to be freed. To be truthful, I was not convinced that in my state of health I myself would survive, but all the same I argued hotly that I would.

Even in camp the doctor was able to go on studying, for though other books were forbidden, scientific publications were available, and so he did his best to keep up to date with modern discoveries in the field of medicine. (This was during the war. Later, when Stalin insisted that all discoveries were made by Russians, foreign books were no longer allowed; but until then there were a good number of them.)

This Estonian specialist was not the only eminent doctor in our camp. There were many other distinguished medical men and scientists, some of whom received awards for their work, after they had been released. The young free Russian doctors attached to the camp made good use of their exceptional opportunity of learning from these prisoners.

One great service which the Estonian doctor rendered us was the obtaining of supplies of penicillin and sulphanilamide. These drugs were available in the Soviet Union but whether they were distributed to any particular camp or not depended entirely on the courage and perseverance of the doctors who demanded them. In principle they were supposed to be reserved for the army, but even at times when there were no supplies in military hospitals some still found their way to Norilsk, where they saved the lives of hundreds of people who were suffering from the various lung diseases which are so prevalent in the Far North.

In 1943, on the eve of Stalingrad, when things looked as black as possible and the doctor, like other Balts, had been completely cut off from all communication with his family for some time, he began to be more than ever convinced that there was no hope left of ever seeing his home again.

At the time I was very ill, but he came to my bedside and we had a vigorous argument. From the moment that the Germans had failed to achieve a lightning victory against Russia I had been certain that in the end they would be defeated. Now that even we had heard of the victory at El Alamein I was sure that Hitler's victorious legend had been discredited and that eventually the whole world would rise up against him. So I told the doctor that the Nazis were going to be beaten and I described the journey he would one day make back to his home in Tallinn.

I succeeded in half convincing him that the Germans would not win the war but he flatly refused to believe that he would survive and be repatriated. 'Let's bet on it,' I said. 'I'll bet you a bottle of wine that you will rejoin your family and that all will be well with you.' And so we wagered a bottle of wine. Whoever got out first was to send it to the other. (Wine was something we never saw in camp. It was forbidden to bring in alcohol. The only people who had any were the free workers who occasionally got a bottle of vodka and for some exceptional reason let a prisoner have a swig at it.)

The years passed, 1944, 1945, 1946. By then the doctor and I were separated by several kilometres, for I had been transferred to a mining camp. Occasionally we got news of each other through the free doctors who visited both camps, but we had no direct contact. Then one day the head of the medical department sent a secret message asking me to come and see him. When I arrived he handed me a note and said that he had something else for me as well but that I must promise not to take the object into the camp; after this he pulled out a huge bottle of red wine. The note said that my friend the doctor, as a reward for his exceptional services to the camp hospital, had had his term shortened and was going home to join his wife and children. He wrote that before leaving he wanted to pay his debt.

In 1947 I received a letter from him, describing the welcome he had had from his family and saying that all was well with him in Tallinn. A year or two later I learned that he had been deported again to the Far North and I tried every means of getting into contact with him, but only managed to hear about him indirectly. Then in 1956 I learned that he had been released again and allowed to return to Estonia. I had greatly enjoyed his friendship when we were in the same camp and I deeply respected him; our meetings stand out in my memory as some of the brightest points in the Norilsk period of my life. Hundreds of prisoners owed their lives to this man. I learnt recently that he died in Tallinn in the early sixties.

*

Weakened by hunger strikes and illness, and the fact that my constitution could never get used to camp food, I spent several of those difficult years in hospital. I was always on the border line between life and death and was continually being told that I would not 'last out' next winter or next month. The doctors were always predicting my death.

One of the big differences between the Hitler and the Stalin systems was the treatment of the weak and sick. A man who fell sick in Auschwitz was at once gassed or shot. But in Stalin's camps, for all their cruelty, the attitude to the sick prescribed from above was, if such a word can be used in this context, almost humane. Mass extermination did go on but it was not really intentional. The idea of death camps was not admitted. I was in the Gornaya Shoriya camp when in the one winter of 1935/6 some eighty per cent of the inmates died. They were building about a hundred kilometres of railway line with several tunnels through a difficult mountain range; the work took years and the men were cut off and ill-supplied in winter. The deaths were not planned. Those who were meant to die were killed outright, but a great number of others died through disorganization and neglect. As I mentioned earlier, daily reports had to go to the central administration of the camps and if the mortality rate surpassed a given level, something was done. Eighty per cent was too much. The camp commandant, Razin, and his whole staff were dismissed; the commandant was tried and condemned either to death or to a long term of imprisonment. The camp system was able to provide workers for remote regions and at the same time isolate those considered dangerous to the State, but it was not intended to kill them all off. The corrective was the medical department. The doctors recruited from among the prisoners were good and devoted men who at great sacrifice saved many people from death. True, there were monsters among them as well, but on the whole the hospitals were islands of humanity.

For years I was able to watch the work of 'mending' those who came into the hands of the doctors and who had to be restored to sufficient health for them to be able to work. Often, particularly during the war, the doctors could do nothing because the patients were brought to them too late and because they lacked the necessary medicines. In the hospitals I could study the process of slow death. I was in the thick of it myself and was often regarded as one of the dying. But if I assume the attitude of a spectator I have to say that to observe others, people of different social strata and various national-ities, as they faced and met death, was most interesting and instruc-tive. One conviction I formed was that so far as Russians are con-cerned, the epigraph from Petrarch at the beginning of Chapter Six of *Yevgeny Onegin* accurately described their attitude to death:

'There, beneath a sad and cloudy sky, live men for whom death is not painful.' Enormous resignation and quiet acceptance were the characteristics which surprised me at first but which I later took for granted in those whose death I witnessed. In 1942 and 1943 I was in hospital at Norilsk after a long hunger strike. I was transferred to a ward with thirty-six beds. In the course of two or three months its population was renewed three times. Very few people were discharged; they had all been sent to this ward because they had been written off. Not only the staff but also the patients showed great indifference to those who came into this death ward. Their treatment was at an end because even the most devoted doctors felt they could do nothing more for them. Some were in the last stages of scurvy, others had haemocolitis (haemorrhage from the bowels) which showed that the patient could no longer digest anything; some had pneumonia and abscesses on the lungs which at that time were incurable – it was only towards the end of the war that Soviet doctors were well-supplied with sulphanilamide which made it possible to cure many lung diseases from which the mortality rate till then had been some eighty per cent.

Thus people came to this ward to die, and they accepted it with utter calm. Whether they had been peasants, workers or employees they all looked alike – as thin as skeletons and as pale as death, but all were peaceful though they thought they might not survive the night. In fact, every morning the attendants found a small number of corpses, pulled them out by the legs and made the beds ready for new patients. The extraordinary thing is that while, for the first few nights, I watched everything with extreme attention, later – because of the general atmosphere – I took it for granted. People knew that they were being brought into the ward to die and their death appeared to them as something wholly natural. They knew that their last wishes would not be carried out, for the camp regulations did not allow the relatives to be informed of the death of a prisoner. His things would not be sent to them and no message would reach them, so a man knew that his life would end in complete isolation, in total loneliness . . . But many thought of death as a relief. When a man came to this last stage it was as if he had thought out everything and made his peace. A few said prayers and crossed themselves, but

they were only perhaps one or two per cent. The great majority
died without a word, having merely finished with their suffering.
Most of them were young – the young died more quickly than the
older people. In any case young people formed the great majority in
these camps in the Far North. I was in my thirties but the majority
were only in their twenties; there was an age limit – I think it was
forty – beyond which no one was sent to this particular camp.

So these people died who should have had their lives before them.
I was the more impressed by their acceptance of death, for they
were people who had been torn out of life and who, living in a
different time, would have lived on and on, and become heads of
families. What was taking place was in fact a massacre of the
people, and it was madness, for they were mostly simple people in
no way guilty of any crime against the authorities, and they could
have been most valuable citizens. This fact, that even before 1930,
and for decades afterwards, simple people perished – not only the
cream of the intelligentsia but also ordinary workers, useful people
with a positive cast of mind, capable of ideals and of heroic achievements, and beside them the grey mass of those simple *muzhiks*[3]
whom no one knew and whom allegedly the Revolution was to
save – the destruction of these people remains most vividly in my
memory.

One of those who died in my ward was an engineer of about
thirty, very well read – there were many such – and either a Party
member or a candidate; he was clearly a 'representative of the
intelligentsia'. His wife decided to get rid of him because she preferred someone else, and did what was done in hundreds of cases:
denounced him by telling the NKVD that in the absence of all
witnesses other than herself he had said this and that about Stalin.
Within a few days he was arrested, interrogated once, tried, condemned in his absence – as happened to tens of thousands – and
sentenced to a term in camp. As he was young and an engineer he
was sent to the Far North. He did what almost everyone did and
kept writing letters to Stalin, continuing to believe that things
would still be sorted out, though the experience of all around him
showed clearly that nothing was ever sorted out and that once you

3. Russian peasants.

were there you were finished. What with hard labour, hunger and cold, within a few months he was in hospital and after some unsuccessful treatment came to the death ward. He felt that he was dying and would not see his family again. He had received a photo of his small son and news that his younger brother had also been declared an enemy of the people and would no doubt share his fate. On his last night, when the only sounds in the ward were the groans and hiccups of the dying, I suddenly heard him say loudly and distinctly: 'Man, how proudly sounds the word.' The man in the bed next to mine went over to him but he died a few moments later. Was it irony? I don't know. It was spoken in a didactic voice, as if it was his final summing up, the conclusion he had drawn from all he had lived through. Of course, if one knew that this was a saying of Gorky that was repeated *ad nauseam* on every possible occasion, it sounded like the wildest mockery. But perhaps this engineer thought it was true, or should be.

While Russians died peacefully, southerners, such as Armenians and Georgians, clung to life with unbelievable tenacity. If you heard a man groaning, struggling or calling for the doctors (who never came as they knew it was hopeless) you could be almost sure it was a southerner who lacked the Russians' stoicism. I remembered discussing this Russian contempt for death in 1939 with another young engineer, who was called Lopatin. He was highly educated and exceptionally observant and clever. He was trying to explain to me the Russians' apparent docility in the face of the inhuman actions of the authorities. He said: 'You have to get to know this people. The Russians will take their place in the sun precisely because they can be satisfied with very little. In no other nation will you find such a capacity to rise above material needs, even the most essential.' He added: 'All you have to do is hold a whip over their heads and feed them as little as possible. If you do that you can reach the Pacific Ocean and conquer the world.' This was the result of centuries of slavery. Stalin's strength lay in his realization of this and in his hatred of the Russians and conviction that you could do anything you liked with them. Lopatin thought Stalin was consciously following the example of Genghis Khan, Ivan the Terrible and Peter the Great: it was no accident that they and he were successful. This boundless cruelty was what the people were used to regarding as a sign of greatness, and they considered it a justifiable means of achieving great aims. Lopatin thought Stalin was the greatest counter-revolutionary ever born because he had crushed all aspirations to freedom and a better life, and while continuing the Revolution in words was in fact continuing the rule to which the Russians had become used over the centuries.

*

Because batches of new prisoners were constantly arriving from the front we, in camp, were extraordinarily well informed about the progress of the war, better indeed than the general public.

The new arrivals were deserters or people sentenced for economic crimes or political propaganda, and after 1942 there were also those who had been sentenced for having been captured by the Germans – they had escaped and returned to Russia but the moment they got home they were arrested on the grounds that since they had survived they could not have behaved with heroism. Jewish service-men were particularly suspect; if they came back alive after being in German hands it was assumed that they must have been traitors and they were treated as such.

As a result of this policy every fighting man had a double threat hanging over him when he went to the front: that of being killed by the Germans and that of the NKVD's vengeance if he became a prisoner and survived. This was a terror measure designed to make everyone feel afraid.

There were some fantastic cases; one I remember is that of an officer commanding a tank unit who fought his way out when encircled, was welcomed back as a hero, and three months later was arrested and tried.

There was always tension between the army organization SMERSH,[4] which dealt with military offences, and the NKVD, which dealt with political crimes. I heard many stories of SMERSH protecting soldiers and even getting them back from the NKVD after they had been arrested. Appallingly as the NKVD behaved,

4. Branch of the Secret Police, organized during the war, particularly concerned with unreliable elements in the Red Army and counter-espionage.

they would have been still worse if the army commanders had not fought them. Throughout the war the NKVD accompanied the army, though they did not normally go very close to the front line and other places where the military were in control. It is also true that after the Russian victories the power of the NKVD was slightly reduced.

In spite of what the régime had done to them there was a spirit of tremendous patriotism and support for the Government among the political prisoners. The criminals had a different point of view. They were violently against all authority and indeed against society as such; they were completely cynical and regarded the fact that they were being punished merely as the measure of their stupidity in having allowed themselves to be caught. They wanted Hitler to win the war and said so. In a few cases their attitude influenced the political prisoners who had to work with them, but these had to keep their mouths shut – otherwise their lives would have been made impossible.

As well as facts we prisoners naturally heard many stories and rumours from the soldier prisoners. They told us of atrocities committed by the Russians but ascribed to the Germans. For instance, if a village refused to support the partisans the people were exterminated and afterwards it was said that this had been the work of the Nazis. We found some difficulty in believing these tales, and in the same way we could not accept the propaganda stories which described small Russian units gaining miraculous victories over large German forces. As the war went on detailed accounts of German atrocities were believed, and they made the political prisoners even more anxious to play a part in the war. Hundreds of thousands of them in camps all over Russia wrote begging to be allowed to serve in the army. But virtually no political prisoners were accepted – only criminals. Deprived of the chance of fighting they were determined to contribute to the war effort as best they could. Voluntarily, they relinquished certain rights, and their work, already hard enough in the Arctic cold, was extended to twelve hours a day.

Once the NKVD became convinced that a prisoner was reliable they made use of his enthusiasm and devotion. To give one instance: when, under Lease-Lend, the Americans provided the Soviet Union with excavators, these were brought by sea from San Francisco to Vladivostok, where there were no Russian specialists available to take charge of them. In our camp, however, there were several prisoners quite capable of doing so. So the camp commandant, an official of the NKVD and an old Party member, Nikolay Vasilye-vich Volokhov, summoned a prisoner who was an expert electrical engineer serving a fifteen-year sentence, and asked him to accompany him to Vladivostok to take over the machines. Whether he had authorization from Moscow to do so I do not know but off they flew together to Krasnoyarsk and from there to Vladivostok, a distance of 6,000 kilometres. The engineer knew English, which the commandant did not, so during talks with the Americans he acted as interpreter. During the six weeks he was away from camp no-one who met him could have guessed that he was a prisoner let out solely for a purpose, and that after this had been fulfilled he would return to his labour camp.

I knew the man, a Ukrainian, very well. He had been in the Komsomol and the Party, and had reached the rank of Colonel in the Engineers, and I can testify that the idea of escaping never occurred to him, not only because he had a wife, children, brothers and sisters on whom terrible reprisals would have been taken had he fled, but also because from the moment he was arrested, in 1937, he was convinced that a mistake had been made and that sooner or later the truth would out and he would be freed and reinstated. He certainly realized that he was one of millions who had suffered injustice and that injustice on this scale would lead to the ruin of the nation, but he regarded all this as a purely internal affair and remained a staunch communist. The idea that foreign powers should meddle in what he considered to be an internal tragedy filled him with indignation. He did not want Stalin in power but still less did he want Hitler.

Another and terrible way in which we in camp could observe the course of the war was by the mass shootings which were linked to the defeats of the Soviet army. I can remember three such massacres at Norilsk. The first was in November 1941 when the Germans were at the gates of Moscow; several dozen people were taken out one night and shot. The next collective shooting was on the 10th of

June 1942, and the third on the 23rd of September 1942, when the news that the Germans had entered Stalingrad was received. Shootings on a smaller scale might take place any night but these mass killings were definitely related to news from the front. I can personally testify only to what happened at Norilsk, but I have heard that the same thing took place simultaneously in hundreds of camps throughout Russia.

The motive was to ensure that the presumed 'Fifth Column' should have no cause for rejoicing. The massacres had a precedent, for after Kirov was murdered, indeed on the day of his funeral, hundreds of people were shot. I remember reading their names in the following day's paper. Some of the victims were important Party members who had been arrested for reasons that had no connection with the Kirov affair. The lists were published in *Pravda* under the heading 'Retribution'. The executions were carried out purely to inspire terror. The NKVD were ordered to kill a given number of people and many of those who died were not even tried.

In ancient times when disaster struck a state many people were killed to inspire fear and deprive internal enemies of the chance for rejoicing. In our times the Soviet Union has revived this primitive practice.

In spite of these horrors most of the inhabitants of the camp remained patriotic even at the worst moments when hunger and epidemics caused innumerable deaths. Spring 1943 was our lowest moment so far as rations were concerned, for even outside the camps there was an acute shortage of all food including bread, and we prisoners got practically nothing to eat. If help from abroad had not come we should all have died, but it was during that summer that American wheat began to reach us and it was thanks to this that a proportion of the prisoners survived. The deliveries were not made without loss, for German submarines were in action and some of the transports were torpedoed. Later, Russian naval units were sent to deal with the raiders and eventually a naval action was fought somewhere near Norilsk.

Doctors from the camp, amongst them a gifted surgeon called Rodionov, were ordered to look after the wounded. Rodionov saved the life of the Soviet Commander and of many others. As a reward he did not have to serve the remaining years of his sentence, but was put in charge of a hospital for frontier guards and NKVD patients.

Towards the end of the war we prisoners lived entirely on American supplies and I can still see in my mind those tins of spam and butter with their labels printed in both Russian and English.

Though deprived of the opportunity of fighting for their country, the political prisoners made a contribution to the war effort that was a remarkable achievement. They built the gigantic industrial complex of Norilsk, with its huge mines and a large foundry that turned out nickel and other metals which were in very short supply. The Norilsk base was immensely profitable; not only did it bring in millions of roubles but it also covered the needs of the army and industry for years ahead.

Being human, the prisoners whose labour brought Norilsk into being naturally hoped that their work and their devotion to their country would be recognized, and that their sentences would be shortened, but I can testify that their primary motive was to defeat Hitler.

At the end of the war what happened was that the free salaried men, who directed the work, received decorations and promotion while some prisoners who had overfulfilled their norms, even some held under Article 58, were let off one, two, three or four years of their sentence. Of course, if they were serving a sentence of twenty or twenty-five years this did not mean very much, but at least it was taken as a good omen. Unfortunately the first post-war years did not bring any real improvement in our situation. In some ways it became worse.

THE POST-WAR YEARS

1948 and 1949 were the years in which a new purge got under way. Its object was to complete the work of the 1937 purge; prisoners such as myself who had survived many years of prisons and camps were to be weeded out and put in 'isolators'. This was how, after nine years, I came to leave the camp at Norilsk and was transferred with two hundred and fifty other veterans to the notorious Alexandrovsk central prison near Irkutsk. We thought that the authorities were deliberating whether or not to shoot us; in fact the move turned out to be just one more measure of repression.

The transfer itself was an appalling experience. We went to the transit prison at Irkutsk and from there left on the last lap of our journey. Outside the narrow door stood a lorry surrounded by guards. As we approached it we were seized and handcuffed in pairs. The job was done hurriedly and roughly, causing us acute pain and making our wrists bleed, but we had no time to utter a word for we were at once pushed so violently into the truck that we fell to the floor. Before we had recovered our breath the next pair was thrown in on top of us and then another and another until the lorry was filled to capacity. We lay like sardines, unable to move and forbidden even to groan. Finally a guard climbed on to the edge of the lorry and counted us as though we were cattle. When he had finished he was handed a rusty chain. We had heard about these chains which, it was said, had lain unused for thirty years in the cellars of the Irkutsk prison and had recently been brought out again. The guard threaded the chain through every pair of fetters and then secured it to the side of the lorry.

It was an early autumn morning but the sun had risen and the air was bright and warm. The man I was handcuffed to had much thicker wrists than mine and as a result the metal was biting into his flesh and causing him great pain. Nonetheless he whispered to me:

'At least those damned sadists have left us some light and sunshine.'

He was wrong. As we heard the driver get into the cabin and switch on the engine the sunlight vanished and we felt something heavy descend upon us and cover us up. It was a tarpaulin. The transport commander told us later that he had received a special order to keep us not only crowded and handcuffed but also in the dark so that we should not know where we were going.

We started off, so completely covered over that no passer-by could have guessed that the lorry was bearing a human cargo. One unfortunate prisoner was in such pain from his handcuffs that he could not refrain from groaning all through the journey. After we had arrived and been unloaded we stood in a row in front of a big iron gate and were told to raise our arms for the guards to take off our fetters. It was then found that this poor fellow's handcuffs could not be removed and his groans changed to heart-rending screams when a saw that had been sent for was used without effect. Finally a hatchet was brought and did the job but by then the man's wrists were a mass of bleeding flesh. He fainted and had to be carried away.

In this prison I met many people who had been intended to vanish from the public scene once and for all. Among them were Nazi VIPs who for one reason or another were not to be tried as war criminals. Some had been seized in Western Germany, others, such as the members of Schulenberg's diplomatic staff, had been in prison for some time. There were also some Japanese who had been captured at Harbin.

In the Alexandrovsk prison the conditions were particularly harsh. No letters or newspapers were allowed. Besides the usual punishments and punishment cells the prison was infested with agents, one to each cell, or indeed usually more than one to ensure that the agents spied on each other. In prison slang they were known as 'broodies' (*nasedki*).

As in other Soviet prisons the mood of the prisoners was one of passive, hopeless resignation. It had taken me a long time to understand how, since most of them were innocent of any crime against the régime, they could bring themselves to this attitude of acceptance. Eventually I realized that they were convinced that they could just as easily have been shot out of hand as imprisoned, so that a sentence of ten, twenty or twenty-five years seemed almost merciful to them.

In fact, given the conditions in the prisons, there was not much to be thankful for; all it meant was that death came slowly instead of quickly. An old Russian proverb says: 'No one can avoid prison or beggary.' It gives expression to the poverty and lack of rights of the Russian people; now it had become truer than ever and I often heard it repeated by old men and boys, by women, by people of all categories – peasants, workers, doctors, engineers, professors. It summed up what we thought of our lot. A comment by a political commissar expressed the same attitude from the point of view of the authorities. 'We are not trying,' he said, 'to bring down the mortality rate.' I shall never forget hearing him say this in the most matter of fact tone of voice.

Although it is true that a few of my companions in the Alexandrovsk prison lived to be rehabilitated and that among the dead some had their reputation posthumously cleared, neither the Russian people, nor the men of other nations who came within the power of the régime, can ever forget the atrocities for which Stalin was responsible, nor feel an easy conscience until the whole story has been told. In the fifties I met one man who had been with me in this prison; he had been given a pension and rehabilitated and was now living out his life, but he said that he could not enjoy it while 'considerations of state policy' forced him to conceal many of the terrible facts that he knew. 'Doesn't this mean,' he asked, 'that there are still people who are thinking of renewing this dance of death?'

*

One of Stalin's last and most dreadful crimes was his campaign of repressions against Party officials in Leningrad. In one sense 1948 was a real turning-point; the country was on the way to recovery after the devastations of the war but it was precisely at this time that many people began to lose faith in the Party and the system. They had partly got over the exhaustion they felt after the years of danger and deprivations, and they expected some significant improvements in their way of life. Not least in Party, military and literary circles, people were asking themselves whether the war had really ended in victory for the Russians or whether it had not rather strengthened Stalin's system of dictatorial rule. Stalin realized that the nation expected something new and better after its enormous sacrifices in the fight against Hitler, and so he and the secret police had to do something to show the population that they had no intention of letting go of the reins. They decided to strengthen the régime by shedding some more blood.

To explain the background to this bloodletting I must stress that both the intelligentsia and the masses were united in their feeling of dissatisfaction and disillusionment. Naturally the NKVD could not countenance the desire of many intellectuals for freedom of criticism and creativity, but the peasants presented, if only inarticulately, demands which would have been even more difficult for the authorities to accept. Many people still placed their hopes on Zhukov,* who was very popular at that time and widely regarded as the man who won the war. It was thought he might either take political power into his own hands or at least exert sufficient pressure to force Stalin to decollectivize the farms. There was a very widespread illusion among the peasants that decollectivization was not only possible but essential, for agriculture was in a simply catastrophic condition. (I know this from my own experience. In the early fifties I was living in exile on a *kolkhoz*[1] called 'The Testaments of Ilyich', where of the several hundred workers only four were men – apart from myself. These were two invalids, a team-leader who was of German extraction and had therefore not been called up, and another person who for some reason or other had returned to the *kolkhoz* after being demobbed.)

There was a second widespread illusion for a time after the war, but it was cherished by the young and the intelligentsia rather than the peasantry. They expected that there would be a significant relaxation and improvement in foreign relations, a *modus vivendi* with the West, and the founding of UNO kept these hopes alive for a little while longer. Allied with this was yet another expectation, shared by many workers as well, that it would surely be possible to diminish the military budget and thereby raise the standard of living to a more tolerable level.

1. A collective farm.

The MGB was well aware of all these hopes and evidently did not like them, but it had to wait for a signal from Stalin before being able to act. The signal eventually came and set the well-known 'Leningrad Affair' in motion in 1948. I learnt the details – from very reliable sources – only some years later.

Stalin had summoned Khrushchev,* now at the head of the Moscow Party organization, and Malenkov,* who was in charge of the Central Committee apparatus. Stalin said he had learnt that some anti-Soviet plots were being hatched in both the Moscow and the Leningrad Party organizations. Khrushchev asked for a few weeks to look into the matter, but Malenkov said he would go to Leningrad immediately and carry out investigations. Khrushchev was playing for time and hoping Stalin would forget about the matter or change his mind; this was the only way of trying to save both his colleagues and himself. He quickly rearranged the Party apparatus, switching people around from one job to another, thereby giving the necessary impression of vigilance. Malenkov behaved very differently and was personally responsible for the subsequent purges and deaths, since he took a personal and active interest in the affair.

There had of course been some earlier purges in Leningrad in the twenties and thirties but it was still widely thought that the problem – the existence of an element of independent thinking and initiative in the local Party apparatus – had not been completely and finally solved. Everything appeared to be quiet and in order, but if some criticism of the General Secretary did begin it would probably be in Leningrad – or so Stalin seemed to think. He had apparently feared that many people there would welcome the Germans in 1941 and felt that it might be better not to try too hard to defend the city and save its inhabitants. If they were destroyed by the Germans the problem of Russian opposition to his rule ought to be solved once and for all.

It is quite possible that in 1948 Malenkov found enough evidence to convince Stalin that something really was wrong in Leningrad and its Party organization and that prompt and drastic action was necessary. It should not be forgotten that this was a time of considerable disarray in the Peoples' Democracies of Central and Eastern Europe. Anti-Stalin feelings could be found in all of them and the lesson of Tito's apparently successful rebellion was clear: everything possible must be done to ensure that such a thing would not happen again. Any potentially powerful disaffected groups in the USSR itself must be nipped in the bud.

As was the custom of the Soviet security service, it preferred not to wait and then liquidate any serious threat to Stalin's leadership but to take prophylactic action to prevent well in advance any likelihood of real trouble in the future. This now involved the decimation of the Leningrad Party leadership, the encouragement of exceptionally widespread mutual denunciation and spying, and the attempt to revive the fears of ten years before so that virtually everyone everywhere would be too petrified even to think of any alternative to Stalin's rule.

I was not surprised when a professor at Leningrad University later told me that after his arrest the investigator asked him if he remembered 1937. He said he did and was informed that this was a good job as '1937 was not a thing of the past'. Indeed, the false and fantastic accusations and the physical as well as psychological torture showed that this was so. On the other hand there was a certain difference which made the 'Leningrad Affair' more like a new St Bartholomew's Night than the mass, nation-wide purges of the late thirties. Although news of the Leningrad purge reached all corners of the country with lightning speed the press and radio had very little to say about it and very few details, either true or false, have ever been revealed.

As in the thirties the families of the accused were made to suffer as well, perhaps in part so that as little definite news as possible got out and the whole business was surrounded by a frightening mystery. In July 1951 I had a good chance to learn at first hand how the State security machine could deal with relations of enemies of the people. On the way to a place of exile after my release from camp I was held for a time at the prison in Krasnoyarsk. When the list of the numerous prisoners in my cell was called out I was surprised to hear the name of Kapustin, for I knew that this was the name of the Second Secretary of the Leningrad Regional Committee, a man who, I thought, had been physically liquidated a couple of years before. However, it was a boy of about ten who answered and I was even more surprised when he later told me that he was the son of the man I had been thinking of. He said that all the families of those who had been executed in Leningrad in 1949 had been arrested by now. He himself was moved to another school immediately after the arrest of his father but then the relations who had taken him and his young sister into their home had been 'repressed' for doing this. Kapustin junior, however, had not been arrested until January 1951, when he was interrogated, sentenced to 'eternal exile' and despatched to Krasnoyarsk where he had already met the sons of many of his father's late colleagues. In the cell we taught him how to write petitions reminding the authorities that as he was still under twelve he was not supposed to be kept in a 'general' prison cell. He wrote some petitions but they were unsuccessful and before long he was sent off into exile in a very remote spot in this part of Siberia, where he no doubt remained until after Stalin's death.

It was soon after this that I learnt a little more about the Leningrad Affair when I was visited by my family and by an old friend of mine who was now a journalist. I had arrived at my place of exile, a collective farm, but for some time I was unable to write home as neither I nor anyone I knew had any money (people were paid only once a year, late in the autumn) and so it was impossible even to get a stamp. Eventually I had enough kopecks to post a letter to my wife, who immediately sent a telegram saying that she and our son were leaving at once to see me. When they arrived I was amazed at what they had to say. Although it was fifteen years since I had last seen them and I had sometimes lost touch with them for long periods I felt that I knew what was going on and what people in Moscow were thinking. I was wrong. In particular I had not realized how much my family had suffered because they were related to me, an enemy of the people (my wife has touched on this in her own memoirs which came out some time ago in Hebrew). My son in particular had completely stopped thinking within a 'Party' framework. Unlike me, he and his mother had broken with Marxist ideology and it was difficult for the three of us to find a common language on many subjects.

One of the things I talked about with my family and with the journalist who also came to visit me (he was a good friend of the writer Fadeyev) was the Leningrad Affair. They told me that the power and cult of Stalin were now greater than ever, but so was the demoralization within the Party, which felt impotent vis-à-vis the secret police. The Leningrad Party leaders had confessed not only to various economic crimes but also to plotting against Stalin himself and to plans for the arrest of many leading officials in Moscow, including men in the MGB, who were to be charged with crimes for which Stalin bore the major responsibility. Some of the accused confessed that they had been encouraged by the defiant behaviour of Tito; apparently they were hanged, not shot.

I was told that one of the chief investigators into the Leningrad Affair (they were specially sent from Moscow as the local ones were considered too unreliable) had earlier played a prominent role in SMERSH and was called Yepishev.* I have often heard his name since then. He helped to liquidate Beria, did well under Khrushchev and still plays a very important part today in controlling dissent both in the USSR and in Eastern Europe. When he visited Prague in the spring of 1968 I felt certain that this indicated serious concern in the Soviet Party leadership at the way things were going. But what my visitors told me in 1951 showed that if a genuine 'revisionist' movement had got under way in the late forties it would quickly have gathered a great deal of support in Moscow itself. It was – and is – the job of Yepishev and many others to ensure that nothing of the sort should come about.

*

From the Alexandrovsk prison I was transferred to Tayshet. In the early days of the Revolution this had been an ordinary 'corrective labour camp', but then, in the forties, it had been turned into a 'special régime' camp and as such was greatly feared. 'Special' camps were those instituted during the periods of mass arrests especially for political prisoners, and Tayshet was said to be the largest of them all.

The régime in these camps was very severe. The inmates were at all times under attentive surveillance, the barracks were locked in the evening, and even during the day the prisoners could not move freely about the camp. They wore a uniform with, on both coat and trousers, identification marks made up of letters and figures which recalled those worn by the inmates of Tsarist penal colonies; these marks made it easy for a warden or guard to see which part of the camp a prisoner belonged to. Correspondence was very strictly controlled; in some camps prisoners were allowed to write home only twice a year, and as a result family ties, which were still to some extent maintained in other camps, were often broken. Few of the prisoners had any hope of ever being released, for most of them were middle-aged or old and were serving twenty-five-year sentences: this was then the maximum penalty for crimes against the State. They were made to work, but whereas in the other camps large construction projects were usually involved and specialists were often put to their own kind of job, in the 'special' camps even the greatest experts were forced to dig, carry railway sleepers or make roads.

At Tayshet, which lies on the frontier between eastern and western Siberia, halfway between Krasnoyarsk and Irkutsk, the prisoners were used to build the railway to Bratsk. (It was begun in the forties and completed only in about 1960.) The work was terribly hard, the climate harsh, extremely so in the winter, and the food was inadequate, but since those to whom this régime was applied were regarded as the most dangerous type of prisoner they were not in any case intended to come out alive.

When I reached my part of the camp I found myself among quite different types of people from those I had been with during my previous fifteen years as a prisoner.

Here, there were no criminals and most of the prisoners were foreigners. Of the Russians many had been in the front line during the war and not a few had held important posts in the army or in the economic administration. The soldiers had been sentenced for making 'counter-revolutionary' (i.e., anti-régime) statements, or for alleged spying on behalf of the Americans or British, or had been accused of collaboration with the Germans. They had been tried under Article 58/6, which dealt with spying but had a very wide application. In the thirties most of the heavy sentences were given under Article 58/8, i.e., for 'terrorism' and anything that could be connected with it.

The great variety of people in Tayshet and all the other 'special' camps reflected the feverish activity of the security organs since the machinery of terror had been charged not only with maintaining 'security' at home but also in the satellite countries, where it instituted purges and from which it gathered new supplies of victims.

The population of the Tayshet camp totalled about 100,000. It was only one of many 'special' camps; there were others all over Siberia, in Kazakhstan and in the Far North; we reckoned that there must be several million people in the 'special' camps, while simultaneously the number of prisoners in the other camps had grown unbelievably.

The camp was divided into several parts, each section of which had its own way of treating the inmates, all designed to help the authorities to carry out their investigations.

It was at Tayshet that I first heard the word *chifir* (the word comes from the Chinese) and learned what it stood for: a drug by which people deprived of all normal tranquillizers or stimulants could reach a state of forgetfulness.

Prisoners were not allowed to drink spirits but in 'general' régime camps, where some individuals still had links with people outside, a few of them sometimes managed to get hold of alcohol and even of drugs such as cocaine and opium; in 'special' camps this was impossible. Instead, the prisoners discovered *chifir*; by the time I reached Tayshet the use of the drug was so widespread that the authorities were using special measures to stop it. *Chifir* is derived from tannin and caffeine; its action is more powerful than nicotine and when used in strength can produce the effects of cocaine or opium.

It is usually made of tea. Fifty grammes of tea are sufficient to make a large number of cups of strong English tea but to get *chifir* you have to boil 400 grammes in so small an amount of water that it makes only three to four cups. The proportion of tannin is therefore very high and its effects are astonishing. Those who drank it became intoxicated or went into a trance and forgot all the suffering they had endured. In their efforts to prevent prisoners from finding escape from their misery in this way the authorities had food parcels carefully checked (each prisoner was allowed only one small packet of tea); searches were made to prevent tea from being smuggled in and punishments were imposed for the use of *chifir*.

In spite of all this there were prisoners who succeeded in establishing a trade in tea, and in some sections of the camp (there were some 500 to 600 prisoners in each section) they managed to set up a kind of club for the enjoyment of *chifir*. Here prisoners used to drink late into the night until they had reached a state of happiness. In my camp the drying room – the place where prisoners coming back from work soaked from rain, sleet or snow left their clothes overnight – had become such a club. It was a low building, part of which was a basement; as a fire was always kept burning the temperature was pleasantly warm. There was a prisoner in charge of every drying room; the post was regarded as one which could be procured only through '*blat*', i.e. 'pull', and was much sought after and hard to get. The attendant in our drying room was an interesting personality. In spite of his Scandinavian surname he was a Russian and came of an enterprising Siberian family which, between the nineties and the First World War, had built up a small fortune. After the October Revolution they became colonists in Korea and this is where Elas was born. His parents gave him a Russian education and he was specifically Russian in his outlook and way of life. He told me that he had always thought of himself as a Russian living in a foreign land and looked on Russia as his home.

He had made some money and since he was young and adventurous decided to travel. He went to China, where he lived in Canton and then in Shanghai, learned the language and got to understand the Chinese way of life. Then, when the Russians took a close interest in North Korea and were preparing to turn it into a People's Democratic Republic, he put himself at the disposition of the administrators. They made use of him, as they did of other Russians, but he soon fell under suspicion because he had never lived in Russia and more particularly because he had been in China under Chiang Kai-shek and had visited Japan, whose forces were then occupying South Korea. In 1947 or 1948 he was arrested and sent to Siberia.

Elas was both unusually clever and businesslike, to which qualities he owed his appointment to the coveted job of attendant in the drying room. This exempted him from hard labour and enabled him to indulge his passion for *chifir*; his craving for it was insatiable. Little by little he organized something like a club. People he had got to know came to his tiny cell, furnished only with a bed and a table, and helped him to get hold of tea and carry on an unending trade in it. In return they shared his feasts and escaped momentarily from the hopelessness of their lives. The tea was sold for a fabulous sum, every packet costing many rations of bread and soup because it brought a forgetfulness which was beyond price.

It was curious that Elas chose a German as his chief assistant. SS Major Gaedeke was a young man of about twenty-seven who had been captured by the NKVD in East Berlin, where he had been in charge of a section of American espionage; he had received a sentence of twenty-five years.

He was tall and thin and had a military bearing, and he had seen far too much in his short life. As a boy he had joined the Hitler-jugend; later he had been in the SS and fought on the Eastern Front. By the time the war ended he was disillusioned with Nazism and, finding himself in the Western Zone, joined the CIA, which used him for espionage in the Eastern sector of Berlin.

He claimed to have had a large number of people working for him, including some very young German boys who were in our camp. They had formerly been in the Hitlerjugend and Gaedeke had recruited them to perform some elementary tasks such as taking down the numbers of cars and spotting the units to which the Russian occupying forces belonged. They were in their teens and when the trial ended they were amazed to find themselves condemned to the same term of imprisonment as their Chief.

Gaedeke stood up well to camp conditions but four of the boys died and when I left some of the others were seriously ill. The few very young Germans who survived Stalin's death were later released.[2]

2. The liberation of German prisoners began in 1953. As far as I know, the last of the German prisoners in Tayshet were set free during Adenauer's visit to Moscow in 1955. But it is not possible to be quite certain, for when a person is led out allegedly to be freed it is still on the cards that something different may happen to him. Although the general order was to release all the Germans, efforts were made to detain those who had spied for the Americans, and some were still in camps in 1956, when their sentences were reviewed (as were those of people who had more recently been engaged in serious espionage deep into Soviet territory) and reduced from twenty-five to ten years. It therefore looks as though any

There were many Germans in our camp; they had lost all their arrogance and were humble and obedient. They were also very polite and concealed any hatred they felt for the Russians who disliked them, despised them and generally treated them roughly. They endured hunger much less well than the Russians and were always ready to jump at the most humiliating job in return for the slightest privilege.

Most of them, including high-ranking officers, were keenly interested in trade and speculation. In their own camps economic crimes had been treated with exceptional severity – a man might be shot for stealing a potato or tortured or beaten up for the smallest act of dishonesty; but though they had inflicted these penalties on others I saw German officers speculating and thieving in a way which made nonsense of their theories that only people mainly engaged in trade, such as Jews and Poles, were dishonest and, because of this, justifiably classed as inferior races.

In the immediate post-war period the Germans were very badly treated by the Soviet authorities; they were beaten up and refused medical help. Our guards were Russian peasants who, when de-mobilized, had preferred to take service in the MGB than return to their *kolkhozes* where people were dying of hunger. They hated the Germans; many of them had seen how the Russian POWs had been treated in German camps and they felt no pity for the enemies who had now fallen into their hands.

Certainly in Tayshet, where there were many Germans, the only people who treated them as human beings and helped them to survive were Jews. For instance, when a German could get no help from a Russian doctor he would go to a Jewish doctor for treatment.

On the whole, the Jews' attitude was basically humane; they stood up for human rights and human dignity and condemned oppression under whatever banner it was exercised. Most of the Russian Jews with whom I talked believed that what we faced in camp was not a national problem but the results of an ideology which denied human rights. Knowing the atrocities they had com-

---

Germans who survived into the middle fifties must eventually have been freed and most of them repatriated.

mitted against the Jews, most Germans were terrified of meeting them and were particularly afraid of the Jews in the Camp Command and the NKVD. Yet, as a rule, even in the case of officials, the only people who showed them any kindness were Jews. Not all Jews were like this, of course; there were Jewish foremen and engineers who had come from the Western areas which had been occupied and who were ferocious in their attitude towards the Germans, but they were a minority.

Because I knew German I talked to many of the German prisoners and in a number of cases I found that we had a common language, and not only in the sense of knowing German; these men were not Nazis and today I am still in contact with some of them. Gaedeke was not in this category, but by talking to him I came to understand something of the vast muddle which was in the minds of the young Germans who had become Nazis and later changed their opinions and tried to find their feet.

Another member of the *chifir* club was a man I will call Vanya; it was he who had introduced me to Elas, and such an introduction was a privilege, for it was very difficult to gain the confidence of a man in Elas's position. Vanya was a fairly well-known author and I had read several of his books. He came of a noble family and had had a pre-revolutionary upbringing. In spite of this, when the February Revolution broke out – he was a young boy at the time – he became an enthusiastic Bolshevik and engaged in revolutionary activities in his home town in Central Russia.

Later he joined the Komsomol and then the Party, of which he was a most loyal member. His articles first appeared in the Pioneers', then in the Komsomol, and finally in the Party press; the views he expressed were always Left-Wing. He became a member of RAPP (Russian Association of Proletarian Writers). Perhaps he did this to stress his proletarian convictions or to bury his aristocratic origins. He wrote novels, essays and literary reviews and had many literary friends.

In the early thirties, though no action was taken against him, he had what he described as 'some misunderstandings with the Party'. He wrote a long novel about the Trotskyists, full of hatred and harsh condemnation. He also brought himself into the book and made full amends for ever having joined the now discredited RAPP; to his astonishment – indeed, all these years later he still could not get over his amazement – the novel was not published. Since the book followed the correct Party line, had been praised by important Party members and had even received the approval of the Central Committee this seemed to him to be inexplicable, and he continually stressed that it was full of praise of Stalin and presented Trotsky and his followers in a hideous light. I suggested to him that at the height of the struggle with Trotsky a novelist with *his* antecedents was not considered a suitable ally and that later, during and after the war, the policy was to keep quiet on the subject of Trotskyism. Moreover, it was then considered a specifically *Party* issue, unsuitable for presentation in fiction or even in memoirs; it concerned Stalin personally as well as the position of the Government, and was thus no subject for *belles lettres*. It was all right to write about collectivization, even in the way Sholokhov did, but when it came to Trotskyism and the mass arrests and killings connected with its suppression, this was something too serious for entertainment. Even to call a non-Party member a Trotskyist, using it as a smearword, not as a deadly accusation, was inadmissible. Either you had to quote the Party press and curse Trotsky as a mad dog in exactly the words that *Pravda* used, or you should keep quiet because there was something religious about this ritual.

This has always reminded me of a passage in the Bible which lays down that not one word may be taken away from or added to the Commandments, and I reflected that when a movement turns into a church it imposes similar sanctions; you may not 'take away' anything from, and you may not add anything of your own to, its statements. This fitted in with my conviction that Stalin wanted to turn the Party into an 'order' and give a sacred and divine character to its resolutions and to his own writings. Something of this attitude remains to this day. Take the struggle with Molotov: the formula was 'Molotov, Kaganovich . . . and Shepilov who joined them'. You may not talk about Shepilov individually; you can quote canon law and that is all you are allowed to do. Vanya's case illustrates this point; Yaroslavsky* and Zhdanov invited him to their receptions but all the same they would not allow his book to be published.

When the war broke out Vanya wanted to go to the front but infantile paralysis had left him with one leg shorter than the other, and he was rejected for military service. In 1942, however, he got a post in Military Intelligence (SMERSH). Ostensibly he was the editor of a Red Army newspaper but his real work was connected with counter-espionage. He kept the job until the end of the war and became thoroughly conversant with its methods. When he was released he went back to Leningrad and returned to writing and journalism. In 1947 misfortune fell upon him. He was very much interested in things foreign and was put forward as one of the writers who were permitted to have contacts with Western Marxist authors. He knew J. Aldridge and J. Lindsay and he met the correspondents of the Italian communist paper *Unità* and the French *Humanité*; indeed, they came often to his home. Vanya's wife was a pretty young actress and she apparently had an affair with one of the foreign correspondents for whom her husband had vouched. Later this man was suspected of spying and expelled. Vanya's wife was arrested. She got a sentence of only ten years and was sent to a camp near Rostov where she was able to join the camp-theatre and thus qualify for lighter work and better food than the other prisoners. That she was treated so leniently suggests that she must have given a lot of information about other people.

Then Vanya too was arrested for involvement in espionage. At first he protested his innocence (and innocent he must have been, for he was later rehabilitated), but eventually he was persuaded to confess to what he had not done. He was sentenced to twenty-five years in Siberia, his case being the more serious because he had been in SMERSH and evidently retained some connection with security afterwards.

Once in camp he came to an understanding with the authorities and acted as an informer. This was one reason which caused him to join Elas's club, for under the influence of *chifir* people often revealed what was on their minds; another reason was that he hoped to get copy for future novels.

He appeared to see nothing wrong in his behaviour. As he had co-operated with the authorities in the past, so he co-operated with them now; he believed that his own case was a special one – a mistake had been made – but as for the rest of us, we were guilty and needed to be closely watched. It was for this reason that he first made contact with me. We all realized that he was an agent and I was warned not to have anything to do with him, but I had learned through my long experience of camp life that evasion was useless. Had I not earlier got into trouble for *refusing* to respond to the advances of an agent who wanted me to discuss Trotsky's death with him? Now I had made it a rule not to avoid such people; the game was risky, but it was interesting. I saw a lot of Vanya; indeed, within certain limits we became quite friendly. He grew convinced that I, like himself, was a loyal communist and that my sentence, like his, had been a mistake and that one day we would both be released.

On one occasion he actually saved my life, for when a new investigation was threatened he gave a good report about me to the authorities and, since he was trusted, they believed him. The disadvantage of being on good terms with him was that it made the other prisoners distrust me, but this was the lesser of two evils. Much about Vanya shocked me, but he was undoubtedly an interesting person.

*

Alipi Andreyevich Kravtsov was another interesting man who frequented Elas's *chifir* club. I first met him at the point where prisoners gathered before being drafted to one part of the camp or another. Alipi's appearance was striking; he was a tall, strongly built man with a typically Russian face who, though beards were forbidden in camp, wore his with such a patriarchal air that he got away with it. He went about in a long black naval coat and attracted attention by his bearing and expressive way of talking. He was then about thirty or thirty-two, and therefore did not belong to the generation to which I devote most of this book, for he was born about the time of the Revolution and had grown up in the Soviet Union. To me he was in some ways representative of his generation, and his fate should therefore be of significance for the generations that will follow his. His self-control and his memory were exceptional and his views were unusual.

Alipi was the son of an Orthodox priest. He was a typical intellectual and by the time he was ten had already learned several languages, but he became as keenly interested in technical subjects as in the humanities and after leaving school he went to a technical college. Though brought up under the Soviet system he joined neither the Pioneers nor the Komsomol and kept aloof from politics. He told me this was because the thirties was a period of purges and trials with which he felt he could not associate himself, even formally. He was one of those who realized that if people who raised their hands did not also raise their voices, this in itself was a form of participation. Alipi stuck to his work and kept away from meetings, but even so he felt that his disengagement did not entirely exculpate him. All the same, he hoped that if he did his work honestly and had no contact with political people, things would turn out all right for him, or as right as was possible. This attitude was characteristic of many of his contemporaries.

Being sent to a labour camp did not make him alter his views, and when he learned that I was one of the few survivors of those Party members who had been arrested in the thirties and that I had worked at the Executive Committee of the Komintern, he began to be very cautious with me.

At first he had taken me for an intellectual, a foreigner, or someone who had been abroad and who had got into trouble on this account, and as foreman of the brigade in which I worked he had been friendly to me. When I told him my story he cooled off, for he had a strong prejudice against people who had taken part in communist politics. This was common to many Russian intellectuals. Later his attitude towards me changed and for sixteen months we were close friends. He told me all about his family, showed me their letters to him and those he wrote in reply. When we heard of political events such as the Korean War he would listen to what I had to say but never make any comment.

Eventually he told me the whole story of his life and of how he came to be in the camp. He was called up at the outbreak of war and by the end of the first year held the rank of Captain; then he was transferred to the General Staff of the Naval Forces. He must have struck his superiors, as he struck me, as being solidly loyal, honest and responsible, and no doubt because of this he was appointed to important and secret work in the cypher department. Next he went to the Far East as Cypher Officer in the Pacific Fleet, a post in which the fact that he knew English well came in very useful.

At that time American ships were running the Japanese blockade and were welcomed by the Russian sailors who were defending Vladivostok. As he was head of the cypher department, it was part of Alipi's job to have contacts with the American sailors who came to the port or who were posted there in connection with the arrival and departure of their ships.

His work was very hard, for cables arrived all round the clock and sometimes he was on duty for twenty-four hours decoding Russian and American signals and intercepting Japanese communications. The strain was great, and he became a chain smoker and a heavy drinker, though never an alcoholic; I think he sometimes took cocaine. Naturally, his work put him in possession of a lot of highly secret material and, as a non-Party man, he realized that this was dangerous for him. He therefore tried to get posted to a different kind of job but was unsuccessful; for one thing, his superior officers had a high opinion of him and had recommended him for a decoration. When he told them that since he did not belong to the Party he was wrongly posted, they replied, 'If that's your only trouble it can easily be put right. Here is a form, make an application to join.' This invitation was one which it was difficult to refuse, but he made a clean breast of his position to the Commanding Officer and told him that whether or not he held a Party Card, he would always, at heart, remain a totally apolitical person. The CO smiled and replied that there were plenty of others who were in the same position and that he himself was not much of a politician either. But, he added, since to carry out the orders of the Soviet Government a man was required to be devoted not only to the Government but also to the Party and to Comrade Stalin in particular, and as in Alipi's case it seemed that he could make such a profession loyally and with a good conscience, it followed that his place was in the Party. Convinced by this argument, Alipi signed his application. Once he had joined the Party he had access to still more secret material and was transferred to the General Staff in Moscow, which apparently meant promotion.

When he arrived in Moscow with his pretty young wife and their child they were lodged at the Government's expense in one of the big hotels (the housing shortage was acute) at a cost of 1,500 roubles a month. In his position as deputy head of a department of the General Staff, Alipi no longer did the cyphering himself but checked the work of his staff. There were no criticisms of his work, though there were some complaints that he was unsociable and reserved and did not go to parties. To this he replied that his job took up most of his time and that he liked to spend such leisure as he had with his family. From his American contacts he had acquired a passion for detective stories and had an enormous collection of them; reading them was his only relaxation. (Even in camp he still remembered some of these stories and told me about Agatha Christie.)

Everything seemed to be going well for him when, one night in 1949, there was a knock on the door, the place was searched and he was arrested. He was accused of treason to the Fatherland and charged under Article 58/1a; it was alleged that he had made contact with American spies during the war and given them the keys to Soviet codes. The accusation was monstrous; if he had really done anything of the sort every coded message would have been read by the Americans and repercussions would have been noticed immediately.

Alipi was interrogated in the Lubyanka prison; representatives of the navy as well as MGB officials were present at the questioning. Since he was innocent and no methods of pressure could extract a confession from him, his accusers reverted to a method which was much used in the thirties and was now again coming to the fore; they repeatedly called in his wife for interrogation and did everything in their power to force her to give evidence which would incriminate him. In the course of these interviews indecent proposals were also made to her, as she mentioned later in letters which she managed to get through to him.

At the time he had no idea that she was being questioned; evidently the plan was to get some admission from her and then confront him with it. His wife, however, held out and his superior officers, so he afterwards learned, stood by him. The only good this may have done him was to shorten the investigation of his case; by the summer

it was over and he was sentenced to three years in camp. The short-
ness of the sentence was proof that neither the MGB investigators,
nor the officers of the Naval Command, nor the *troyka* (special
commission) had found any evidence against him; but once the
MGB had started proceedings against someone it was regarded as
impossible for them to admit to a mistake.

In one of his last talks with him the interrogator actually hinted
that they would do the best they could to soften his fate but that
they could not possibly admit that he was innocent since this would
discredit the officer who had arrested him, the superior who had
signed the order and the official of the Ministry who had confirmed
it – and in the case of someone doing secret work the confirmation
had to come from very high up. Alipi could not accept this argument and when the interrogator told him that even the Minister
himself might get into trouble he replied that it was quite right that
he should, for suspecting a man like himself. Probably at first they
had genuinely suspected him, and his posting to Moscow may have
been arranged in order to simplify investigations. It was characteristic of the time that anyone who had had any contact with the Americans should be under suspicion, and Alipi, to whom they had given
tobacco and detective stories, spoke of them as human beings and
not in the orthodox Party fashion. It is also possible that his move
to Moscow was intended to make him break all contact with them.

Some time after meeting him I was able, through friends of mine,
to help him to get in touch with his wife. At first he was very happy
when he received a letter from her, but later I noticed that after the
arrival of each letter he became more and more gloomy. When the
fifth letter arrived he showed it to me. In it, she asked why he was
not doing anything to obtain his release, and remarked that whenever she met his former chiefs, colleagues and friends they enquired
why, if he had been wrongly condemned, his case was not being
reviewed?

In his reply he tried to hint at the cause of his detention and
stressed that he had done all he could to prove his innocence, but
when her answer came it was obvious that she had not understood
anything about the tangled web in which he had been caught up.
She insisted that if he wished his child to survive and assure the

future of his family, he should not keep quiet until the end of his sentence but insist on his case being reviewed and on being set free. He wrote back that while he was in the Tayshet camp he could do nothing and that to justify himself he must wait for his release. Her reply to this was threatening: 'It's one of two things,' she wrote. 'Either you are guilty, in which case I must draw the proper conclusions from your sentence, renounce you and have no further contact with you, or else it's all a mistake, in which case how is it possible that you cannot prove your innocence?'

Alipi spent hours reading and re-reading his wife's letter, often showing it to me and asking my advice. It seemed that his wife was now making it a condition that he must not only get his sentence revised but positively prove his innocence, if he were to be able to look forward to any home life in the future. Eventually Alipi managed to arrange for a well-informed friend of his to visit his wife and explain to her the circumstances of which he was a victim and try to make her realize the madness of her demands.

After some months this woman wrote to say that she had been to see Alipi's wife but had not been able to make any impression on her. It was ironical that her attitude must in part have been the result of conversations he himself had had with her in the past. She was as unpolitical a character as he and when he was in the cypher department and wanted to impress on her the need to be careful about security and observe the rules of his job, he stressed that the MGB was right to be suspicious and that one had to trust them. Also, when she had questioned him in his office about purges and events of that sort he had replied that it was better not to think too much about such things since they were being carried out by people who had been trusted by Comrade Lenin himself.

In consequence, he had inculcated in her a spirit of unquestioning loyalty to the Party and its organs and could not now think of a way to convey to her what the situation really was.

Towards the middle of 1950 Alipi fell seriously ill and was sent to hospital; as a result I saw less of him. When he recovered he pulled every possible string to be made the statistician of the hospital, a post which entailed keeping the charge sheets on which were entered the date of admission of the patients and the record of their past illnesses and of the treatment they had received. At the time I was surprised that he wanted the job, but later on I understood why.

In the late autumn of that year I was subjected to the most terrible experiences of my twenty-two years as a prisoner and as a consequence became a patient in this hospital. Orders had been issued to maltreat prisoners. There were cases of out-of-hand shootings, beatings-up and other forms of torture.

I was beaten about with rifle butts, dragged around in the snow, had rifles discharged just over my head, and one day I was made to undress and wade into the river, which was full of floating ice. There I spent two hours filling buckets of water and carrying them ashore to provide baths for the guards. As a result of this treatment I developed pneumonia followed by pleurisy and spent twenty days lying between life and death in the hospital. Even when I was over the worst I was still in great pain, could not sleep and was in mental agony, so one evening I got out of my bunk and went to the office where Alipi was working. When he saw me, sallow, emaciated and in despair, he was horrified. I told him that he must help me, and he knew at once that what I needed was a drug which would make me sleep. He had access to such drugs but he evidently believed that what I really wanted was not just to fall asleep but never to wake up again.

He then began to speak and what he said later came to have a special meaning for me. He knew that I had been a prisoner for over fifteen years and he positively implored me, using the strangest expressions, to do everything I possibly could to remain alive. He begged me to try not to think of all the suffering I had endured and to turn my mind away from the pain I was feeling at that moment. He said that in hospital he saw many innocent people die and he knew what a torment it was for people to go on living in the conditions to which we were subjected, so he well understood why people wished to put an end to their lives. But he believed that there were individuals, and that I was one of them, who, having survived so many years of this inhuman experience, having seen so many people suffer and remembering many of their names and their stories, had a duty to remain alive so that one day they would be able to talk about them to people who did not know but who should

know these things. He explained that it was because of this conviction of his that he had talked to the medical staff and ensured that
all the new medicines would be used to save me. They had done so
and now he urged me to live on at whatever cost to myself.

His words were so gentle and friendly that they made me feel even
physically better, and perhaps because of this I managed to live
through the night and the days that followed. A fortnight later I was
discharged. That I am alive today, although I still have cavities in
my lungs and occasional pain, is therefore largely due to him.

In December Alipi, who had joined a theatre group, got them to
put on *The Forest* by the nineteenth century dramatist Ostrovsky.
He chose his own part, that of an actor and philosopher, a figure
through whom the author expresses his indignation at a way of life
in which there is no place for an honest man. It is a play that was
often put on in the Soviet Union and was generally much liked
because it hinted at the unsolved problems which faced the people
of the Soviet Union under its new social structure. Alipi proved to
have great talent as an actor – indeed he excelled in his part. It was
difficult to get invited to these performances and as a rule I did not
try, for I felt that in the circumstances in which we were living they
were humiliating. But most of the jailors and prisoners who formed
the audience enjoyed them and appreciated the efforts of the so-
called cultural and educational department of the camp which
occasionally put on concerts, poetry readings and plays.

On the 31st of December the play was staged as a sort of New
Year celebration and Alipi insisted that I should ask Vanya for a
ticket. I did so in the hope of having a talk with Alipi afterwards, for
since our conversation that night in hospital I had had little opportunity of speaking to him. In fact, I never got there as a friend of
mine, who was in great distress and was afraid of going mad, asked
me to spend the evening with him. He was a writer, a man of sixty
who was quite unable to adapt himself to camp life; recently he had
received a parcel containing a book, a German classic, and he
suggested that we should read it aloud to each other. In the end we
went on talking until it was too late for me to go to the play, but I
still hoped to have a chance of seeing Alipi after the performance. I
met Vanya who told me that the play had been a great success,

Alipi had been marvellous and the civilian officials of the camp (these were salaried free men and occupied most of the front rows, having no theatre of their own) and the camp commandant had been delighted with everything and particularly pleased with Alipi's performance. He added, however, that Alipi had been very tired and had gone back to the hospital to sleep.

New Year's Day 1951 was a holiday, and we were even allowed to stay in bed a little later than on other days. I intended to take the opportunity of going over to see Alipi but while we were having breakfast the doctor came in looking very upset. He told us that Alipi had not appeared that morning and that when they had gone to find out what the matter was they had found his door bolted. The doctor had knocked and when he got no answer had broken in. He found Alipi lying on his bed, dead.

A commission was appointed to determine whether his death was due to natural causes or not. The doctor told us that Alipi had taken a large number of sleeping tablets and that as his heart was weak this had been the cause of his death. If it had been proved that he had committed suicide the medical staff and the Camp Command would have got into a lot of trouble, which would have had repercussions on all the prisoners, and investigations would have been made as to how Alipi had been able to get hold of so many sleeping pills. Thus, everyone was relieved when the verdict came that he had died from natural causes – a heart attack. He left no messages and no letters were found in his room.

Had he lived until Stalin's death he would no doubt have gone back to normal life; he might even have been able to make it up with his wife, but he could not endure for so long.

His fate was the fate of millions. He was a wonderful friend to me and a very fine man. This is the first time I have told his story.

*

I must now add a few words about the rest of the members of the *chifir* club, all of whom felt the death of Alipi as a mortal blow. His fate was of course discussed by us when we met at the club, where the place in which he had sat listening to others' stories, his blue eyes full of sadness, was now empty. When we became drunk on *chifir* it seemed as if he was again there in his long black coat, or invisible but close to us.

But the days of the club were numbered. Soon after Alipi's death Elas was summoned and taken from the camp to an unknown destination. The circumstances of his departure showed that he was about to be investigated again. A new wave of terror was starting – this was 1951 and from the beginning of that year the machinery of the MGB was harder at work than ever; in particular it had been ordered to dig out of the camps all sorts of people who might provide some new evidence about something or other. As Elas had many contacts and knew Korean and Chinese his help was needed in organizing the espionage apparatus in Korea. He hinted before he left that he expected to be taken close to the Korean border so that with his knowledge he could be consulted by MGB employees in their task of making a thorough purge in that country. Incidentally, he did not expect his sentence to be softened. He thought he would be lucky if his assistance enabled him to be released when he had served his term. I learned nothing of his later fate.

As for Gaedeke, he had tuberculosis. He was able to keep going thanks to his light work in the drying room. Later that year I heard he had started to spit blood and was in hospital, where I think he died – though I never got definite news of this.

Vanya got safely through 1951 and 1952. If Alipi was the figure of ill-luck, Vanya was the lucky one. He went on writing and helping to produce plays. There was a vogue for spy plays and one of his, a dreadful piece of trash called *At the Crossroads*, was put on in the camp; it was a story about some diversionist who bribed Party members, with secret meetings and revolver shots. It had the more success because there were many in the audience who, if they had not taken part in such plots themselves, had signed confessions saying that they had and had been sentenced on the strength of them. Immediately Stalin died, Vanya made every effort to get out. He was among the first to have his case raised, and he was fully re-habilitated. He went back in triumph to Leningrad and was warmly welcomed by his friends. He contributed to the more conservative literary journals and continues to write novels. I am only curious to know if he made it up with his wife.

As for myself, the fourth in this strange quartet, one night I was called from my cell and transferred to another section of the camp. It turned out later that this was not by accident. It was three months before my release from camp and when I was transferred to this other section – and thus lost touch with my friends – I was kept under careful supervision by the agents of the MGB. A new case was being prepared in which I was to be one of the accused, but Stalin died before it was ready. About a dozen of my friends had been arrested, charged with 'Trotskyist agitation' in the camp, and given another five or ten years. These were old people who had by then served most of their twenty-five-year sentences; the blow of the additional sentence was all the harder for them to bear. The trial itself was a monstrous travesty – the accusations were ridiculous, no defence was allowed and the whole investigation was conducted in an inhuman fashion. The sentences were passed in 1952 and a year later they were among the first to be revised. But some of those implicated in the case did not live to see this. For some of these sick, elderly men who had been on the point of release the disappointment of the added sentence was too much. But those who survived saw not only this last sentence revised but all their earlier sentences as well, and when I came to Moscow in 1956 I rang most of them up and found them well and living on a pension.

As I have said, my own case did not come up in Stalin's lifetime. I was therefore able to leave the camp when I had served my term, but had to remain in exile in Siberia until I was rehabilitated. This should have happened in 1955 but in fact it took a year longer. When I was finally summoned by the regional KGB chief he received me very civilly, coming towards me and shaking my hand. He then said he must apologize – not for the whole of my captivity, since others were responsible for that – but for this last year. They had hung on to me because the KGB could not find any convincing proof in my dossiers that it was safe to release me.

My wife had gone to the authorities in Moscow as soon as the revision of cases began. The judge showed her my enormous dossiers and spread out his arms: it would take time. But meanwhile some Polish communists intervened on my behalf and at last an order came from the Central Committee which finally released me.

THE POST-STALIN YEARS

IN 1953 Stalin's prestige with the masses was at its height. A general atmosphere of deification prevailed, as though there was an inward acceptance of the idea that he was the Almighty Leader, the Tsar, the Pontifex Maximus; as though the life of the Soviet Union, its destiny in the world and the fate of each Soviet citizen was bound up with his existence and achievements. Into this climate burst the news of his illness, which was at once recognized as an announcement of his death. The impression it made was overwhelming, probably unique.

To many Soviet citizens he was indeed God, and since the idea of God leads to that of immortality, he had come to be regarded as immortal. Propaganda did not disassociate itself from this view. On the occasion of Stalin's seventieth birthday he was toasted in the words, 'May Comrade Stalin live forever', and when the toast was quoted in the press hardly anyone dared even to smile.

Like many Oriental despots, Stalin was not interested in establishing a dynasty or concerned with what would happen after his death. Even though he had had at least one heart attack, and it was thought that the next one might prove fatal, he did not make a will. He seems to have believed that he still had many years to live; nevertheless, he was frightened by the thought of death. After my release in 1956 I was told by a man who had been a visitor to Stalin's villa near Sochi that on one occasion when the Albanian leader Enver Hoxha was staying there he remarked on a change in the landscape which had taken place since his last visit: a fine plantation of cypresses had been cut down and semi-tropical plants put in their place. Hoxha enquired why this had been done. In answer Stalin made a long speech to the effect that one should always be surrounded by plants that symbolized life, not death. For the same reason, so I have been told, other funereal-looking plants were also uprooted. His fear of death assumed more dangerous forms of expression as well. A man who was very high up in a Ministry, a very crafty and observant fellow who had managed to avoid trouble at all times, assured me that people in Stalin's entourage had told him that he took the closest interest in his health and consulted many doctors. They gave him a régime to follow, but once observed that man's power to keep death at bay is limited. Stalin's fury when he heard such an admission coming from those whose business it was to keep him alive was, my friend believed, at the basis of his persecution of the doctors which culminated in the alleged 'Doctors' Plot'.[1]

Another manifestation of Stalin's horror of death was that in his last years he suspected everyone; as a result he lived in complete isolation and hardly ever appeared in public, only summoning individuals to interviews when he wished to give them orders. A remarkable result of this complete breakdown of trust was exemplified by the fact that he would not delegate the control of the NKVD even to Beria but appointed people who had to report personally to him. Also, although he had plenty of men to do his dirty work for him, he directed all the harshest measures of the Terror himself. Even Poskryobyshev, who acted as his executioner and played the role sometimes ascribed to witches at the end of the fifteenth century, did not know all the plans Stalin had in mind for that machine of annihilation, the secret police.

One way in which he ensured the good behaviour of his subordinates was by taking hostages. I was told that two or three years before his death Stalin even had Poskryobyshev's wife arrested. I have not been able to check this fact but it would be characteristic of his methods. The story was told me by a man who was arrested in 1951 and who had heard it from a close relation of Poskryobyshev. He said that Mrs Poskryobyshev had been sent to Eastern Siberia on Stalin's personal order and that for a long time her husband dared not even mention this fact to his master. However, in the end, he could bear it no longer and cautiously made a plea for her release; at this Stalin gave him such a look that he apologized for his in-

1. In 1952 some doctors, mainly Jews, were accused of the attempted murder of several Soviet leaders. The accusations were dismissed as false after Stalin's death.

discretion and never again mentioned the subject until after Stalin had died.

Whether or not this is true it is certainly a fact that Molotov's wife was expelled from the Party and deported from Moscow. The charge was said to be that she had spoken Yiddish to the Israeli Ambassador.

Molotov, it appears, was even more frightened than Poskryoby-shev and it was not until 1956 that Mrs Molotov got her Party card back. The terror which Stalin inspired in all those around him was also well illustrated by the behaviour of Kaganovich; a close relation of his was in the camp with me. For many years he had been protected by Kaganovich but in 1949, when the post-war purge was at its height, he was arrested. His wife at once tried to see their influential relation, whom she previously had often visited. Now it took her nine months to get an interview. When she came into the room Kaganovich, who was usually very reserved, received her warmly but before she was able to make her request he said, 'Do you think that if there was anything I could do for your husband I would have waited for you to ask me? You must realize that there is only one sun and that the rest of us are only very distant, very small stars.'

In fact, Kaganovich did help the woman and her children in various ways, but about her husband he felt that he could not do anything, and that making any attempt even to enquire about him would only be putting himself in danger.

Stalin was a man who had acquired limitless power, and his reputation as a divinity caused people, even those in leading positions, to feel that there was no way of influencing him. As a result they developed an attitude of complete impotence. As for the wretched masses, although Stalin was their executioner they succeeded in closing their minds to this fact and worshipped him.

When the news of his death reached Siberia the scenes of grief in the village on my *kolkhoz* surpassed anything I have ever witnessed, and I understand that this small hamlet faithfully reflected the mood that swept through the country. The people's sorrow was sincere and crushing; they behaved as though their own beloved Father had died, the protector behind whose backs they had sheltered. I saw old peasant men and women who could not have put on an act, and had no reason to do so, looking quite distraught. They lamented, 'Who will defend Russia now? The Germans will fall on us. The foreigners will attack us. Russia is lost.' These simple people spoke of civil war, famine and chaos; they were in despair. The behaviour of the children was particularly extraordinary. All the schools were closed, indeed all life had come to a halt, and out into the village street poured children from the age of six to sixteen, their eyes red from crying as though they had indeed been orphaned. Around them was a crowd of men and women, sobbing hysterically; even Party members, even the members of the local Party Committee, were weeping. At one moment the District Secretary of the Party called out, 'Enough tears', and for a short time the weeping stopped, but then it started up again. We, in exile, had no cause for mourning, so I was astonished to hear that at a meeting at which tributes were paid to Stalin (I did not go to it) a former Party leader, a woman who had been in the labour camps for fifteen years, had cried more violently than anyone else and had even torn her hair and clothes. Since I knew what she really thought about Stalin I went to see her, to enquire about this. She was still crying as she told me: 'Don't you understand, I'm not weeping for him. I'm crying over my own fate and over the suffering of all the others.' Her tears were falling because Stalin had not died twenty or thirty years earlier.

This made me wonder whether among the millions of people throughout the length and breadth of Russia who were at that moment expressing their grief, many were not in fact weeping for themselves.

Of course, our main concern, as victims, was to learn what would happen next. We sat glued to our loudspeakers listening in to Moscow. The first Government proclamation came on the 5th of March, the day of Stalin's death. I missed it because I was on my way to see a friend, an intelligent man who had spent some seventeen years in camp but had retained the ability to think clearly. When I got there he had heard it and summed it up in the following words:

'He is dead, he will be buried, and we shall go on to other business.'

This made me realize that with Stalin gone something new and unknown was about to take shape, that every idea so far held would have to be examined in a new light.

Naturally, we believed, with very few exceptions, that the change must be for the better.

I made a round of my friends and dropped in on an old Bolshevik who had once been Procurator for the Vladivostok region; arrested in 1937, he had suffered terrible punishments during his interrogation and had been sentenced to death. He had however been reprieved and was now working on a nearby *kolkhoz*. His wife, a simple peasant from near Irkutsk who had formerly been a school mistress, was visiting him. I found him looking most upset and unable to find words to express his feelings. When his wife came in with the tea she took a look at him and said, 'Calm down, after all it can't be worse; it can only get better.' In the event she proved right, for her husband was rehabilitated and given a pension.

While Stalin was alive there had been a complete paralysis of public opinion. No two people could speak freely to each other; few indeed had courage enough to face even their own opinions. This attitude was so general that later, when Khrushchev described how he and Bulganin* had discussed politics on their way to and from the Kremlin, no one believed him, for it was assumed that Khrushchev was much too prudent to talk to anyone, even to Bulganin – and certainly the latter never confirmed this story. But now that Stalin was dead even we prisoners engaged in endless discussions about the future – and not only with our friends.

The funeral took place on the ninth. Not only the whole of Moscow came to have a last look at Stalin but people walked tens of kilometres from outlying villages into the capital. The result was a stampede; generals and other high-ranking officers linked arms, spoke to the people and ordered them to move back. In spite of this hundreds were crushed to death. Of course, we did not hear of this till long afterwards.

Into this atmosphere of grief a photograph in *Pravda* burst like a flare. It showed all the members of the Praesidium standing on either side of the coffin. A row of melancholy figures, among whom Malenkov stood out strikingly, his feet wide apart and a broad grin on his face. The caption might well have been: 'At last!'

All that could not be said in articles, speeches and proclamations was uttered in this picture. It made a great impression and was reproduced in all the other papers.

We waited with much anxiety to see who would come out on top. The speeches we heard made it obvious that no one was actually claiming to be Stalin's direct heir, but it was clear that Malenkov thought of himself as the natural leader. Molotov and Beria also spoke and when we heard Beria's resolute and challenging words we were inclined to think that he too was a man who meant to stay in power and that he would see to it that his power was sufficient for this. On the whole we expected Beria to win.

However, when the Government's plans became known we realized that no member of the Praesidium was going to stand in Stalin's shoes; this in itself was reassuring. Cut off as we were, to a great extent, from the outside world, it was by a sixth sense that we became aware of various changes which did in fact take place – as we were to learn later on.

For a short time after Stalin's death the full-time operators of the NKVD stopped work. Then, by the middle of March, they were again back on the job, there were a few more arrests, and investigations were continued. But the machine was no longer operating in the same way. When Stalin died the power which made the operators work was switched off, so, although everything *looked* the same, we knew that something had changed. Later, people who had been in the Lubyanka prison in Moscow at this time and whose fate was still undecided told me that they too had sensed the change even though they had little factual evidence to go on.

Our hopes were confirmed by the fact that so few new people were being 'gathered in'; if a lot of fresh prisoners had arrived it would have been obvious that directives from the top had remained unchanged and that it was pointless to think of release. After the 15th of March 1953, there were no more interrogations in our area and I later learned that this was the case in most of the Soviet Union. Here was evidence that Stalin himself was totally responsible for those measures which were often thought to be 'the work of Beria'.

When, on the 27th of March, Voroshilov proclaimed an amnesty, we had our first real proof that a deep change had taken place. This measure did not apply to political prisoners; all the same, it affected millions of people, and to us it came as a message which seemed to say: 'Now Stalin is dead we are concerned about the fate of prisoners and we are doing something about it.'

A category which benefited by the amnesty was that of the prisoners under the age of eighteen. In 1935 Stalin had a law passed by which children from the age of twelve upwards were to be treated as criminally responsible and suffer the same punishment as adults for certain crimes. They could even be shot – and during the Terror of the thirties many were, including the children of the Trotskyists. Later, this law was made less harsh, but many measures of the original act remained in force. Under Voroshilov's amnesty these children were released; so were people serving sentences of less than three years and others who had already had their sentences reduced.

To us it was of immense significance that the first important act of the new Government had been to grant an amnesty, and this at a time when there was no precedent for granting one. In the past, the coronation of a new Tsar had often been accompanied by an amnesty; now people made joking allusions to this practice.

To be honest, some of the effects of freeing a large number of criminal prisoners were unfortunate. A wave of murders and robberies followed their release. As late as June, when the trains were still full of ex-prisoners, there were stories of passengers being robbed and thrown out of the window. Policemen too were attacked. These criminals saw in the fact that they had been freed a proof of the weakness of the Government and, believing that severe measures would no longer be taken against them, they did just as they pleased. There was banditry in Leningrad and Moscow, but as the freed men could return there legally the authorities did not know what to do about it.

Among us the amnesty aroused mixed reactions. Many people were naturally indignant that it did not apply to political prisoners. Since Stalin personally had been responsible for their incarceration it was felt that they should have been the first to be let out. Beria was blamed for the failure to free us and some people suggested that he had let out the criminals first in order to produce a reaction of fear among the population and discredit the idea of further releases.

But to most of us it seemed that once an amnesty applying to certain types of prisoners had been proclaimed things could not remain at this level, and that now the new Government had shown its intention of reversing *some* of Stalin's measures, it must in time free us too.

Then, on the 2nd of April, the radio and also *Pravda* announced that the case against the doctors had been dropped, and we knew that this meant the end of the world as we had known it and that anything might now happen. This was the first admission that security officers could make mistakes and even act from criminal motives. During the Revolution, under Lenin and under Stalin, it had been taken as axiomatic that the security organs were always in the right. The fact that now they were accused of having fabricated evidence and that a case they had initiated had been dropped caused a real change in the outlook of innumerable people, for it now appeared that the Government was not only disassociating itself from Stalin's crimes but even begging our forgiveness for them. The behaviour of the press, which from one day to another made no mention of Stalin's name, was also a good augury. True, his body lay in the Mausoleum on Red Square, but no one had dared to inscribe over it the dictum that was used for his predecessor: 'Lenin is dead but his work lives on.' Had this slogan been used for Stalin we should have regarded it as an extremely bad omen.

*

To right the horrifying wrongs done in the purges immediately raised two problems: how release and rehabilitation were to be carried out, and how blame was to be apportioned among those of Stalin's henchmen who were still alive.

The first of these questions was obviously of paramount interest to exiles like myself. Many thought that a general amnesty would be the best method but realized that this in its turn would raise the problem of how rehabilitation was to be effected, for it was obvious that following a general amnesty the courts would be flooded with applications. Which priorities should then be established? On this subject many different views were voiced. It might seem logical that the cases should be examined in the order in which the applications came in. But this would result in great injustice, for it would mean that the quickest off the mark, or those who had influential connections, would be the first to be heard, while the cases of workers and peasants, the immense majority of prisoners, would be delayed.

Then there were those who felt that since the people who had been shot or died in prison had suffered the greatest injustice, and their numbers far exceeded that of the survivors, their rehabilitation should have priority. There was also the claim of the more recent victims of Stalin's reign, such as those of the Leningrad affair, and of his recent campaign against cosmopolitans and Jews. Their wounds were still fresh.

To release and rehabilitate in chronological order, beginning with those arrested in the thirties, seemed a reasonable solution but one which for various reasons would be very difficult to carry out systematically. For one thing the decision regarding priorities would be taken at the top where there were people whose principal concern would be to cover up their involvement in what had happened; this applied not only to the most recent purges, though Malenkov, for instance, had a vested interest in delaying investigation into the Leningrad affair. Indeed his anxiety to conceal his role in it had a bearing on his eventual removal from office. People, especially abroad, were astonished that he did not put up a fight; after all, he had carried out reforms in foreign policy and had passed measures which had benefited the peasants, and these had been marked up to his credit. There had also been efforts to popularize him by spreading rumours that he was Lenin's nephew or even illegitimate son. The fact that in spite of his prestige he went quietly was because he knew that if he put up any resistance his initiative in the Leningrad affair would have come to light. As many of its victims were still alive they would have been able to bear witness against him, and as he was very deeply implicated in the repressions of 1949 he would have had no chance of extricating himself.

His case was quite different from that of Kaganovich and Molotov, who had certainly been implicated in what happened in the thirties but not in more recent crimes. Malenkov's responsibility for the Leningrad purge is proved, if proof is needed, by the fact that as soon as he was removed the matter was quickly cleared up. My own attitude towards Malenkov was that as he had been so closely associated with Stalin's atrocities I refused to address my application for release to him (he and Voroshilov were the two people to whom such letters had to be sent), and I was not the only one in our area who felt like this.

In spite of the disagreement at the top about the way of effecting the release of prisoners, an enormous number of people were quickly freed. For thirty years train-load after train-load of captives had moved east, but now the trains were moving west, filled with former prisoners. I remember one such man whom I had first met in the prison at Krasnoyarsk in 1951, when his views reflected the state of desperation in which we had lived for decades but which it is hard for people who were not victims of the purges to conceive.

He came of a family of miners in the Donbas, but himself had worked on the railways. He was an honest, practical man, not much concerned with theories; for a time his honesty gained him advancement, but then it caused him to become suspect. In 1937 he was arrested and sentenced to fifteen years. During the war his loyalty and abilities gained him his release, but after a year of freedom he was re-arrested and condemned to life-long deportation, in spite of the fact that no new charge was made against him. He was now thirty-five, and his attitude was one of utter despair. Nor was he desperate only about himself – he believed that all his generation, whether imprisoned or free, had had their lives wrecked for good and all.

During the short time in which he had been free he had settled in a remote Siberian town, worked on the railway and married a young Siberian girl. This was his second marriage. (Almost all prisoners who had not previously been married, or whose marriages had broken up, married as soon as they were released.) He had insisted that his fiancée should accept one condition – they were never to have any children. When he told me this I was horrified, and I said to him that I considered his demand inhuman. Quite unmoved, he replied: 'I don't want to be the father of slaves. I don't want to have children who will have to live in the same misery that I'm living in.'

I tried to convince him that his hopelessness was monstrous, that sooner or later the people would have more freedom and live in less frightful conditions. I spoke with real conviction, and used many good arguments. When I had finished, all he said was: 'That's a very pretty speech, but life has taught me better . . . I know that our fate is to perish in our misfortune, and our children will be branded and equally unfortunate. That's why we have no right to have children.' He also remarked that the river Yenisey was as likely to flow upstream as my dreams for the future to come true. His outlook was shared by many prisoners.

Four years passed, and I was still in exile. Then one day this man came through my village on his way home to the Donbas, called on me and said, 'Well, it seems that rivers *can* flow upstream.' Later I heard that he had got his job back and also his position in the Party. He had been able to readjust himself to normal life, but before the releases took place we wondered how many prisoners would be capable of doing this.

There was one great difference between the position of the men released now and those who had been freed under Stalin. In his day no one had been allowed to protest or argue about the evil doings of the State or even to refer to them, so a man who had been arrested, interrogated, tortured and then released was always made to sign a paper promising that he would not even reveal the fact that he had been arrested to anyone. This created a stifling, graveyard atmosphere.

Men came back to their wives after years of imprisonment and never referred to the way in which they had passed the time. Occasionally, usually when drunk, ex-prisoners did talk about their experiences, and if it became known they had done so they were liable to get a sentence of up to ten more years in prison. The effect of this wall of silence was two-fold. In the West, when Vyshinsky described life in camp as a rather happy experience, he attacked Kravchenko, who had defected and written a good account of the Soviet system. Many intellectual and progressive people believed that Vyshinsky was telling the truth. Within the Soviet Union the uncertainty and ignorance about the conditions in which prisoners were held had the effect of terrifying people. They imagined that the worst conditions and the most horrible tortures prevailed everywhere and all the time. Of course the authorities had a vested interest in promoting this belief, and they were so successful that people arrested for the first time were often brought to the point of confessing to crimes they had never committed by the interrogator simply remarking: 'Well, now you are in the hands of the Cheka.' This statement could be enough to break the man down. Today this technique is still used but not on the same scale.

After Stalin's death prisoners were no longer made to sign a promise to keep silent. I am not sure if this was always the case, but I was not asked to sign any papers (I had decided that if I was I would refuse), nor were the other prisoners whom I knew.

The reaction of the young towards returned prisoners was very interesting. Komsomol members and students in particular were deeply affected by the coming to life of those who had till then been mere abstractions to them. They approached the ex-prisoners with great curiosity and respect, for, over the decades, a legendary image of those in the camps had grown up. The effect of the official propaganda line about them had been to present them as people who had tried to oppose Stalin in the name of something else. When these young people were told, by the repatriates themselves, that practically all of them were innocent of any political activity and that deportation was something that could have happened to anyone for no reason, they refused to believe it, for they naturally assumed that Stalin's victims must have been his declared, or potential, enemies. A freed man would be asked with sympathy what the essence of his opposition to Stalin had been, and when he asserted that his arrest was without any cause, his questioner would say: 'Don't be afraid – there's no longer anything to be frightened of', or, perhaps, disbelievingly, 'But you can't have been arrested for no cause at all, there must have been a reason?' So after decades during which the prisoners had spent their time trying to convince the authorities of their innocence and loyalty they now had to prove the same thing to these young sceptics.

When hundreds of thousands of men and women had been

imprisoned and tortured began to talk, this struck the greatest blow ever to the cult of personality, and the stories told by the ex-prisoners became an important factor in the preparation for the Twentieth Congress. If they had not talked, the authorities would not have been able or obliged to unmask Stalin. As it was, they did not feel that they could tell the whole truth immediately, and it only came out gradually and has still not been disclosed in full. Strangely enough, there were even prisoners who were frightened of the effects of a too rapid rehabilitation and of the liquidation of the cult of personality. Because of the backwardness of the Russian masses, some thought that not to hold them firmly in hand might lead to disastrous consequences.

Apart from the shock that the truth about Stalin would cause to the Russian people, if the majority of them had been totally un-prepared for the revelation, and the possibility that they would not have believed it, there were friends of mine who felt that to tell the whole story would mean the destruction of all the communist Parties in the West. They knew of course that in the long run all would be known, but they were anxious that as much as possible should be hidden for at least a number of years. This was not my view; I thought it was impossible to be silent any longer, and impossible to go on building something on a lie. I believed that the Twentieth Congress had to settle accounts with the past and in particular with Stalin.

Of course, attempts were going to be made to shift the blame, other than Stalin's, from Peter to Paul, and indeed where exactly the blame lies is a most complex question to which we shall not know the answer for many years, if ever.

For my part I found it difficult to accuse people who had lived through the era of the purges but were now doing what they could to make amends. One could say to them, 'What were you doing during the Terror, what did you do against the policy of the purges?', and they could not reply, 'As for that, what were *you* doing?' A woman member of the Party who had been in a camp wrote me a letter after her release, which preceded mine, in which she described what some communists felt about this question of guilt:

. . . My generation of communists everywhere accepted the Stalin form of leadership. We acquiesced in the crimes. We endorsed them. This is true not only of Soviet communists, but of communists all over the world. We, especially the active and leading members of the Party, carry a stain on our consciences individually and collectively. The only way we can erase it is by making sure that nothing of the sort ever happens again. How was all this possible? Did we all go crazy or have we now become traitors to communism? The truth is that all of us, including the leaders directly under Stalin, saw these crimes as the opposite of what they were. We believed that they were important contributions to the victory of socialism. We thought that everything which promoted the power politics of the Communist Party in the Soviet Union and in the world was good for socialism. We never suspected that conflict between communist politics and communist ethics was possible. We know better now. Now I realize that any application of force which violates the principles of truth, justice and humanity constitutes a betrayal of socialism.

On the other hand, I personally feel that there is a difference between criticizing people for having accepted Stalin's policy, which many communists did not do, and blaming them for not having prevented his crimes. To suppose that this could have been done by any individual, however important he might have been, is to misunderstand Stalin's Byzantine tyranny. My belief is that neither Bulganin, nor Mikoyan,* nor Khrushchev, nor Molotov, nor Kaganovich could have altered the course of events. Any attempt to disagree would have ended in disaster for themselves and all their circle without any good having been achieved. It was because I realized the appalling predicament of those who were near to the source of power but without any possibility of influencing it that, even at the worst moments of my life, I was thankful that by the time the purges came I was one of the victims and not one of the hangmen. I felt this reaction especially strongly at the time of the Hitler-Stalin Pact; I was thankful to be a prisoner and not a free man acquiescing, even passively, in what was taking place. It returned to me when I saw the victims of the Finnish War and of the purges of the forties – rather imprisonment or even death than a share in the responsibility for what was going on. Yet, in spite of this, I think one should differentiate between sadists, traitors and careerists on the one hand, and, on the other, those who were forced to take a share in Stalin's crimes because they were not strong enough to resist him.

This attitude made it possible for me, and others who felt this way, to accept the fact that the people who were carrying out the process of rehabilitation were often those who, in the first place, had condemned us to prison.

This is my attitude, but there was no unity of opinion then or later among the leaders, the prisoners or the rehabilitated as to whether to pardon or to try those who had brought Russia to this pass. Eventually the Government went some way in the direction of punishment. A certain number of sadists were arrested and some were shot, but neither these deaths nor the well-deserved liquidation of Beria, Abakumov* and Bagirov,* gave any real satisfaction. The scale of the crimes that had been committed made nonsense of the punishments inflicted. As to Stalin, the chief author of all the atrocities, he was dead and everyone agreed that his body ought not to remain in the Mausoleum on Red Square. Eventually it was removed – but what relation did such a gesture bear to fifty million deaths?

On the other hand, a policy of forgiveness was not generally acceptable, for this suggested not only toleration of the criminals but also of their crimes. Most people thought that so long as these men remained alive they would continue to act within the framework of Stalinism and secure their own privileges by bringing misfortune on others.

Perhaps if a disaster such as the one that marked the end of Hitler's rule had brought Stalin's reign to a close – for instance, if he had not died in his bed of natural causes but had been assassinated, the changes after his disappearance would have been more radical. Perhaps there might have been an upheaval, but, given the ferocity of the security machine, such a revolt would have been immensely costly; perhaps it is better that things happened in the way they did.

I certainly believe that history will blame Molotov, Kaganovich, Malenkov and also Khrushchev and Mikoyan for what they did while Stalin was alive. But the fact that once they ceased to be slaves some of them did what they could to undo the injustices, seemed to me, and to others, to make it more constructive to assist these leaders in their present task than to blame them for their past misdeeds. They were trying to reconcile two aims: to find a sufficient number of scapegoats and not to disrupt the state by terrorizing those who ran it. Thus there was always the implication that the security machine had not outlived its usefulness and that repression was not wrong in itself, though in the past it had often been used against the wrong people.

Presumably this attitude arose from the predicament with which Khrushchev was faced: the alternative of clearing up the whole mess and thereby being deprived of certain people and cadres whom he needed, or of going slow. Adenauer was faced with a similar situation. Khrushchev, however, had to go particularly slow because he could not make a complete break with Stalinism and had to do what he could to prevent comparisons being made between Nazism and Soviet Communism. He was, in fact, a sort of caliph for an hour. The striking characteristic of the 'Khrushchev era' was the distinctive part he played at the beginning of his rule and his complete bankruptcy towards the end of it, after the Twenty-Second Party Congress in 1961.

He was promoted to the highest office not because he was the strongest member of the Central Committee apparatus and not, of course, because of any charismatic qualities he was thought to possess. Quite the opposite – he was appointed First Secretary precisely because he was exceptionally weak as a leader, had no experience of traditional political struggle (he joined the Party a year after the Revolution) and had no deep roots in the group that took power after Stalin's death. The apparatus had learnt something from the last twenty years, notably that the First Secretary of the Party should execute decisions made by others and not aspire to a position in which he could completely disregard the views of his associates. It was difficult to find a person who might not try to seize personal power over the Party. The safest man in this respect seemed to be Khrushchev.

All this sheds light on what happened later, both for better and for worse. At first he was regarded as a latter-day 'Tsar-liberator', especially when he tried to appease the widespread popular discontent by releasing and rehabilitating tens of thousands of innocent people. Later on, however, his limitations and political illiteracy – Leninist ideology was something completely foreign to him, as a typical Russian of peasant origin – became intolerable for the other Party leaders. Failures both in foreign policy (especially the break with China) and in home affairs (in particular, agriculture) were leading the country and the system up a blind alley. Khrushchev's idea of dividing the Party into two – this would in reality have amounted to the end of Party dictatorship – showed that he had completely lost touch with the upper echelons of the Party apparatus, which in due course cast him, weak and isolated, out of all his positions of power and influence.

*

What happened to political prisoners when they were released, in terms of reintegration in the life of the country? If they were simply freed but not rehabilitated they remained deprived of many civil rights: they could not move about freely, they could not enter certain towns and they had no claim to accommodation. The first step towards re-acquiring these rights was to get themselves re-habilitated. To do this they had to have their sentences quashed. In the case of Party members they could also demand to have their Party card restored to them and insist that they should be reinstated in the Party with the seniority which they would have acquired had they not had their card taken away from them when they were sent to prison. This is what I did.

Obviously the released Party members belonged to many different categories. With the exception of the first and last of the six types into which I have rather arbitrarily divided them, virtually all applied for readmission to the Party.

1. Those who had been conscious opponents of the Party and of the régime and not only of Stalin and Stalinism.

2. Chance victims of Stalin's Terror machine who, though they had not committed 'crimes' against the régime, had no chance of being freed while Stalin was alive.

3. The few loyal old Party members who were still alive after the great purges of the thirties.

4. People who had been imprisoned during the war or soon after it ended.

5. Party members who had been arrested more recently.

6. A small number of former Party members who said that after what they had seen they thought it impossible for the Party to reform itself and felt that this being so they could not ask for readmission. They were few and exceptional, but it was a sign of better times that they were allowed to get away with this attitude.

As well as the first group there were also some conscious opponents of the Party who had never joined it – a few hundred Mensheviks, Socialist Revolutionaries and anarchists who had survived decades in prison and whose situation was so desperate that even they themselves doubted whether they would benefit from the new measures. That they were in fact freed shows that a genuine change of policy had taken place. After their release they were obliged to live for some time in prescribed places, but even some of them were in time reintegrated into normal life.

For instance, I knew an old woman, Irina Konstantinovna Kakhovskaya, who, as early as 1905, was a member of the Socialist Revolutionary Party. She had been in prisons and camps ever since the early thirties. At one time she was in a camp in Central Asia with her friend 'Marusya' Spiridonova, who had been at the head of the so-called Left Socialist Revolutionaries and plotted terroristic action against the Bolshevik leaders. A cousin of this woman was in exile with me; she corresponded with her and after a time I too began to write to her. At first our letters were about literature and other abstract subjects, but after a while we also wrote about current events.

At the age of seventy, after well over twenty years of detention, she was freed. After my release I went to visit her in her little house, 120 kilometres from Moscow, where she was writing her memoirs, which were extremely interesting. No promises had been extracted from her to keep silent about her experiences and she had made no ideological concessions. Yet in 1959 I read an extract from her memoirs in *Novy mir* No. 3, where it was highly recommended in an editorial note which mentioned various biographical details but not where she had spent her last thirty years or so.

Another case of an active enemy of the régime being allowed to take part in the life of the country is very different but also interesting; V. Shulgin, who a few years ago published even in *Pravda*, was the leader of the extreme Right-Wing of the Duma, and was the virtual embodiment of reaction. During the Civil War he was editor of a 'white' newspaper which called for pogroms and was fanatically anti-Bolshevik; in the twenties, as an émigré, he was one of the chief organizers of counter-revolutionary movements inside Russia. Until 1944 he remained a member of émigré anti-Bolshevik organizations. Then he fell into Soviet hands and was put in prison. Three years later we heard that he was still alive but that while maintaining his loyalty to the Tsarist régime and his position as a nobleman he had announced that the way in which the Bolsheviks had conducted the war had convinced him that they were worthy leaders of the Russian people and that in future he would therefore cease his activities against them. While Stalin was alive the most he could achieve was to avoid being shot, but under Khrushchev he was released, went back to the town of Vladimir and began to write articles on peace and disarmament. He did not deny his past or his anti-Semitism, but in other respects he wrote and spoke like the average Soviet citizen. His case has been used, particularly abroad, as propaganda suitable for émigrés.

How are we to view such a case? It seems that releases were not related to the gravity of the so-called crimes committed by the prisoners. This is because basically Bolshevik policy is always keyed to expediency. I believe that Khrushchev's idea was for the KGB to prevent any threat, however small, to the security of the State and the stability of the régime, but not to use repression for other ends. If this is so it is a return to the framework established by Dzerzhinsky and Lenin and explained in a famous passage in a letter from Lenin to Kursky (May 1922) in which he suggests that crimes punishable by shooting should be defined in such an elastic way as to make it possible to prevent well in advance any attempt at counter-revolution. This use of repression is different from that employed by Stalin, who used the NKVD to settle accounts with his personal enemies and who gave boundless power to the security organs for 'prophylactic action' against people who were not hostile towards the régime.

That Khrushchev was prepared to use repression against former enemies of the régime who, it appeared, might still be dangerous is shown by what happened to Fricis Menders. He had been a leader of the Latvian Social Democrats and was arrested and imprisoned. After Stalin's death he was released and repatriated but soon he was re-arrested by the KGB allegedly because he was writing his memoirs in which he described the repressions. It is far more likely that, given Menders's prestige in his country, the feeling of local nationalism prevalent in Latvia and the existence of an underground movement, the authorities feared that Menders would become a spring-board for the Latvian Social Democratic Party.

But under Stalin there had been prisoners who were arrested simply because their name was on a list or by some other accident. They were innocent at that time of any anti-Soviet feeling, and later this was sometimes even admitted to them, but with the rider that since their mistaken arrest they had obviously ceased to be harmless and could therefore not have their sentences quashed. Thus a whole class of people who had done no wrong to the régime had become pariahs simply because they knew how rotten the system was. Not unnaturally the years spent in corrective labour camps quite often had the effect of turning them into genuine opponents of Stalin.

Under Khrushchev, these people were rehabilitated and paid compensation, and efforts were made to create conditions in which they could work. None the less, like many other innocent prisoners, they also met with hostility from diehards who continued to be distrustful of anyone who had been in a camp or who were just wary of having any contact with them in case at some time in the future the official line would change. To some extent this attitude also prevailed in regard to old Party members, the category in which I have most friends, though on the whole directives enabled them to find work and sometimes even to go back to their old job. Galina Serebryakova, for instance, who, in the twenties, began to write a biography of Marx and was a friend of several leaders of the Party, was arrested in 1936, tortured and kept in prison for twenty years, but after her release she was asked to continue her biographical studies of Marx and Engels. A lot of use was made of such people for propaganda work, as among them were some who had taken part in the Revolution and Civil War; they were asked to record their experiences. Indeed, many writers whom I had known in camp were, when freed, strongly urged to tell their stories, no doubt because they were among the few gifted people who could remember the early days of the Revolution and because it was believed that they were capable of inspiring enthusiasm and loyalty to revolutionary ideals among the young.

Strange as it may seem, these people carried and still carry out their task with great conscientiousness, describing their work for the Bolshevik Party under the direct leadership of Lenin, rarely mentioning the Stalin period, but hinting at a relationship between the Lenin era and the present régime. They are of course allowed to speak and write only within the framework established by the present leaders and possibly for this reason some of them have withdrawn altogether from politics and have made no public statements.

It is among Party members who were not old Bolsheviks but for the most part were formed during the Stalin period that one sees those who have most quickly recovered their jobs and their places in society. In general, they seem anxious not to appear different from anyone else; the views they express are conservative and they show great confidence in the Party and all its doings. On the other hand, there are a very few exceptions who demand that rehabilitation should go much further than it has and even suggest that not only should the memory of Zinovyev, Kamenev, Pyatakov, Bukharin, Radek and many others be cleared of slander but that their works should be published.

In fact, the pace of rehabilitation was slow, and this is not surprising since the officials concerned were, for the most part, those who had actually passed the sentences that were now being quashed, and so they naturally found it difficult to pronounce on questions of guilt and innocence. Nor in many instances would it have been possible for them even to discover the motive behind the arrest.

Take my case – none of those in charge of rehabilitation ever found any reason for my expulsion from the Party, and could only conclude that it had been ordered as the result of a telephone call, which in those days was a good enough reason not only for expulsion from the Party, but even for being shot. To make things more complicated, there were cases where a man had been sentenced to prison but never expelled from the Party.

Was the rehabilitation of some of the victims inevitable? This is a question that is often discussed today. I think that it was inevitable, for after Stalin's death the disappearance of this dreadful figure from primeval history made it essential for anyone who wished to remain in power and to avoid an upheaval to disassociate himself from his predecessor's crimes and to support the rehabilitation of at least a proportion of his victims.

Yet even between the years 1953 and 1957 the policy of rehabilitation met with considerable opposition from within the Party apparatus itself. It came not only from leaders whose part in Stalin's crimes was likely to be disclosed, but also from minor members of the Party. They, of course, were the people who had operated the penal machinery under Stalin. I had a personal reason to notice this for when I came to be readmitted to the Party the woman who had to draw up the papers for my reinstatement and the annulment of all the previous decisions against me happened to be talkative and told me that at the age of seventeen she had actually handled the papers for my expulsion. With complete detachment she had now brought the dossier, which more than twenty years earlier she had used to expel me, over from one office to the other for the purpose of rehabilitation.

*

When we thought about the future of the country, three categories of the population seemed to be involved – the masses, who were stirring in their sleep; the Party and State *apparatchiki*, who were still working, albeit half-heartedly, according to their old instructions and if they got no new ones would soon be overcome by inertia (they were to be distrusted since, if they came once more under strong control, they would undoubtedly function as before);

finally there were the new authorities who were to direct the *apparatchiki* and who had not so far taken on any recognizable form.

The vital questions to which we could not forecast the answers were: how would the people as a whole react to the new circumstances once they had recovered from the shock of Stalin's death? Would the Praesidium arrive at an agreed policy? Who would become our Master?

In the event, by remaining inactive the people missed a great opportunity. At first everybody 'talked'. The Government seemed to welcome this awakening and the press began to write of a heightened sense of responsibility and of the wish of the people to control their fate, but soon habits inculcated by years of repression sprang up again. Before expressing their opinion, people read the leaders in *Pravda* and *Izvestiya* and when they eventually gave their views it was easy enough to see where these had come from.

For some time we had no indication of what the Government was planning to do. All we learned was that the Central Committee was dealing with 'urgent problems' and we understood very well that it must be much easier for them to consider urgent concrete problems than long term policy – it was decades since these men had been asked to think about policy so that by now they were capable only of carrying out orders.

The one thing they had in common was the desire to avoid being terrorized in the future as they had been in the past. To make sure of this it was necessary for them to see that no one succeeded Stalin in his role of tyrant.

A great deal of speculation went on among us as to what would happen at the first meeting of the Praesidium after Stalin's death. We still do not know for certain what took place, but the account which I regard as the most likely to be accurate says that Molotov put forward a number of simple points with which all the members of the Praesidium would probably agree and which were in fact to become the basis of Soviet policy. Foreign policy was to aim at peace not only by words but also by deeds. An alliance with the peasants was to be sought and therefore they were no longer to be abused and persecuted. Russian chauvinism was to be jettisoned and a foreign policy based on the equality of other nations was to replace it and be validated by deeds as well as speeches. The insistence on action rather than words showed that these men knew their place in history, though, of course, it did not prevent them from continuing to make high-sounding and meaningless declarations. But even these were not the same as those made in Stalin's time, when words were always used to conceal facts which were in complete contradiction to them, so that a speech about disarmament was taken to mean preparation for war and a reference to successful collectivization signified agricultural disaster – although no one dared to question the glittering phrases out loud.

Later we learned that during March, April and May 1953 there had been a fair amount of unity within the Praesidium, but of course a struggle for first place lay below the surface, though not all who could have aimed so high did so. Molotov, for instance, when he declined the post of Chairman of the Council of Ministers, gave notice that he was not in the running. He said that he was too old, but no doubt his main reason was that he felt he had been too closely associated with the past régime. Kaganovich was in the same position. Since two of the most crucial questions before the leaders were how to undo Stalin's work and which people were to be entrusted with this task, it was obvious that those who had been prominent in the thirties were not suitable candidates.

The three men who wanted power were Beria, Malenkov and Khrushchev. Under Stalin the Minister of Home Affairs, with his control over the secret police, was as powerful a man as any except the Leader himself. When Beria accepted the challenge he was obviously making a bid for supreme power, but he certainly realized that he would be able to exert it only indirectly, for he was a Georgian, as Stalin had been, and it was clearly impossible for one Georgian to succeed another. It seems therefore that he intended to use Malenkov as his figurehead and that it was lack of support from Malenkov at the critical moment which explains what later happened to Beria.

There is now a view in the West that he was a 'liberal' and that he was removed because it was thought that he would make too many concessions. This is as absurd as the opinion, sometimes heard in Russia, that he spied for the West.

His liquidation had at least two very simple reasons behind it. First, with him went one of the three rivals; secondly, a strong blow was dealt to the secret police, for which the other members of the Praesidium felt an almost physical hatred.

What happened was that Beria, having failed to get Malenkov's support, went to Berlin in a panic to deal with disorders for which the secret police was blamed. Soon after this he was arrested and given no chance to defend himself. His removal involved a military action, tank units were brought in, and had the police tried to resist they would have been overcome. In fact they did nothing to defend their chief because they had no orders to follow, and being a purely executive machine were incapable of taking the initiative.

The military hated the security forces and were delighted to be able to act against them; indeed in many places they now took over the KGB's work. For instance, the Lubyanka prison was closed for three days and a soldier stood at the gate checking passes and refusing entry to the secret police. The latter did not argue, but went off quietly, probably into hiding.

The impression made by the removal of Beria was enormous: people who had not been entirely reassured by the amnesty or the rehabilitation of the doctors[2] now took heart. The Government won great prestige, and it was achieved at considerable risk, for Beria had been very near to supreme power and the fearful MGB had been his instrument. The Government now exploited the theme that after Stalin, Beria was the man most responsible for the atrocities of the past years, and since he *was* deeply involved in Stalin's crimes, this was as credible as it was convenient.

New arrests caused a number of Beria's relations to arrive in our part of the world. One was his sister, another a high-ranking official of the Ministry of Transport whose only crime seemed to be that his name was Beria – Georgia had been combed for members of the family. The police was being used against its late master's kith and kin and to some extent for its own liquidation. Most people approved of these actions, but the more thoughtful among the prisoners wondered where this continuation of secret police methods would end.

2. See Footnote, page 235.

Although the period between the second half of 1953 and the beginning of 1955 seemed outwardly calm, the struggle for power, which had not been settled by Beria's death, went on.

Malenkov and Khrushchev now stood out as the obvious candidates and one or the other seemed certain to become our Master, for though in theory no supreme ruler is allowed by the Soviet Constitution, we knew very well that in due course we should have one. This gave rise to a lot of discussion among us as to whether Russians needed a 'Master', and if so, why? It reminded me vividly of a conversation I had had in the early twenties with a Russian émigré. He then told me several things which at the time I did not understand, which twenty years later I began to realize had some truth in them, but which even today I do not completely comprehend. The conversation took place at the time when I was drawing near to communism; the Soviet Republic had been proclaimed, and I believed that this was the natural form of government for the Russian people. But my friend insisted that by virtue of their history, traditions, upbringing and temperament, the Russians were incapable of approving a Republican structure for their country, and he added that such concepts as government by the people and the submission of the minority to the majority, and the idea of an intellectual élite which would keep its links with the people, were utterly alien to them. I refused to believe him and argued that the very idea of socialism excluded the notion of one-man rule and that any return to Tsarism was unthinkable. He replied that he believed every nation has its own conception of leadership and that, regardless of the outward form of its institutions, it will function on this basis. The English, for instance, he considered to be innately Republican in spite of having a monarchy, and the Russians to be innately monarchic in spite of having a Republic.

For him the only question was how Russia was to find a good Tsar, one who would enjoy the confidence of the people and in fact do their will. He thought that Lenin's great mistake had been not to proclaim himself the Tsar. Later I met many people who believed that had Lenin done this all would have been well, and that the misfortunes that came upon Russia were solely due to the elevation to power of a false Tsar in the person of Stalin, one who had no links at all with the people and who, if he was heir to anyone, was heir to Ivan the Terrible.

And now, in exile, so many years later, when we were discussing this very subject, I heard a professor say jokingly: 'So what you want is a constitutional monarchy?' And the answer came in a chorus: 'Yes.' I think that many people in the present ruling circles of the USSR probably also hold this view: that is to say, they want a break with the past. They hope that progress will be evolutionary, and for this to come about they consider it a *sine qua non* that the 240 million people of the country should not overturn the present régime.

When I was again a free man I found that discussions about the political future of the USSR outside the camps had followed a course nearly parallel to those going on within them.

There was, however, one difference – our ideas were bolder. This was natural, for we had nothing to lose, whereas a professor who collects pictures and has a carpeted flat in a new block of flats tends to reject conclusions which endanger the privileges he has fought for and obtained; and it is people such as this who are at the head of the army, of industry, of the academy of sciences. Without them and their essential loyalty to the régime it is impossible to imagine government by the Party and its apparatus.

Sometimes I am asked why the new Master must inevitably arise from inside the Party. The answer is simple: promotion of an outsider would be extremely dangerous to the positions of those now in power, and the generation which grew up under Stalin is more afraid of losing its privileges than of anything else. Even Soviet Trotskyists who have survived by a miracle say that if Trotsky were still alive he would agree that as millions had been killed in the Civil War, the war against Germany and the purges, more lives must not be lost, and that development must therefore be peaceful, even if this means that it will be very slow.

It is always assumed that the ruling strata will never give up power and therefore that all progress must come through them. Perhaps when a generation which has no knowledge of the Stalin period grows up there may be some hope of a broadly-based popular government being at least discussed, but at present nearly everyone feels that reform must come not by way of violence or by pro-clamation, but gradually. When I left the Soviet Union in 1956 most people seemed reasonably satisfied with the then Party leader. Since the October Revolution, as the current joke put it, they had been ruled by a titan, then a tyrant, and now a tourist. Khrushchev was good enough for the time being.

If one asks how it is possible that after all they have been through Russians should come out of the experience with an attitude of acceptance, it may be useful to point to Dostoyevsky. He who had preached revolution, served a term of forced labour in Siberia and written *Notes from the House of the Dead*, ended by preaching loyalty to the Tsar and became a supporter of the régime which had con-demned him. One may well ask why he did not come out of the 'house of the dead' three times more rebellious than before. The reason is no doubt the same as that which has caused twentieth century Russians, who have had similar experiences, to react in a similar manner. Certainly they think that repression and arbitrary rule should cease, but many of them believe that the system itself must not be touched, because out of all the bloodshed something has been gained for the people, and to jettison this by rebellion would, besides destroying some concrete gains, also write off millions of recent deaths as a total waste; this is something which hardly anyone is prepared to face. For these reasons a form of organic development is their only hope and this, they believe, can take place only under the rule of a 'kind master'.

A question which the more thoughtful among us never ceased asking was why in our life-time political activity in the USSR had developed in a way so contrary to Lenin's ideals. It is easy enough to defend his theoretical notions, e.g., his ideas about class govern-ment, class dictatorship, the transformation of the State as it pro-gresses towards communism and its eventual withering away. Theoretically, socialist economic development should also be reflected in forms that become increasingly more democratic. That these ideals have not been fulfilled is no doubt partly due to the fact that the necessary economic conditions did not come into being, but it is also because the trend has never been towards self-government. This is because at every step a new privileged stratum was formed which governed not on behalf, but instead, of the people, and it was one which was incapable of instituting democratic reforms. In many spheres, government by a group which pays lip service to the abolition of all government put an end to the idea of self-government. Also it is plain that in the battle between democracy and bureaucracy, bureaucracy will always get the upper hand. The crucial problem of how to ensure checks from below had worried Lenin and he even referred to it in the last article he wrote, *Better Fewer, But Better* – his spiritual testament. He hoped that, by a fusion of Soviet and Party, mutual control from below would be established and would gradually increase its power. He believed in the possibility of a separation of powers; popular control on the one hand, and executive control on the other. This is the old idea of the basis of power being subject to independent control, but the conception was strangled at birth by its own machinery. Indeed, as early as the twenties the positions were already so entrenched that it would have needed a revolution to offer an opportunity for control to be exerted from below. Perhaps if, as my émigré friend had suggested, Lenin had proclaimed himself Tsar and had appealed to the people against the Party he might have achieved it, but for him this would have been unthinkable.

Such an idea was not unthinkable so far as Mao Tse-tung was concerned, and I should like to point out here that his predicament thirty to thirty-five years after Lenin's death was in some ways similar to Lenin's situation in 1921–1924. Lenin had initiated the wide scale economic reforms known as NEP and begun to rely not only on his Old Bolshevik supporters but also on the newcomers of 1917–1918. This was the time of Trotsky's unambiguous approval of NEP and of discussions about the need to change Soviet policies both at home and abroad – in brief, democratization within and rapprochement with the West. Only insignificant numbers of the Old Bolsheviks (for instance, the Workers' Opposition of Shlyapnikov and Kollontay and the so-called Democratic Centralists led by Sapronov and V. M. Smirnov) wanted fundamental changes in the dictatorship of the proletariat at this juncture. The problem that Mao tried to resolve thirty-five to forty years later in China was more complicated. He began to struggle against a powerful opposition from within the Party, at the head of which Liu Shao-chi was trying to use practically the whole apparatus of the Party against the leadership of Mao. Then Mao put into practice the conclusions to which Lenin had come but did not dare to implement. Mao proclaimed the Cultural Revolution which *inter alia* had the object of opposing the authority of a single leader to the apparatus of the Party. It looks as though political power in China had shifted by the end of the sixties to a new apparatus based on the personality cult of Mao, which is in fact a continuation not of Lenin's but of Stalin's practices in the world communist movement. The full implications of the Chinese Cultural Revolution are not yet clear but there is one point which is of tremendous importance for the Soviet Union and all the other communist Parties throughout the world: the deeply nationalistic character of the Mao Tse-tung régime, which is based predominantly on the Chinese Army.

To return to Lenin, I think it is obvious that the reforms he planned were based on his belief that a new society was going to emerge. He did not imagine that the masses would be perfect. This was an idea which was developed later with much hypocrisy by Stalin, but Lenin thought that once the former ruling classes had been eliminated from their control over religion, education and administration, the people would be able to rule themselves. He did not look on the Party as a mystery of faith, though later there were people who assumed that he did. Also, while the concept of a multi-party system was inconceivable to him, he did not believe that differences of opinion (as distinct from class interests) could be eliminated, or that they were necessarily harmful, and unlike Stalin he never considered that the dialectical process was going to end with the triumph of the socialist revolution. On the contrary, he held that the dialectical process would always continue.

Since the October Revolution, and more particularly since Stalin's death, the fact that unanimity of thought is irreconcilable with human development has been made abundantly clear. This is a different premise from the one on which the structure of Stalinism was based, the aim of which was to destroy variety and to replace it by the concept that there is only one view which is admissible and right. Not that Stalin invented this theory; even at the inauguration of the First International heated arguments revolved round this theme, and the socialist and workers' movements were constantly fighting to establish the notion that all right ideas proceed from one premise and from one centre, and that they alone can be accepted. It is this view which over the years gave rise to a type of communist theology and eventually to the monstrous repressions of the purges.

An important factor in the development of the Soviet régime has been the innate contempt in which the rulers have held their people. Contempt for the people was the hallmark of Stalin's character, and it followed naturally that those who regard Stalinism as preferable to an alternative which involves risk usually refer to the people as dirt. It is not however fair to say that Stalin was responsible for originating this attitude or that it distinguished him from many other Bolsheviks in important positions; Trotsky, for instance, was one of those who clearly shared it.

The one leader who did not, I believe, despise the masses was Lenin. Contempt may be implied by some of his ideas but he certainly never drew any such conclusion from them and there is no word of contempt for them in his writings. Naturally he recognized that the peasants were the most backward part of the population but he disapproved of the use of force against them and tried to raise them to the level of the workers and lead them towards constructive achievements from which they would benefit. His faith in man and his belief that good must triumph over evil amounted to idealism, perhaps to utopianism.

Very different were the run-of-the-mill little bureaucrats with their Party cards who felt like giants because they knew that they had armed force at their beck and call. I can still see them now as they were in the thirties and forties, striding about with revolvers which they were happy to pull out of their pockets on every possible occasion. They were convinced that they were fulfilling the will of the Party and Government and that they had a right to impose themselves on the masses.

I think that the spread of this arrogant attitude arose from the fact that the Soviet régime quickly fell under the control of a handful of people most of whom (quite contrary to the legend that

Bolsheviks were a special race) were not of outstanding intellectual calibre.

It is this contempt for the people which seems to me to be the link between Stalinism and Fascism.

And it is not confined to Russia. For instance, when, at the time of the Hungarian rebellion, I was in Poland, I became very conscious of it. Talking to 'responsible people' I argued that the Hungarians wanted something other than what they had got, and I went on to say that their wishes should be considered and that they had a right to decide their own destiny. Whereupon the 'responsible people' replied: 'You needn't talk to us about the masses. We know them. Tell them that things are going to be like this or like that and they will all clap and agree. Then a month later someone comes and tells them the exact opposite and again they clap and agree. As a Party member you have no business to talk about what the masses want. They will want what we want.'

In Russia even some of the political prisoners were infected by this view. I remember one of my friends, who had been a Trotskyist and spent many years in camps, insisting that rehabilitation should be carried out slowly and the cult of personality liquidated gradually. He thought that because of the backwardness of the people and the fact that for years they had been ruled with incredible inhumanity and totally cut off from the peoples of the West, they must, at least for the time being, be held very firmly in hand if order were to be maintained and such advances as had been achieved were not to be jeopardized. I argued that it was impossible to go on for ever talking about the will of the people while regarding them with utter contempt, and that such a contradiction was a sinister and corrupting lie. I urged that if the will of the people was held in any respect it would be possible to envisage free elections with several political parties in competition. But when I said things like this I realized from the replies they provoked that the very conception of genuine democracy was lacking in such people. Though the régime might give up dictatorship in theory, the idea that it should give up supervising the thoughts, words and actions of the people was wholly unacceptable. No doubt it was partly because the system was considered to be insufficiently strongly established for this to be possible without the risk of chaos. An example of this feeling of weakness is illustrated by the continued jamming of some foreign radio-stations, though it is surely a monstrous thing that over half a century after the Revolution there is still no freedom of information. My belief is that so long as this control over the masses is exerted there can be little progress not only in the political field but even in agriculture and industry.

Yet in spite of all I have said, I think that if by the stroke of a magic wand democratic methods could be introduced with a guarantee that there would be no upheaval but only a change of government, many of those now, and even then, in power would be and would have been prepared, and even glad, to give up some of their power. I also believe that the majority of the fourteen million Party members are not inherently conservative, but what makes the very idea of the introduction of democracy quite un-realistic to them is, on the one hand, their conviction that such is the hatred of the masses (the workers as well as the peasants) for the régime that even partial reforms would cause it to be overthrown; and, on the other hand, the well-known resistance to change of those in entrenched positions, whose only aim in life is to move up the ladder of the bureaucracy and who therefore have a vested interest in maintaining the present structure.

The fact is that, after Stalin, Russia is like a country devastated by nuclear warfare. The destruction is not only physical but also moral and intellectual. To prove this one has only to read the leading Soviet philosophical and economic journals. In these the lack of originality, the low level of thought and the incapacity to understand the problems treated is agonizingly apparent. The only field in which some evidence of widespread creativity was seen fairly soon after Stalin's death was that of lyric poetry, probably because this can arise spontaneously.

In all other areas there was complete confusion after 1953 and the only people who were able to camouflage their ideological bank-ruptcy were those already in power. They could carry on their activities without producing an attractive long-term plan, but if any of their opponents attempted to displace them they would have to put forward a clear alternative programme. Perhaps if Trotsky had survived he would have conceived a plan; however, not only he but also his followers of any calibre had been exterminated. So had the intellectuals who had been followers of Bukharin, and so had the Trade Union leaders such as Tomsky. It is also quite possible that no blue-print was put forward because in the first years after Stalin's death anything of the sort was simply inconceivable. I had some confirmation of this view a little later in Western Europe when I met a few Russian émigrés who followed Soviet affairs very closely. I found that none of those with whom I spoke was able even to imagine a programme for the immediate evolution of the Soviet Union's political machinery.

The only people in Russia who might be prepared to take the risk of an upheaval are the young, who have no recollection of the purges or of the 'old' methods. When assessing their chances, however, one should not forget that the bureaucrats are becoming more and more intelligent, and as the democratic forces grow in strength so too does the bureaucracy. Little in any case can be achieved without a proper knowledge, analysis and understanding of the past, and this can hardly be attained by many Soviet people in present conditions.

So far as the all-important question of Soviet youth is concerned, I have come to the following conclusions:

1. When we speak of the young generation we should have in mind people who are now no more than twenty years old, in other words people who are completely untouched by the period of Stalin's rule.

2. Representatives of this generation are continuing the tradition of young Russian rebels of the past who acted as 'locomotives' of revolution. They are becoming a more and more unruly element in society, questioning more and more of what they are told by the official Soviet apparatus. It is not yet clear what this rebellion is based on and what direction it will take.

3. Although this new situation seems to have some similarities with Western protest movements it would be misleading to draw any parallels. The basic motives of the young Soviet dissidents are very different from those of students and others in the West.

4. A distinguishing feature of Soviet young people is their passionate interest in the past – particularly in what has happened to Russia during the last few decades and in the path their own parents have taken through life. This is where they come up against a huge knot of contradictions which they can neither untie, nor cut through, nor simply ignore.

Will it ever be possible to discover and discuss the historical and objective truth about the last seventy years of Russian history? We often discussed this sort of question in the camps and prisons in the thirties, especially with reference to the English and French revolutions. It was often said that the interests of the present, and possibly future, classes which had taken over from the nineteenth and twentieth century revolutionaries in Russia would make it impossible for those who were trying to get at the truth of what had happened to make any headway for decades to come.

Since then the official line of the CPSU in this respect has changed and changed again and still no firm interpretation has been decided on. The new official history of the Party has been coming out with great delays and has still only got to 1929, but even so it has aroused passionate discussion and violent arguments among the intellectuals. It is not least the young people who are dissatisfied with the compromises and omissions of the professional historians. A typical attempt to dispose of the problem for the time being was made by S. S. Smirnov in *Komsomolskaya pravda* on the 16th of November 1966. In a letter to a young friend he claims that it is impossible, so soon after the events of 1937 and 1938, to see them in perspective, and it would be premature to make any judgments about what took place at that time. I doubt whether many of Smirnov's young readers found this a very satisfactory answer, for it shows that although it is no longer possible to deny much of what went wrong, there are still such powerful forces blocking the way forward towards the truth that the individual who wants to discover what happened cannot be given much advice on where and how to set about his task. This situation obviously leads many young people – and not only young people – to one dead end after another.

These young people are, however, the hope for the future.

МВД СССР

Управление МВД
по
Красноярскому краю

16 апреля 1956 г.

№ 26730

Вотам паспорт
XI—IIА 691790

Видом на жительство не
служит. При утере не во-
зобновляется.

С П Р А В К А

Выдана гр. БЕРГЕР Иосифу Михайловичу, 1904 года
рождения, уроженец гор. Краков. Гражданину СССР, по
национальности еврей в том, что он осужден Особым
Совещанием при НКВД СССР 2 апреля 1935 года за
КРД на 5 лет ИТЛ. Особым Совещанием при НКВД СССР
от 29 июня 1937 года срок наказания понижен до 6 лет
тюремного заключения. Вторично осужден Таймырским
окружным судом 22 сентября 1943 года по ст. ст. 58-10
ч. II УК и 58-II УК РСФСР на 10 лет ИТЛ, с поражением в
правах на 5 лет с поглощением неотбытого срока.

Определением судебной коллегии по уголовным делам
Верховного Суда РСФСР от 28. II. 1944 года приговор суда
по ст. 58-10 ч. II оставлен в силе, а обвинение по ст.
58-II УК РСФСР из приговора исключено.

После освобождения из лагеря направлен в ссылку
в Красноярский край 25 июля 1951 года. Постановлением
МВД, КГБ и Прокуратуры СССР от 27 февраля 1956 года
Постановления Особого Совещания при НКВД СССР от
2 апреля 1935 года и от 29 июня 1937 года отменены,
дело на основании п. "б" ст. 204 УПК РСФСР прекращено.

Постановлением Президиума Верховного Суда РСФСР
от 23 марта 1956 года, приговор Таймырского окружного
суда от 22. IX. 1943 года и определение судебной коллегии
по уголовным делам Верховного Суда РСФСР от 28. II. 1944 г.
отменены и дело производством прекращено за недоказан-
ностью предъявленного ему обвинения.

Из ссылки освобожден 29 марта 1956 года.

Справка выдана для получения паспорта по месту жи-
тельства.

НАЧАЛЬНИК ОТДЕЛА УМВД

НАЧАЛЬНИК ОТДЕЛЕНИЯ

Москва 1956 г.   Апреля мес. 27 дня.   Первая
Московская Государственная Нотариальная контора
свидетельствует верность настоящей ФОТО копии.
Взыскано государ. пошлины 5 руб. Реестр 2 Ф. № 10264

Нотариус

TRANSLATION OF THE RELEASE DOCUMENT

USSR MVD
Office for the Krasnoyarsk
    Territory
16 April 1956   Passport Issued
No 26730   XI–IL 691720

Not a residence
permit. Not
renewable in event
of loss.

CERTIFICATE

issued to citizen Joseph Mikhaylovich BERGER, date of birth 1904, born in the town of Cracow, citizen of the USSR, by nationality Jew, *that* he was convicted by a Special Board of the USSR NKVD on 2 April 1935 for counter-revolutionary activity to 5 years in a corrective labour camp. The term of punishment was extended by a Special Board of the USSR NKVD on 29 June 1937 to 8 years confinement in prison. Convicted for a second time on 22 September 1943 by the Taymyr District Court under articles 58/10 pt. 2 of the Criminal Code and 58/11 of the Criminal Code of the RSFSR to 10 years in a corrective labour camp with deprivation of rights for 5 years, the sentence to run concurrently with the unserved period of the [previous] sentence.

The judicial division for criminal cases of the RSFSR Supreme Court on 28.2.1944 resolved that the sentence of the court pertaining to art. 58/10 pt. 2 be confirmed but that the charge under art. 58/11 of the RSFSR Criminal Code be dismissed.

After release from the camp he was sent into exile to the Krasnoyarsk Territory on 25 July 1951. By a ruling of the MVD, the KGB and the USSR Procuracy of 27 February 1956 the rulings of the Special Board of the USSR NKVD of 2 April 1935 and 29 June 1937 were vacated and the case under point 'b' of art. 204 of the RSFSR Code of Criminal Procedure was discontinued.

The Praesidium of the RSFSR Supreme Court on 23 March 1956 ruled that the sentence of the Taymyr District Court of 22.9.1943 and the decision of the judicial board for criminal cases of the RSFSR Supreme Court of 28.2.1944 be repealed and the case discontinued as the charge brought against him was not proven.

Released from exile 29 March 1956.

Certificate issued for the purpose of receiving a passport at the place of residence.
Chief of Section of Office of MVD
Chief of Department

Office for the
Krasnoyarsk Territory
of the MVD.

Moscow, 27th day of
April 1956. First
Moscow State Notary Office
confirms the authenticity
of this Photo-copy.
Stamp duty of 5 roubles
exacted.
Register 2 F. No. 111244
Notary

Epilogue

As I complete this book I realize that I have not included in it by any means everything I should have told the reader. When I began writing my memoirs, thirteen years ago, I was sure that I would be able not only to shed some new light on the events to which I was a witness but also to draw some general and possibly far-reaching conclusions.

This latter turned out to be much harder than I had expected, although some of the conclusions I arrived at before leaving the Soviet Union do not, in my opinion, require any revision in 1970. In particular, I did not then and do not now wish to defend or accuse anybody. None the less there is much that can be learnt by humanity in general from what actually took place in the USSR in the twenties, thirties and forties of this century (I deliberately do not use equivocal and hackneyed phrases like 'the personality cult' and meaningless generalizations like 'Stalinism' which are often used to cover over the actual facts). Now that I have again been living in the West (including Israel) for nearly fifteen years I feel I ought to add something to what I would have said if I had been publishing this book immediately after my release. I write in the spirit in which the ancient Jewish sages interpreted the phrase 'Let the sinners be consumed out of the earth' from Psalm 104. The sages suggest that we interpret this to mean 'Let the sins be consumed out of the earth'. If we are to draw some lessons from this dreadful period of Russian history we must, I think, concentrate on the terrible sins that were committed and leave the question of the sinners for future generations to examine.

The tragedies I have written about in earlier chapters represent of course only a microscopic part of the sufferings borne by the Soviet population and thus by a section of humanity, and they are only a small fraction of the calamities I observed and heard about myself.

But these memoirs are intended as a contribution towards the establishment of the truth about what happened and why; this is something in which everyone should be interested, and in particular those for whom the Soviet system is a model which should be emulated. During the whole twenty-two years I spent 'outside society' (a phrase used by the investigators to describe the status of people who represented a danger to the little group of people concentrated around Stalin) I heard endless conversations to the effect that once the truth about conditions in the USSR became known abroad the idea of saving humanity through socialism would be discredited for ever, and the main idea of the October Revolution, which Lenin saw not only as a national revolution but as the beginning of the liberation of all humanity, would be rejected and disproved.

But what happened in reality? In the Soviet Union there were a few feeble attempts to correct 'mistakes' here and there, but then the very officials in charge became frightened at their own courage. I should mention here that after twenty-five years of unimaginable terror and mass liquidation virtually the only people left in positions of authority were those who, because of their low intellectual level, were incapable of thinking at all or who had been broken and were no longer capable of making or even suggesting a fresh start. The Twentieth Congress (1956) did not lead on to anything new. What followed was only a game, for there was no real inner change in the leaders, and this was required not only because of the multitude of their crimes and the number of their victims but also because of the difficulties of finding a new way forward while bearing in mind the experience of the past.

But even more terrible to a person like myself is what has happened outside the Soviet Union. The world communist movement has of course been breaking up but public opinion and the workers' movement in the West have not come to the conclusions which we in the prisons and camps considered obvious and inescapable. Indeed the second half of the sixties has brought into the limelight a considerable number of people who regard rebellion against Western society as their basic mission. I have been following the ups and downs of the revolutionary movement for a little over

fifty years now but I have never in any period witnessed such confusion and absurdity as is to be found in the so-called 'New Left'
movement in a variety of countries at the present time. The worst
forebodings of the 'lost generation' of revolutionaries, to which I
belong, have been exceeded in some of the events of the last few
years, in particular in a number of universities in the West.

It appears as though all of us who were victimized during the last
twenty-five years of Stalin's life were also the victims of a great
illusion – the illusion that, once the facts about the degeneration of
the Soviet Communist Party and the crimes that were being committed against the people became known abroad, any further
bacchanalia of lies and deception by 'socialists' there would be
impossible. The most one can say is that the process of 'sobering up'
is an extremely slow one, especially in countries like France and
Italy, and I hope that these recollections may do a little to offset the
powerful apparatuses of deceit and obscurantism which are still
continuing to operate in the West.

What, then, were the 'sins' which in my view brought about the
catastrophe which beset the revolutionary generation in Russia?
First of all, disregard for the basic values of humanity. 'Revolutionary expediency', to which we communists in the twenties were
ready to subordinate everything else in our political activity, turned
out to be a concept so dangerous that it opened the way to counter-
revolutionary expediency and was used in order to mock and
humiliate the best representatives of a whole generation. The first
sin, then, was the sin against humanism.

The second was hypocrisy, dissimulation, which displaced all the
aims and ideals of those who had dreamed about a better future for
humanity. What is known as revolutionary propaganda is now not
only full of glaring contradictions but is in itself a crime against the
fundamentals of human consciousness, a crime against truth, and it
undermines every possibility of an honest discussion between people
of different views.

The third sin is the sin of mystification, when a rational approach
to problems is forsaken and various so-called 'innovators' enjoy
themselves by fostering the maximum development in their subjects
of certain instincts or emotions. In particular the instinct of national-

ism has not only proved to be stronger than Nazism, which developed it to the absurd, but even now divides mankind into opposing
groups and permits the exploitation of prejudices in order to commit
a whole variety of crimes. I could say a great deal about anti-
Semitism in this context.

These, then, appear to me to be the three most deadly sins which
still endanger the future of humanity. Are those who struggle against
them just dreamers, without any chance of success? As I write the
last lines of my memoirs I want to say that the future seems to me
not to be entirely devoid of hope. It seems to me that there is a
profound process of spiritual rebirth going on within the youngest
generation now growing up in the USSR. This process is not
limited only to the students or intellectual élite, but is spreading to
various levels of the working class and even to some parts of the
peasant youth. What is striking is the depth of thought at which
some of the young workers and peasants are arriving in the process
of rethinking the old standards and values which were accepted for
so many years by their elders. I have the feeling that the conclusions
to which the new generation in the Soviet Union is coming will be
more far-reaching and more surprising for most outside observers
than anything that has been written or said on the subject until now.
This, anyway, is the conclusion I have reached and I would like the
reader to share it with me.

Tel-Aviv.
June, 1970.

INDEX

SELECTIVE INDEX

Abakumov, Viktor Semyonovich (?–1954; head of SMERSH 1942–6; Minister of State Security 1946–52; arrested and condemned to death 1954), 248

Adenauer, Konrad, 218n, 249

Agranovsky, Abram Davydovich (1896–1951; 'feature-writer' in Norilsk camp), 35–9

Aksakov, Sergey Timofeyevich, 51

Akulov (special investigator), 23

Alymov, Sergey Yakovlevich, 42n

Andreyev, Leonid Nikolayevich (1871–1919; dramatist and novelist, author of *The Seven that were Hanged* 1909, *The Red Laugh* 1905; settled in Finland where he remained after Revolution), 150

Anvelt, Jaan, 190–1

Arakcheyev, Colonel, 55

At the Crossroads ('Vanya'), 232

Babel, Isaak Emmanuilovich (1894–1941; outstanding short-story writer; arrested 1939, died in camp, rehabilitated after Stalin's death), 45

Bagirov, Mir Dzhafar Abbasovich (1896–1956; First Secretary of Azerbaydzhan 1933–53; tried in 1956 after the Twentieth Party Congress and sentenced to death for treason, terrorism, etc.), 248

Bakayev, Ivan Petrovich (1887–1936; became a Bolshevik in 1906, spent several years in prison before October Revolution; member of 'Leningrad Opposition' in twenties, tried in 1936 with Zinovyev (q.v.) and Kamenev (q.v.) and sentenced to death), 156

Belousov (Mariinsk prisoner), 66–78; and Metal Workers' Union, 67; friendship with Kalinin, 67, 68–70; on mood of workers after Civil War, 68–74; arrest as counter-revolutionary, 74–6

Ben Gurion, David, 131

Beneš, Eduard, 139

Berger, Esther (wife), 7–10, 213

Beria, Lavrenty Pavlovich (1899–1953; head of NKVD from 1938, Marshal 1945, member of Politbureau and Deputy Chairman of Council of Ministers 1946; arrested and shot after Stalin's death, allegedly for spying for Britain), 38, 44, 88, 114, 235, 239, 240, 248; liquidation, 214, 258; bid for power, 257–8

Better Fewer, But Better (Lenin), 262

Blok, Alexander Alexandrovich (1880–1921; leading Symbolist poet, author of *The Twelve*; after Revolution active in various cultural enterprises started by Maxim Gorky (q.v.) under aegis of Lunacharsky (q.v.), the People's Commissar for Enlightenment; became disillusioned with Bolshevism), 46, 150

Brede, General Herbert, 190, 191, 192

Bryusov, Valery Yakovlevich, 46

Bukharin, Nikolay Ivanovich (1888–1938; member of Bolshevik Party